THE
PRESIDENT'S
SPEECHES

THE

PRESIDENT'S

SPEECHES

BEYOND "GOING PUBLIC"

MATTHEW ESHBAUGH-SOHA

LYNNE
RIENNER
PUBLISHERS

BOULDER
LONDON

Published in the United States of America in 2006 by
Lynne Rienner Publishers, Inc.
1800 30th Street, Boulder, Colorado 80301
www.rienner.com

and in the United Kingdom by
Lynne Rienner Publishers, Inc.
3 Henrietta Street, Covent Garden, London WC2E 8LU

Library of Congress Cataloging-in-Publication Data
Eshbaugh-Soha, Matthew, 1972–
   The president's speeches : beyond "going public" / Matthew Eshbaugh-Soha.
      p. cm.
   Includes bibliographical references and index.
   ISBN-13: 978-1-58826-410-7 (hardcover : alk. paper)
   ISBN-10: 1-58826-410-6 (hardcover : alk. paper)
1. Presidents—United States. 2. Presidents—United States—Messages. 3. United
States. Congress. 4. Political leadership—United States. 5. Political planning—United
States. 6. Public policy (Law)—United States. I. Title.
JK585.E74 2006
352.23'80973—dc22

                                                                    2006011623

British Cataloguing in Publication Data
A Cataloguing in Publication record for this book
is available from the British Library.

Printed and bound in the United States of America

 The paper used in this publication meets the requirements
of the American National Standard for Permanence of
Paper for Printed Library Materials Z39.48-1992.

5 4 3 2 1

To Michelle

CONTENTS

TABLES AND FIGURES

Tables

Figures

PREFACE

SCHOLARS OF THE PRESIDENCY AND US POLITICS LOOK AT ME SIDEWAYS when I argue that presidents do not use their speehes to rally the American public in support of their policy goals. "But how," these scholars ask, "can the president successfully influence Congress without supportive voters pressuring their legislators on his behalf?" A better question might be, "how can a president ever hope to be successful by relying on a disinterested US public to govern?" It is well-known among political scientists that two enduring characteristics of the American people are their scant knowledge of politics and their disinterest in learning more; they'd rather be entertained by cable television than watch the president of the United States speak about the nation's pressing problems. In other words, it must be possible for presidential speeches to have an impact on the policy process—whether the adoption or implementation of public policy—which is independent of direct public involvement.

I began exploring questions on the president's public leadership when I read Samuel Kernell's *Going Public: New Strategies of Presidential Leadership.* Kernell's was (and still is) the dominant paradigm used to explain the impact of the president's speeches on his legislative success. Despite its elegance and consistency with broad notions of democratic presidential governance, it appeared to me that only Ronald Reagan had been influential under the going-public model: speak to the American people and they will coerce their representatives in Congress to support your policies. It also appeared to me that no one had directly tested the effects, by way of public opinion, that presidential speeches have on congressional actions. And given more recent research by George Edwards in his *On Deaf Ears: The Limits of the Bully Pulpit,* it seems unlikely that presidents can successfully lead Congress in this fashion, in part because presidents have so much difficulty leading the public in the first place.

Yet, presidents continue to speak often about policy. I argue that when presidents speak, they provide legislators and bureaucrats with cues about their policy preferences. Indeed, going public really isn't about speaking to the public at all. If the president's speeches affect the policy decisions of legislators and bureaucrats, then presidents may achieve their policy goals regardless of public involvement. Undoubtedly, public support is at work throughout the policies that legislators, bureaucrats, and presidents debate and pursue. Presidents may even take advantage of conditions under which the public already supports the president's preferences. But the president need not rely on a disinterested public in order to use his public speeches to affect his policy success in either Congress or the bureaucracy.

* * *

In researching and writing this book, I have received help from many along the way, particularly George Edwards, Ken Meier, Jim Anderson, and H. W. Brands. I also thank many other members of the Political Science Department at Texas A&M University, including Roy Flemming, Pat Hurley, and Dan Wood, who taught me time series. I thank the staffs at the Lyndon Baines Johnson and George Herbert Walker Bush Presidential Libraries who aided me during my stays. In addition, I recognize the Program in American Politics in the Political Science Department at Texas A&M University for providing grant money that aided in the research and development of this work.

Writing the draft manuscript was the easy part. Turning that mess of ideas and data analysis into a coherent and publishable book required much more thought, dedication, and effort. Fortunately, Leanne Anderson and others at Lynne Rienner Publishers saw enough promise in the manuscript to offer me a chance at publication. I thank Leanne especially for specific suggestions about content, organization, and the title. Thanks also to Karen Schneider for marketing the book and to Lesli Athanasoulis for ushering the manuscript through production. Two anonymous reviewers deserve thanks for offering suggestions about the perspective and contribution of this book and for pointing out numerous oversights. Thanks to Jun-deh Wu, my research assistant at the University of North Texas, for some last-minute data requests and for help in preparing the manuscript. I also thank the University of North Texas Office of the Vice President and Research Technology Transfer Office for a small grant that I used to offset the cost of indexing the book. Naturally, all errors are my own.

Many others have helped me become a relatively productive scholar, even though they may not know it. I thank the Rafenelli Winery for making the best Zinfandel on the planet. Wine must be a necessary ingredient to successful political science research, although I do not have the scientific data to support that claim. Music also seems vital to a successful research agenda, given our discipline's rare moments of insight, but usually laborious and sometimes tedious workload. With that, I gratefully quote Jay Farrar: "Smile upon the chaos streams, turning point calm awaits you." I am also thankful that I chose to research agriculture policy. Although this book may not win any additional accolades, it is to my knowledge the only political science book that mentions karnal bunt fungus.

Last, I thank my family—the Sohas *and* Eshbaughs—which has always provided me with the support and encouragement I needed to pursue and complete my Ph.D. and to secure a job that would allow me to continue my research. I thank Ethan Orion, who has taught me to work more efficiently so that I can spend even more time listening to him laugh. Deepest thanks go to my wife, Michelle, who listens to me explore ideas aloud and who—unbeknownst to her—provides me with motivation to strive to become as good a writer as she is. It is to her I owe the greatest thanks, for she inspired me on a chilly Ohio evening to dedicate my life to researching political phenomena.

—*Matthew Eshbaugh-Soha*

1

WHY PRESIDENTS
SPEAK ABOUT POLICY

THIS BOOK IS ABOUT SPEECHES AS A SOURCE OF PRESIDENTIAL POWER.
It examines the president's reasons for using speeches and whether they
improve his ability to lead Congress and the bureaucracy. It explores the
conditions under which the president's signals—speeches presidents
make about their policy preferences—may increase his influence in
Congress and the bureaucracy and notes when they are unlikely to do so.
It develops the importance of public policy to these relationships and
argues that presidential influence through signals varies systematically
by policy type. It adds to our knowledge about how presidents attempt
to influence legislation and control the bureaucracy. But even though a
great deal has been made of the "bully pulpit" in the modern presidency,
we do not know enough about how or to what extent speeches directly
affect the adoption and implementation of public policy.

Presidential speeches are central to the power of the modern presidency. Through them, presidents attempt to influence legislation before
Congress, cultivate public support, and set the media's agenda.
Presidents use their speeches as another tool, another opportunity
increasingly available to modern presidents, to achieve their goals in
spite of the difficulties of presidential governance. The centrality of
presidential speeches to the legislative and, as I will argue, bureaucratic
processes leaves little doubt that presidents must use their speeches to
affect these institutions. The pervasive question is not whether the president speaks frequently about policy but how these speeches might
increase the president's governing powers.

The dominant paradigm in the literature that explains the president's
use of public speeches is the "going-public" argument. "Going-public"
scholars put forth an indirect link among presidential speeches, the public, and legislative success. Facing Congresses driven to recalcitrance by

1

divided government and the gridlock that follows, presidents attempt to break this logjam by enlisting the public—the core and fundamental justification for representative government—as an ally in their pursuit of legislation. In other words, the president uses his speeches, a tool unique to the modern presidency, to put public pressure on legislators to succumb to the president's wishes.

The most recent quantitative research, even though it finds some evidence of presidential influence in Congress through speeches (Barrett 2004; Canes-Wrone 2001), does not provide adequate support for this version of the going-public model. Primarily, presidents have much difficulty in consistently enlisting the public to pressure legislators to support their legislative priorities (Edwards 2003). They even have difficulty increasing an issue's salience or expanding "the scope of conflict," a precondition to moving public opinion (Edwards and Wood 1999; Eshbaugh-Soha and Peake 2004, 2005). As a result, the president's means of affecting legislation through speeches may not hinge on public support for the president's policies. Instead, presidents may directly influence the decisions of legislators by sending signals that legislators need to make efficient, yet relatively informed, decisions. The success of direct signaling, as I will detail throughout this book, depends heavily on the policy area under debate.

Presidents may also use their public speeches to influence the implementation of public policy. After all, the same conditions that encourage presidents to "go public" in the first place—gridlock and divided government—also push them to achieve their policy goals in the bureaucracy (Nathan 1983). An environment that simultaneously motivates presidents to use speeches to affect policy in Congress and turn to the bureaucracy for policy successes when the legislative process stagnates may also encourage presidents to use these same speeches to increase their influence over the implementation of public policy. When presidents mention publicly a policy or an agency, those working on the policy may feel a sense of gratification toward the president and work even harder than they normally do to implement their policy mission. Clearly, each bureaucrat has her own preferences to which she will give priority and therefore could ignore signals when they are not relevant to her decisions. But public recognition of a policy area and direction by the president present bureaucrats with a unique sense of support that arguably, given the president's allure in the Oval Office and without, motivates them to do more of what they already do. Signals may be even more effective than individual meetings as an informative and persuasive policy tool, given the decentralization and "thickening" of federal institutions (Light 1995).

This book offers a reexamination of this crucial aspect of presidential power and contributes to the literature on US political institutions and public policy in three ways. First and foremost: How do speeches increase the president's success in Congress when the public—a vital component to going public—is typically unmoved by presidential attempts at leadership? I maintain that presidential signals directly influence legislators by providing them with information they need to make efficient, yet relatively informed, decisions. Although the public may increase the likelihood that a legislator will respond to a president's signals, the president does not need to actively mobilize the public to be successful in Congress, a precursor to presidential influence in the going-public model. In other words, it matters little if the president's words go unheeded by a disinterested public, so long as the president's speeches directly influence the decisions of policy actors in Washington, D.C.

Second, presidents will use direct, informative signals to increase their influence over policy in the bureaucracy. Like legislators, bureaucrats also need information from the president to set priorities in the face of limited time and agency resources. Presidential signals, particularly positive ones, motivate bureaucrats to implement their missions more vigorously than they would without public support from the White House.

Third, public policy plays an important differentiating role in US politics. This study bridges the link between public policy and US institutions and revisits the notion that public policy is a necessary means to wholly explain the ends that are processes of US political institutions. Specifically, variation by policy type is a strong predictor of whether or not presidential signals may be influential in either Congress or the bureaucracy. Ultimately, two questions guide this book: (1) *How* do presidential statements affect the president's influence over public policy in Congress and the bureaucracy? (2) *Did* presidential signals, from 1950 to 2004, affect legislative and bureaucratic activity?

My argument is clear and direct: presidents need to inform legislators and bureaucrats of their policy preferences in order to lead them and to exert influence over their policy decisions. Given the decentralization and individualization of Congress and the thickening of the federal bureaucracy, signals are the most efficient way for presidents to communicate their policy preferences to the most public officials. Besides, presidents must make public statements to meet high public expectations. It is only rational for presidents to speak about policy to influence it, just as they speak to appear presidential. Legislators and bureaucrats also need leadership from the president, provided through policy signals. By expressing their policy preferences through signals, presidents supply legislators and bureaucrats with mental shortcuts, cues they need to make efficient, yet relatively informed, decisions amid institutional environments that limit the time and resources they need to pass and implement public policies.

The Public Presidency and the Permanent Campaign

Presidents of the modern era have at their disposal a tool—speeches and their appeal to public sentiment—that has become inseparable from their abilities to govern, yet one that was unavailable or at least not used by presidents of previous eras. Unlike the framers' understanding that presidential power is derived from constitutional authority, the Wilsonian model proclaims that "power and authority are conferred directly by the people" (Tulis 1998: 113–114). Reliance on popular sentiment, arguably a central component to presidential governance since the Theodore Roosevelt administration, discourages presidents from leading only those institutions responsible for making policy (such as Congress), moving them instead to appeal for public support to achieve their policy goals.

This change in presidential leadership is not without its critics, as cultivating public support may undermine presidential leadership over the long run. According to Jeffrey Tulis (1987: 181), as presidents rely on "crisis politics" to generate interest and increase the effectiveness of their rhetoric, they may face a credibility problem as citizens become less able to determine when a crisis is genuine. Presidents who rely upon the "dynamics of public opinion" (Tulis 1987: 178) to craft public policy will ultimately undermine sound deliberation and create bad policies (Tulis 1998: 94).

Despite these and other complaints that the president's power of public governance encourages presidents to "pander" to public opinion (but see Jacobs and Shapiro 2000), offer superficial policies to appease the whims of public opinion, and otherwise "personalize" the presidency (Lowi 1985), thereby reducing the president's capacity for true leadership, presidential speech making and the cultivation of public support that follows are central components of modern presidential leadership. Indeed, public speech making and leadership are at the core of modern presidential governance, with presidential speech making increasing markedly over the past thirty years. As shown in Figure 1.1, speeches have increased considerably since the first year of Richard Nixon's administration.

Figure 1.1 Yearly Presidential Speeches, 1949–2004

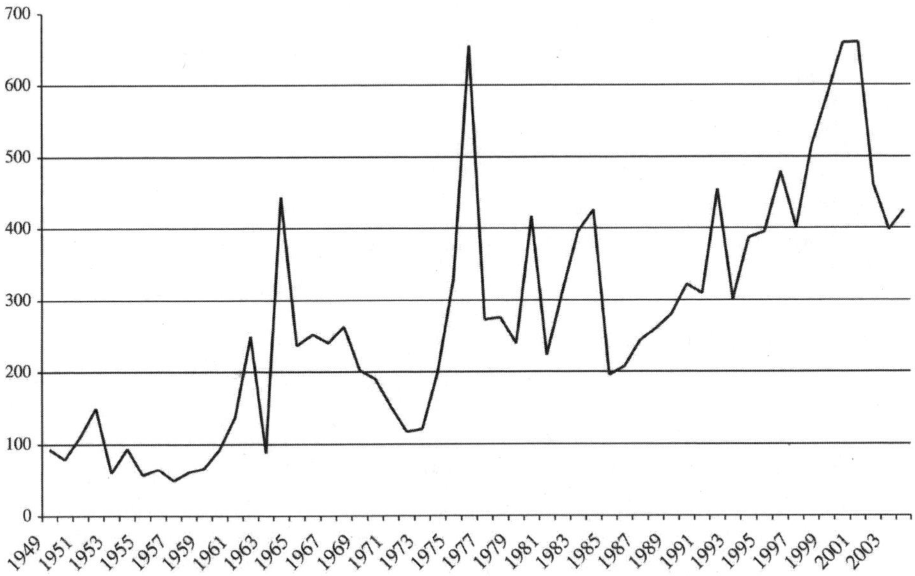

Source: Ragsdale (1998); 1998–2004 estimated by author from electronic version of the *Public Papers of the President.*

Along with the rise in presidential speech making has come the end-less pursuit of public support, otherwise known as the permanent campaign. Presidents rely increasingly on private polls to tap public opinion (Jacobs and Shapiro 2000, 1995) and then use these data to cultivate support for the administration in general, for specific policies, or for aspects of the president's personality. Just as President George H. W. Bush commissioned more polls than Ronald Reagan, so too did Bill Clinton rely on polls more heavily than Bush did. It is well known that President Clinton even polled the US public to help decide upon a summer vacation spot.

Despite these efforts to understand and lead the public, more and more research demonstrates an utter lack of presidential success in such leadership. According to the information in Table 1.1, public approval ratings have not increased, on average, since Eisenhower (see Eshbaugh-Soha 2004), even though efforts to cultivate them—through public speeches—have increased substantially. Successful efforts to cultivate public support directly, through national addresses, are also waning. Brace and Hinckley (1992) demonstrated that Presidents Dwight Eisenhower through George H. W. Bush could expect an increase of about 6 percent-

Table 1.1   Average Presidential Approval Ratings by Administration

President	Average Approval	Maximum	Minimum
Eisenhower	65	79	48
Kennedy	71	83	56
Johnson	56	79	35
Nixon	48	67	24
Ford	47	71	37
Carter	47	75	28
Reagan	52	68	35
G. H. W. Bush	62	89	29
Clinton	55	73	39
G. W. Bush	59	90	37

Source: Gallup Polls, various years.
Note: Numbers for G. W. Bush are through November 13, 2005.

age points in their public support following a nationally televised address; Ragsdale (1984) showed a similar 3 percent increase. Presidents since then, in part because of declining viewership (Baum and Kernell 1999) and other constraints, have not been able to count on comparable increases in public support following their national addresses (Edwards 2003).

Other research has demonstrated that presidential approval ratings are a time-varying parameter and that the influence of this key indicator of presidential prestige is lessening over time. Wood (2000a) and Bond, Fleisher, and Wood (2003) contended that Edwards's (1989) earlier optimism about the impact of presidential approval ratings in Congress was not complete, as the effects of presidential approval ratings on the president's success rate in Congress have declined for recent presidents. Since 1981, moreover, presidents have given more speeches in reaction to declining approval ratings but have not given more speeches to increase them (Eshbaugh-Soha and Andary 2004). This was not the case between 1969 and 1980, when approval ratings had little, if any, impact on the president's speech making.

Presidents do not typically lead the public on specific policy issues either. Two presidents generally known as good communicators—Presidents Reagan and Clinton—were not overly successful at affecting pubic opinion on even their core policy priorities (Edwards and Eshbaugh-Soha 2001; Edwards 2003). Support for increases in defense spending, for example, peaked before Reagan took office, only to decline significantly while he was in office and actively campaigning for additional funding (see Edwards 2003: 56). Despite Clinton's initially convincing nearly 60 percent of the US public that his health care plan was right for the United States, public support for the administration's health care plan rapidly dropped, to the point where Congress never even voted on it (see Edwards 2003: 37).

The continual increase in public speeches, presidential use of public opinion polling, and other tools to cultivate public support has not sustained or improved presidential leadership of the public. This poses a problem for going-public scholars (as argued in Chapter 2), who maintain that presidents must enlist the public as an ally in their quest for legislative success. These conflicting trends, moreover, suggest two potential answers for why presidents persist in their pursuit of public support when their prospects for gaining it seem to be diminishing.

First, presidents give more speeches not to move the public but to maintain the support they already have. Because expectations of presidential leadership are also on the rise, presidents must make numerous speeches simply to avoid a loss of public support.[1] Indeed, presidents spend much of their time appealing to those who already agree with the president (Edwards 2003: 244). Changing the public's mind is a rare event indeed and can only be expected as presidents exploit opportunities when they arise (Edwards 2003: 249).[2]

Second, presidents do not use their speeches solely to influence the public. Instead, presidents signal their policy preferences through their speeches to also affect policy elites. Presidential leadership on policy through their public speeches leads to increased access to congressional and bureaucratic institutions, thus increasing the president's potential to influence and persuade members of these institutions to support his policy preferences. Undoubtedly, the president's public speeches help him maintain public support and meet increasingly higher public expectations. But it is the focus of this book to argue that this power of the modern presidency, these speeches, signals, or public communications, are designed also to move elite policy actors—to persuade them—to respond to the president's preferences so that he may achieve at least some of his policy goals while in office.

Presidential Signals

Signals are the means by which presidents express their preferences to other actors in the policy process. Signals communicate the president's support for, opposition to, or commitment to a policy area. According to Matthews and Stimson (1975: 51), a cue or signal is "any communication . . . that is employed by the cue-taker as a prescription for his [decision]." A signal is a source of information and acts as a cue so long as one uses it in one's decision. Presidents inform others of their policy preferences through their public signals.

Presidential signals may convey any amount of information, so long as a policy actor uses them in his or her decisions. Presidents may signal general support for or opposition to a policy without providing a policy proposal. Signals may be broad calls for a reduction in welfare rolls. Presidents can also request specific policy changes, such as a 10 percent reduction in the alternative minimum tax over three years. For the purposes of this book, presidential signals may be spoken or written. Although the vast majority of signals sent by presidents are spoken words, the written memos that presidents occasionally deliver to legislators and bureaucrats are publicly available. Often, these different forms of communication work in tandem, providing policymakers and implementers with a clear and precise indication of the president's preferences. A president may speak about a new proposal for air pollution regulations, for example, and then send a written fact sheet to leaders in Congress detailing the president's proposal. Multiple signals—whether spoken or written—are most likely to convey that the president wishes to lead on a policy and that he is concerned with and committed to a policy area.

Informing policy elites of their policy preferences is the first step that presidents must take to affect the adoption and implementation of policy. Presidential signals are potentially the most efficient means that presidents have to communicate their preferences to policymaking elites. Such signals can effectively penetrate multiple layers of a federal bureaucracy and reach the most legislators in a decentralized Congress. A concerted effort on the part of presidents to deliver multiple signals on a policy is synonymous with presidential leadership in the modern era. Thus, this book focuses on the effects that signaling *attention* to a policy area has on the president's influence over Congress and the bureaucracy in part because legislators and bureaucrats are most likely to respond to the president when he leads on policy. This basic diagram of presidential signals and their direct impact on congressional and bureaucratic activities is presented in Figure 1.2.

The Role of Policy

This book is not only about the relationship between the president's speeches and the decisions of legislators and bureaucrats. It is also about the role that public policy plays in these interinstitutional arrangements and the questions raised by a theory that, more or less, downplays the public's role. For too long, scholars have neglected the relevance of public policy to explaining power relationships in US and presidential politics. It is the policy itself that shapes the prospects for success or failure. It is the policy that conditions whether presidents will attend to or ignore a problem that a well-crafted policy may solve. It is the policy

Figure 1.2 A Simple Diagram of Presidential Signaling

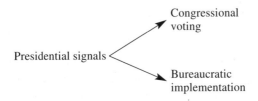

itself that shapes whether a president will discuss it publicly or conceal his preferences behind closed doors. And it is the policy that guides whether the president will prioritize it through legislation, its implementation, or both. The role of public policy is central to the theory of presidential signaling developed in Chapter 3.

Consequences for Democratic Governance

The theory of presidential signaling, furthermore, has numerous consequences for our conception of presidential power and of the role presidential speeches play in policymaking and implementation and for notions of democratic presidential leadership. If presidents need not communicate with the public, if a disinterested public is not vital to the policy success of the modern president, but may only magnify the impact of a signal occasionally, then is signaling a theory devoid of democratic accountability? After all, Wilson (1885) and Tulis (1987) would have us believe that presidential attempts to speak directly to the American people have made the office more democratic, despite some of the deleterious and unintended consequences of the public presidency. Is it an affront to democracy to claim that presidents need not use their speeches to actively cultivate the support of the American people or to use those speeches to affect public policy? Or does the theory of presidential signaling rely on a subtler and potentially more accurate portrayal of how the president's governing authority is derived from the American people? Indeed, it is because the president has a responsibility to each federal institution, agency, policy area, and the people that the president does not use his speeches solely to communicate his policy preferences to the American people. The thesis of this book not only adds to the literature in several ways by explaining the direct impact of presidential speeches on public policy but also raises issues that might seem counterintuitive to a system of government founded on the consent of the governed.

Focus and Organization

This book investigates the impact that presidential signals have on the policy activities of Congress and the bureaucracy. Its central purpose is to determine whether presidents influence the policy outputs of Congress and the bureaucracy through their public statements and how these relationships vary by policy area. Arguably, presidents use their public statements to signal their policy inclinations to influence the decisions of legislators and bureaucrats without also requiring the threat of public sanction. Derived in part from theories of cue taking by political actors (see Mathews and Stimson 1975), the theory of presidential signaling is based on the president's rational need to use public statements to affect the adoption and implementation of public policy. Presidential signals are an efficient way for presidents to express their policy positions, whether a broad desire to reduce crime or specific requests to fund 100,000 new police officers. Moreover, legislators and bureaucrats should respond to the president's preferences because legislators and bureaucrats need him to achieve their own policy goals. Yet policy, which offers different incentives for political leadership and responsiveness (Gormley 1986; Lowi 1972), conditions the effectiveness of presidential signaling. I investigate each of these claims through time series methodology and data.

Chapter 2 lays the foundation for presidential power and influence through speeches. Even though the going-public argument is the dominant explanation for the impact of presidential speeches, it describes insufficiently the relationship between presidential speeches and legislation. Presidents are typically unable to move public opinion and thus cannot rely on the public to pressure legislators to support their policies. Going public is also limited in explaining the policy process because it neglects (1) the impact that speeches might have on bureaucrats and (2) the conditioning role that public policy itself may play. Placing the president's speeches in the larger context of presidential power and policy is a necessary first step in explaining why and how presidential signals affect the adoption and implementation of public policy.

Chapter 3 develops the theory for this book. Presidents have many means of influence over the policy process. Research shows, however, that traditional means of power have not noticeably enhanced presidential success in Congress. Presidents are successful in Congress, nonetheless, and presidents' signaling authority is one factor that may help explain why they are. Signals may be an additional means of influence for presidents in the bureaucratic arena. That legislators and bureaucrats need and respond to signals frames why presidents use signals to influence the policy process and why they should be successful doing so. Both legislators and bureaucrats have rational needs to listen to and respond to presidential signals. Chapter 3 concludes with a discussion of the conditioning effects of public policy, that presidential signals should be more or less effective depending on a policy's salience and complexity. Specifically, civil rights, clean air, and domestic farm policies provide test cases to see if different policies affect the signaling relationship between the presidency and policy outputs. This chapter presents the basic, quantitative models used to test the influence of presidential signals in Congress and the bureaucracy. These models make direct reference to the presidential influence in Congress and presidential control of the bureaucracy literatures discussed in Chapter 2.

The next three chapters develop three policy areas to assess whether presidents are successful at affecting policy through signals. Each empirical chapter begins with general expectations for presidential involvement in a policy area characterized by salience and complexity dimensions. A brief history of presidential interest and involvement in each policy area follows. Together, these descriptions suggest why presidents will or will not have success using their signals to affect a specific policy. The three empirical chapters provide evidence of the president's attention to the policies, how signals influence bureaucratic outputs, and whether signals influence legislative outputs as well.

Chapter 4 explores a policy that, based on its salient and uncomplicated characteristics, should facilitate presidential influence in Congress and in the bureaucracy. As such, presidents are likely to affect civil rights policy through their signals, whether over the Civil Rights Division of the Department of Justice or civil rights roll-call votes in both houses of Congress. This chapter is replete with archival evidence that supports the quantitative analysis, including historical data that demonstrate substantial presidential interest in civil rights policy.

Chapter 5 concerns the adoption and implementation of a policy area that has characteristics that promote conflicting possibilities for presidential influence through signals: air pollution regulations. These conflicting characteristics—salience, which promotes presidential influence, and complexity, which does not—mean that signals are most likely to be influential when clean air policy is salient. In short, salience clearly matters to the effectiveness of presidential signals. The Environmental Protection Agency (EPA) and the Clean Air Act are the descriptive focus of Chapter 5. If presidents are to influence clean air policy through their signals, modeling the effects of signals on EPA clean air enforcements will show this. I assess presidential signaling in Congress in terms of the president's public statements on clean air and their relationship to clean air roll-call votes. I made special provisions to control for periodic cycles of environmental issues that may influence clean air policy.

Finally, Chapter 6 examines a policy area that should preclude presidential influence through signals: domestic aspects of the Agriculture Adjustment Act. Like all other policy chapters, the success presidents have on roll-call votes depicts congressional outputs, whereas government payments to farmers comprise bureaucratic outputs. Because agriculture policy is also mired in subgovernment politics, presidents should have little influence over agriculture policy in Congress or the bureaucracy.

In Chapter 7, the conclusion, I tie all policy areas together, assess the adequacy of my theoretical expectations, and recognize some limitations to this and other research on presidential influence over the policy process. In particular, the concluding chapter reflects on all hypotheses, their support, and the reasons why some hypotheses were supported more or less than expected. Although this project supports presidential signaling as an alternative theory to the going-public argument, it does not eliminate the feasibility of a going-public strategy for presidents. I close with some suggestions for future research to build upon this book's conclusions and to test the going-public argument more directly.

Notes

1. This was the consensus of scholars who attended a conference on the public presidency at Texas A&M University in College Station, Texas, in February 2004.

2. Arguably, President George W. Bush did just this after the September 11, 2001, attacks. An opportunity presented itself for the president to lead on terrorism, to set the public and congressional agendas on terrorism, and to maintain public support for his war on terrorism. It is very unlikely that Bush would have been able to accomplish these objectives (nor may he have wanted to) without having exploited the opportunity presented by the September 11 terrorist attacks.

2

THE NEED FOR
PRESIDENTIAL SIGNALING

ON APRIL 28, 1981, IN A NATIONALLY TELEVISED ADDRESS BEFORE A JOINT session of Congress, Ronald Reagan warned of the wrath of the American people if Congress did not pass his economic recovery program. He claimed, "The American people are slow to wrath, but when their wrath is once kindled, it burns like a consuming flame." Congress responded to this implied act of coercion and passed Reagan's proposals in the Gramm-Latta budget reconciliation. Several months later, Reagan called on the American people, imploring them once again to contact their representatives and tell them to pass his tax cut plan and ensure continued economic recovery. Reagan signed his tax cut proposals into law later that year.

Reagan's national addresses in 1981 and their influence over Congress have spawned a significant body of literature that explores the impact that presidential speeches have on the president's success in Congress. This literature holds that presidential speeches are central to the power of the modern presidency. Through their public speeches, presidents attempt to influence legislation before Congress, cultivate public support, and meet high public expectations. Presidents see the cultivation of public support as providing an opportunity to achieve their administration's goals in light of other difficulties with Congress. As a result, scholars have argued that presidents must "go public" with their policy goals to increase their likelihood of success in the legislative arena (Kernell 1997).

Building upon Reagan's success in early 1981, going-public supporters hold that the president's public statements have an indirect, yet positive, impact on his success in Congress. Kernell (1997) argued that presidents go public because the congressional environment has changed. As party control weakened, congressional power became less

centralized, committee chairs relinquished decades of control, and legislators began to pursue individual goals such as ensuring their own
reelections by meeting constituency needs. Whereas presidents used to
call upon party leaders and committee chairs to force less senior legislators to follow the president's lead, institutional changes precluded bargaining as a reliable means of consistent presidential influence. Instead,
presidents must expand the scope of conflict for an issue, which puts
public pressure on Congress to act. Presidential speeches expand the
scope of the conflict to raise the consequences for legislative inaction.
Once the public supports the president's position, legislators will feel
public pressure to vote in favor of his position. That is, presidents use
"the aid of a third party—the public—to force other politicians to accept
their preferences" (Kernell 1997: 3). This indirect linkage model is illustrated parsimoniously in Figure 2.1.

Quantitative research has been building support for Kernell's fundamental suggestion, that presidential statements increase presidential success in Congress. Barrett (2004) showed that when presidents speak
publicly on legislation before Congress, they increase the probability
that they will be successful on roll-call votes. Peterson (1990) and Fett
(1994) demonstrated that the higher priority a president gives a policy,
that is, the more a president speaks about an issue, the greater the president's legislative success will be. Specifically, "the place an issue holds
in the president's publicly revealed legislative agenda can affect legislators' voting decisions" (Fett 1992: 510). In addition, presidents increase
their success on budget votes through national addresses (Canes-Wrone
2001).

These works clearly uphold Kernell's assertion that presidential
statements will increase the president's success in Congress but are
inconsistent with Kernell's theory for two reasons. First, the authors do
not test the impact that the president's speeches have on public opinion
and then what impact public opinion has on legislative activity.[1]
Although Barrett (2004) inferred that presidents can count on their
speeches to increase the salience of an issue before the public, and Fett
(1994) ignored this point completely, Canes-Wrone (2001) tested an

Figure 2.1 A Simple Causal Diagram of "Going Public"

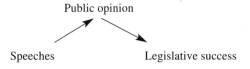

Public opinion

Speeches   Legislative success

alternative model entirely—what affects the president's propensity to deliver a speech and then what impact this has on the president's success in Congress—while asserting that presidential speeches expand the scope of conflict, aiding the president's success rate in Congress. If the bulk of the quantitative evidence does not match the theoretical expectations put forth by Kernell (1997), but relies on them to connect three pieces in a puzzle, then even though we may think that presidential speeches increase the president's legislative success, we still do not know why.

Second, a growing body of literature shows that presidents have much difficulty moving public opinion or even increasing the salience of issues before the public, a precursor to moving public opinion and a requirement for expanding the scope of conflict. Although evidence shows that legislators respond to constituency preferences on salient issues (Hill and Hurley 1999; Miller and Stokes 1963), there exists little proof that presidents typically affect public opinion through their speeches (Edwards 2003). Moving public opinion requires the president to change the public's mind, to make a coherent, yet simple and convincing argument to a disinterested public. Yet research is skeptical of the president's ability to move public opinion (Edwards and Eshbaugh-Soha 2001). Indeed, Edwards (2003) showed that even though presidents may be able to speak to maintain public support, they are not adept at changing the minds of the voting populace. At most, "even 'great communicators' usually fail to obtain the public's support for their high-priority initiatives" (Edwards 2003: 241). If the president cannot achieve majority support for his policy priorities, how can we continue to maintain that presidents speak to enlist the public as an ally for increased success in Congress? Why would legislators listen to a public that the president has not moved to support him? Where are the costs of noncompliance to legislators who resist presidential overtures when the president's power to lead public opinion is either nonexistent or fleeting, at best?

Moreover, only limited evidence shows that presidents increase the public salience of issues (J. Cohen 1995), yet mounting evidence indicates that presidents cannot do so. Edwards and Wood (1999) demonstrated that presidents cannot typically affect media attention (a common measure of salience) to a range of domestic and foreign policy issues. Although Eshbaugh-Soha and Peake (2004) showed that presidents have some influence on media attention and that this influence varies systematically by policy area, they further demonstrated (2005) that presidents do not consistently affect media attention to the economy, the policy issue most central to a president's political success. Peake and Eshbaugh-Soha (2003) also showed that even the president's best tool to increase media attention to an issue, the nationally televised address, is influential only about one-third of the time and that this impact is fleeting.

Overall, going-public scholars assume that presidents can expand the scope of conflict without support from other research (whether on moving public opinion or affecting media attention) and without demonstrating themselves that presidents can do so. Moreover, the anecdote that gave rise to the idea that presidents move the public to increase their success in Congress—Reagan's early success in 1981—is the only clear example to support Kernell's (1997) model as he envisioned it.[2] If the president has difficulty moving public opinion, yet presidential statements increase his success in Congress as these works demonstrate, then Kernell's theory, as Figure 2.1 depicts, may not be complete in its characterization of how presidential speeches influence Congress.[3] In turn, we should revisit the reasons why speeches aid the president in his quest for policy achievement in Congress. It is the contention of this book that a president is not required to move a disinterested public to support him in the legislative arena but that presidential signals can directly increase the president's success in Congress for numerous reasons.

In addition, this literature limits its analysis to presidential influence in Congress alone, even though presidential power operates similarly in the bureaucracy (Neustadt 1990; Waterman 1989). Presidents hope to influence a policy's implementation as much as they do its adoption. As I argue in subsequent chapters, the president's speeches should directly influence bureaucratic and congressional policy outputs. It may be that presidential signals influence bureaucratic implementation and affect legislation for similar reasons: presidential signaling directly affects legislative and bureaucratic activity contingent upon several conditions of influence.

Signaling in the Bureaucracy

Going public has long been considered an effective strategy for presidential success in Congress. As a way to overcome conditions of divided government and the gridlock of recent legislatures, presidents may go over the heads of legislators and enlist the public as an ally in their efforts to persuade legislators to support their policy priorities. Much research has explored this argument, finding that presidential speeches increase the president's legislative success (Canes-Wrone 2001; Fett 1994).

Concomitant with the growing appeal of going public as a governing strategy has been the rise of the administrative presidency. Just as
presidents have relied on public support to affect their fortunes in
Congress, so have presidents jettisoned the idea of just influencing the
adoption of legislation. In the face of divided government and legislative gridlock, presidents have turned to the bureaucracy as a means of
influencing the *implementation* of public policy and securing their policy goals through the federal bureaucracy (Nathan 1983). Presidents have
had some success "controlling" the direction of policy outputs in federal
agencies through appointments or budgets (Wood 1988; Wood and
Waterman 1994), but what impact have the president's signals or
speeches had on the policy activities of federal agencies?

Only a handful of studies have explored the impact of presidential
signals on bureaucratic activities. Without concerning themselves with
developing a theory for influence, Wood and Waterman (1993) showed
that presidential statements on the environment influenced EPA outputs. Carpenter (1996) examined the impact that a nonverbal budgetary signal might have on federal agencies. He found that a single
budget shift was not sufficient for budgetary control of the Food and
Drug Administration and the Federal Communications Commission.
Instead, several budget moves "cascaded" to enhance presidential or
congressional control of agency behavior. Krause (1996) held that
presidential and congressional budgetary signals to the Securities and
Exchange Commission were interdependent: a signal from one institution did not necessarily lead to political control if the other principal
did not send a similar signal. More recently, Whitford and Yates
(2003) demonstrated that the president's drug policy signals have an
agenda-setting effect over the number of prosecuted federal drug
crimes. Indeed, the president's rhetoric on policy is a common source
of information for agencies that seek to know the president's policy
priorities (Shull and Garland 1995). Cabinet-level secretaries (Regan
1988: 142) and career bureaucrats responsible for the implementation
of policy (Agency director interview 2005) use the president's public
statements to ascertain the president's policy preferences (see
Whitford and Yates 2003).

Despite the implication that presidents may affect bureaucratic
activity through signals, the paucity of research on this subject requires
some theoretical development as to why bureaucrats may respond to a
president's policy signals. It is one of the tasks of this book to meld the
rise in presidential speaking with the increasing desire of presidents to
affect the implementation of public policy. After all, presidents wish to
achieve good public policy, whether in Congress or the bureaucracy, and

speeches may be a way for presidents to increase their control over bureaucratic policy outputs. This book explores whether presidents use their rhetoric to influence the bureaucracy and whether they have been effective doing so. Indeed, as Figure 1.2 illustrated, presidential signals should have a direct impact on both.

The Importance of Public Policy to Signaling

Scholars have long recognized that public policy plays an important role in the relationships among US national institutions. Yet since Lowi (1972) proclaimed that public policy is vital to our understanding of US government, scholars have not systematically explored differences in their studies of institutional phenomena. The presidency-Congress literature has examined the broad differences between presidential influence and success on foreign and domestic policy initiatives but has not explored systematic differences within these broad categories (Bond and Fleisher 1990; Edwards 1989). Even scholars investigating the presidential control of the bureaucracy, who examine the effects presidents have on policy-specific federal agencies, do not generalize across different types of agencies or public policies (Wood and Waterman 1994). Fortunately, Paul Light (1993) has reasserted policy's importance in the systematic study of presidential politics, noting that employing policy as a dependent variable is a just way to explore the complex processes of interinstitutional relationships (see Eshbaugh-Soha 2005).

Despite the dearth of research that explores policy impacts on institutional relationships, policy has a clear impact on political processes, which should help explain variation in the effectiveness of presidential signals. Legislators take cues depending on policy characteristics (Clausen 1973), Supreme Court justices rely on different issues as cues in their decisions (Perry 1991), and presidents speak often about policy (Eshbaugh-Soha and Peake 2004). If the goal of presidential signals is to affect congressional voting and bureaucratic implementation, then presidents will likely signal on specific policy areas. Even though different policies produce different political outcomes (Edwards and Wood 1999; Lowi 1972; Hill and Hurley 1999), and the broad contours of public policy influence a president's decision to go public (Lewis 1997), scholars of presidential rhetoric typically ignore variation by policy type. To account for different effects across policy dimensions, this study of presidential signaling examines variation by a policy's salience and complexity (Gormley 1986), analyzing civil rights, clean air, and domestic farm policies.

Power in the Modern Presidency

Presidential power is the power to persuade, to convince others of the merits of the president's position because he cannot rely solely on his office to govern effectively (Neustadt 1990; see Dahl 1957). Because of their limited constitutional authority, presidents need to use their advantages—whether public support, a strong reputation, or a favorable contextual environment—to influence the policy process. Indeed, presidents cannot command legislators to do their bidding in the US system of separated powers (Neustadt 1990), nor can they expect expert bureaucrats to simply follow their policy aspirations.

It is not through speeches alone that presidents attempt to persuade and exert their power. Indeed, there are numerous means besides speeches by which presidents can affect the policy decisions of legislators and bureaucrats. It is these means, furthermore, that shape the likelihood that presidents will be effective communicators and determine whether their signals will have a desired effect.

Presidential Influence in Congress

In the legislative arena, presidents can build support for their policies if they have a strong reputation and act skillfully. A president's reputation, which is related to his leadership skill, is an important yet elusive source of influence. Indeed, "any President who valued personal power would start his term with vivid demonstrations of tenacity and skill in every sphere, thereby establishing a reputation sure to stand the shocks of daily disarray" (Neustadt 1990: 54). Reputable or skilled presidents may therefore be more successful in Congress than unskilled presidents, even though skills are clearly not a determining factor for presidential success or failure (Bond and Fleisher 1990). Even skilled presidents, nevertheless, must take advantage of favorable conditions within the political environment to succeed in Congress. The president's knowledge of Congress, his ability to compromise and consult with legislators, and his use of resources to persuade members to support his policies are important "interpersonal skills" (Bond and Fleisher 1990: 30–31). Moreover, the president's success acting early in his tenure, in capitalizing on a favorable honeymoon period, is important to his legislative influence. Early success may lead to later success, and as Neustadt (1990: 54) argued, being perceived to be a skilled president can be invaluable in smoothing a typical president's rocky tenure.

Public opinion is another potential resource that may aid the president in his dealings with Congress. Beginning with Neustadt's (1990:

78) claim that prestige may "affect the likelihood [of success] . . . and is strategically important to [the president's] power," scholars have conceptualized prestige as the president's public approval. Many have inferred that the more popular a president is, the more likely legislators are to support him. Despite evidence to the contrary (Bond and Fleisher 1990), presidents, Washington insiders, and some researchers concur that the president's job approval ratings play a role in presidential-congressional relations, at least at the margins (Edwards 1997; Rivers and Rose 1985; Ostrom and Simon 1985; but see Wood 2000a).

Because reputation and prestige often operate in the background, presidents need a favorable congressional environment in order to influence legislators and secure passage of their legislative agenda. Indeed, the number of seats the president's party holds in Congress is a reasonable baseline from which to assess the president's potential to succeed in Congress. Presidents can count on same-party support nearly two-thirds of the time (Edwards 1989: 40) because members of the same party share similar policy goals, and they tend to run on the president's record. Logically then, if the president's party has majority status in Congress, he is more likely to be successful than if his party were in the minority. Conversely, divided government can be detrimental to presidential success in Congress (Edwards, Barrett, and Peake 1997). Because party may at times conflict with ideology, a Republican president cannot always count on support from a Republican member of Congress (Bond and Fleisher 1990: chap. 4). Furthermore, the highly decentralized nature of US political parties means that members of Congress are free to oppose the president on any piece of legislation (Edwards 1989: 68).

Presidential Control of the Bureaucracy

Presidents need to persuade members of the vast federal bureaucracy if they expect to further their administrative policy objectives (Neustadt 1990; Waterman 1989). Several formal powers aid the president in this task. First, presidents have the constitutional authority to appoint like-minded individuals to key posts in the federal bureaucracy. Presidents have used appointments to shape the direction and outputs of several agencies (Wood and Waterman 1994, 1993), including the Environmental Protection Agency (EPA) and the Antitrust Division of the Department of Justice (Wood 1988; Wood and Anderson 1993: 28; but see Eisner and Meier 1990).

Second, presidents may increase or decrease an agency's budget to guide its policy priorities and maintain political control. Slashes in the

EPA's 1982 fiscal appropriations by the Reagan administration led to a decrease in EPA enforcements (Wood and Waterman 1994; Wood 1988). Budgets shifts in the 1970s and 1980s also changed the Equal Employment Opportunity Commission (EEOC) in a manner consistent with presidential preferences (Wood 1990). Of course, a single budget cut may not elicit bureaucratic responsiveness (see Carpenter 1996), especially if the president and Congress support conflicting budgetary allotments (Krause 1996). In contrast, serious budget cuts can eliminate the potential for presidential influence. If the president cripples an agency through drastic budget cuts, that agency will find it difficult not only to oppose but also to support a presidential directive (Durant 1992).

The president's removal power is an alternative means of control. If unhappy with an agency's leadership, the president may remove his political appointees and nominate another. Reagan removed Anne Burford as director of the EPA and James Watt as secretary of the interior after their contentious tenures heightened congressional oversight. Because removing appointees is politically costly (not to mention the additional expenditure of capital needed to push a replacement through the Senate confirmation process), removal powers do not typically promote presidential influence (Waterman 1989: 177; Wood 1988). Although more cumbersome and difficult to measure, presidents also have the power to reorganize agencies in accordance with their policy inclinations (Wood and Waterman 1994).

Overall, appointments tend to elicit the most responsiveness from the bureaucracy, and budgets are influential but less so (Moe 1985; Wood 1988, 1990; Wood and Anderson 1993; Wood and Waterman 1994). Presidents can expect to influence the bureaucracy because career civil servants tend not to be hostile to presidential goals (Pfiffner 1988). Nathan (1983) even argued that presidents *should* actively use their constitutional authority, including appointments, reorganizations, and budgets, to administratively control the bureaucracy (see Redford 1969).

The Limits of Presidential Influence, Absent Leadership

Leadership is the cornerstone of presidential success, so that all means of influence in Congress and the bureaucracy are limited in the absence of presidential leadership. Without sufficient leadership, presidents are unlikely to achieve many legislative goals, whether or not the president is popular and his party controls Congress. The Carter presidency provides a perfect anecdote. Jimmy Carter arrived in Washington with a

Democratic majority in Congress rivaling Lyndon B. Johnson's combined 191-vote margin. Carter also had relatively high approval ratings during his first year in office. Nevertheless, he is generally regarded as a failure in the legislative arena because he did not focus on a select few policies crucial to his agenda (Hargrove 1988; Rozell 1990). In other words, President Carter did not lead Congress; he did not show commitment, nor did he provide clear direction for legislators. Of course, leadership does not guarantee the president success, given a lack of party unity throughout the latter half of the twentieth century (Cooper, Brady, and Hurley 1977; but see Cox and McCubbins 1993: chap. 6). But leadership is a key condition that facilitates presidential influence over the adoption of public policy.

Absent presidential leadership of the bureaucracy, the president's formal tools of control do not guarantee him influence. Appointees may be ineffective administering the president's agenda if presidents do not lead the agency into action. Presidents, not political appointees, are the ultimate authority over the bureaucracy. If agency heads suggest a change in policy without the president's support, they may be unable to sustain a change in agency direction (Edwards 2000; see Wood 1988). Appointees need presidential leadership and authority to ensure that career bureaucrats implement the president's program. Even though appointees are loyalists who intend to administer the president's program, they may not have the "skills necessary to enact those agendas successfully" (Edwards 2000: 25) without the president's direction. Sufficient presidential leadership should enhance appointees' effectiveness in administering the president's policy objectives and contribute to effective control of the bureaucracy.

Budget appropriations alone are inadequate to ensure bureaucratic compliance to presidential prerogatives. Primarily, budgets do not reflect solely the president's preferences. The budget is a product of the preferences and compromises of the presidency and Congress. If an agency has allies in the Congress, the budget may not be altered as the president desires, undercutting the budget as a tool of presidential influence. Moreover, if Congress and the president do not have the same budgetary preferences, budgets will not adequately affect bureaucratic behavior (Krause 1996). Even when Congress and the president agree to cut or increase an agency's budget, a series of increases or decreases is required to elicit a change in bureaucratic behavior (Carpenter 1996). Presidents, therefore, must supplement their budget cuts or increases with sufficient leadership of an agency to enhance their control over it.

Finally, formal policy change, through executive order, directive, or statute, is inadequate to ensure that bureaucrats will implement the president's policy goals. Bureaucrats simply cannot and will not follow all presidential directives. Bureaucratic discretion, inertia, agency goals, and the agency's mission may guide bureaucratic action absent clear and consistent policy leadership. Without presidential direction and leadership, bureaucrats may shirk their responsibilities arising from a change in policy, given their own discretion as well as limited time and resources to carry out presidential orders. Presidents who do not lead policy change with consistency and commitment may fall short in their policy goals (see Edwards 2000: 9). Only a change in policy coupled with presidential leadership is a sufficient strategy to ensure that bureaucrats implement policy orders. Indeed, presidents must not only use their formal powers effectively, they "must [also] bargain and compromise in order to increase their influence over the bureaucracy" (Waterman 1989: 170).[4]

Signaling as a Source of Power

One source of presidential power, and one that can provide the leadership for modern presidents not present in other forms of influence, is the president's power to signal. Presidents cannot act alone in the separated system of US government; they must rely on others to ensure that they achieve their goals (Neustadt 1990). Therefore, presidents must be able to present their policy preferences in a persuasive manner to those who can help them secure their policy goals. A potentially effective way for presidents to influence policy is through the broad persuasive power of the president's public signals: when a president publicly states his policy preferences, he is trying to secure his policy goals by influencing others' policy actions.

The idea that presidential speeches are important to the presidency is not new to scholars. Neustadt (1990) once observed that "publicity" is important to the president's power. Edwards (1989) noted that leading the public is essential to the modern presidency. In addition, Kernell (1997) and others (Barrett 2000; Canes-Wrone 2001; Fett 1994) have suggested that public statements can influence legislation indirectly by mobilizing public support. Presidents definitely use statements to project their policy preferences (Grossman and Kumar 1981). The important question is whether presidential signals are a source of presidential power and how they influence policy.

Neustadt (1990) suggested an answer to this question. He underscored five conditions under which presidents would be successful in ensuring compliance from others: (1) an actor must realize that the president has spoken; (2) the president's request must be clear in meaning;

(3) it must be associated with publicity; (4) the president must have the legitimate ability to carry out the request; and (5) compliance with a president's position is enhanced when there is "the sense that what he wants is his by right" (Neustadt 1990: 18–23). Conveniently, the first three of these conditions of influence are met by the nature of signals: presidential signals are informative, clear, and covered by the news media. The latter two conditions suggest that policymakers will be responsive to presidential signals if the president has legitimacy and can act on his request. Because signals are an effective way for presidents to encourage compliance, those who may need information from the president may respond to signals.

Whereas Neustadt inferred that signals are a source of presidential power, cue theory (Matthews and Stimson 1975) provides the foundation for explaining the relationship between presidential signals and legislative and bureaucratic policy outputs. Simply, individuals with limited information use cognitive shortcuts to make decisions in an environment constrained by limited time and resources. Because they need reliable information sources that they may use in their policy decisions, legislators and bureaucrats may respond to the president's policy cues—his signals—given an auspicious political environment.

Presidential signals are an aggregate form of persuasion. Presidents signal not to influence just one legislator or bureaucrat but to affect the collective policy outputs of Congress and the bureaucracy. Signals indicate presidential leadership and commitment to a policy, and they are a way for presidents to inform others of their policy positions and persuade as many policymakers and implementers as possible. If presidents are successful at signaling their policy preferences to members of the legislature and the bureaucracy, we should witness a shift in policy outputs based on the direction and number of signals presidents devote to a policy area. From the bully pulpit, presidents inform, lead, and attempt to persuade other policy actors to adopt their policy preferences. I develop this argument in Chapter 3.

*   *   *

The president is an influential figure in US politics. Although scholars recognize that the president's public speeches may affect his success in Congress, the going-public argument offers an unsupported indirect theoretical link among presidential statements, public opinion, and legislative success. Instead, even though that research finds that public statements have a direct impact in Congress, it ignores presidential statements and their power over the implementation of public policy.

Moreover, it does not explore the important and varying impacts that policy has on political processes.

No study has yet developed a theoretical argument for why presidents signal their preferences on public policy to inform and influence the actions of legislators and bureaucrats. It may be, as I maintain, that presidential public statements are a source of power that presidents use to directly affect legislation and bureaucratic outputs. If presidents can use the bully pulpit to inform others of their policy preferences, then, under favorable political circumstances presidents should be able to translate their signaling prowess into influence over policy in both Congress and the bureaucracy. The dearth of theoretical research on this question requires first that an argument be made as to why we should expect presidents to use signals to influence the policy process and why this relationship should differ by policy area. The next chapter explores this linkage, centering on the argument that political actors look for cues to make efficient and informed policy decisions. Because of this, presidential signals should help the adopters and implementers of public policy make policy decisions with a clear indication of the president's preferences.

Notes

1. However important, these works are limited in several other respects. For instance, studies may not adequately explain why presidents are rational to use a public strategy (Canes-Wrone 2001; Fett 1994); these works just assume the rationality of a public strategy. Or a study may only use State of the Union address speeches (J. Cohen 1995), nationally televised addresses (Canes-Wrone 2001), or first-year presidential data (Fett 1994).

2. My interview with a former member of Congress confirmed this (Member of Congress [Texas] interview 2005). Although the representative suggested that presidential speeches act as informational policy signals for legislators, he only mentioned one instance where the president successfully motivated the public to contact him to support a presidential policy to which he was initially opposed. Not to my surprise, this anecdote was Reagan's national address on tax and spending cuts in 1981.

3. The theory itself may be time-bound. After all, Reagan may have been able to coerce legislators to support him through public pressure owing to the sheer number of cross-pressured seats in 1981, seats held by Democrats in districts that went strongly for Reagan. As those southern seats have become Republican, recent presidents have had less opportunity to sway legislators to support them as Reagan once did.

4. A lack of presidential leadership to motivate action by the Privacy and Civil Liberties Oversight Board—ordered by Congress as part of recommendations by the September 11 Commission—is at the core of criticisms that have been made by members of Congress and civil rights advocates. The board,

designed to protect civil rights in the aftermath of September 11, 2001, was slow to meet and lacks significant enforcement powers because "it's not a top priority for the administration," according to Christopher Shays (Conn.), Republican member of the House of Representatives (Drees 2005). The implication is that if the president prioritized this, it would be functioning actively and properly. This is but one of many recent examples of the importance of presidential leadership to the implementation of public policy.

3

DIRECT SIGNALING

PRESIDENTIAL POWER, AS RICHARD NEUSTADT (1990) SO ELOQUENTLY defined it, is the power to persuade. Unfortunately for presidents, the opportunities and resources available to wield power have diminished just as public expectations about presidential performance have increased. Congress has become decentralized and more parochial as political party weighs less on the minds of the participating electorate. To influence Congress, therefore, the president must persuade not just a handful of committee chairs and party leaders but also numerous legislators with individual preferences and a primary concern for reelection. Presidents understand that if they are to avoid being "irrelevant" (as Newt Gingrich claimed of the Clinton presidency after the 1994 congressional elections), they must adapt to changing circumstances and use multiple means of influence.

Concomitant with the decline in presidential power has been the rise in the public presidency. The public expects presidents to deliver a strong economy and national security yet avoid bickering with an increasingly partisan Congress. Presidents must lead Congress to appease the public, even though conditions of divided government make this a difficult task. Presidents need to use their speeches to influence legislation because so many other tools of influence prove futile and ineffective. The strategy by which presidents inform members of Congress of their policy preferences and then follow up through a campaign of repeated public attention and commitment is relatively new to the US presidency.

This signaling strategy differs from that argued by going-public scholars, not so much as to why presidents speak publicly, but as to how speeches may influence legislation. Instead of presidents' needing to expand the scope of conflict and rely on a disinterested public to coerce legislators into action, signaling is a way for presidents to provide cues directly to elites in government, to provide information and incentives—not coercive threats—to secure their policy goals through legislation. Presidents use signals as part of a strategy that takes advantage of conditions and policies that may aid their leadership of Congress. Although the current literature finds evidence of a direct link between presidential statements and the president's success in Congress, it relies on an untested assumption that presidents can typically increase an issue's salience.

The president's pursuit of influence and the strategy of signaling are not exclusive to the president's relationship with Congress. As the federal government has become more involved in the policy problems of US citizens, the federal bureaucracy has grown beyond the president's control in steering it to implement his policy goals. Signals may be a way for a president to "rein in" the bureaucracy as it has expanded and to efficiently direct its implementation of policy. As a result, presidents intend to directly affect the implementation of policy through signaling just as much as they mean to influence its adoption.

The existing literature presents a puzzle: presidential statements do not typically increase an issue's salience or move public opinion, yet presidents "go public" to increase their success in Congress. Some research, which finds that presidential statements positively influence the president's legislative fortunes, relies on a theoretical argument supported by a sparse body of empirical evidence. Moreover, the literature does not explain the impact that speeches may have on the implementation of public policy. This is striking because the same conditions that encourage presidents to go public in the first place—conditions of gridlock and divided government in Congress—also encourage presidents to pursue their policy goals in the bureaucracy. It seems logical, then, that presidents would also use their speeches as a tool of influence of both the adoption and implementation of public policy.

This chapter develops a rationale for why speeches may directly affect the adoption and implementation of public policy. Simply, presidents hope to influence policy, and signals may help them do so. Both legislators and bureaucrats, moreover, desire policy success, and the president's support—expressed through signals—may help them achieve their own policy goals. Because they operate with incomplete information, legislators and bureaucrats need signals, as mental shortcuts, to process a vast amount of information in a relatively efficient manner. Just as the president's signaling authority will vary by policy type, I also suggest how speeches may at least set the congressional agenda, one step toward increasing the president's success over policy adoption.

The chapter is organized as follows. To begin, I argue that the reason presidents signal in the first place is first to inform, then to lead other policy actors to achieve their many goals as president. Showing commitment and concern to a policy, as expressed through signals, is how presidents lead the policy process in the public presidency. Next, I show how the theory of presidential signaling borrows from cue theory, in that people have a need for information shortcuts. Applying cue theory to congressional and bureaucratic behavior, legislators and bureaucrats use mental shortcuts and will respond to presidential signals because the president is a legitimate and important actor in the policy process who can help them achieve their own goals. Finally, I discuss how public policy should condition the effectiveness of presidential signaling. Policy affects political processes, and this corollary should be no different for the effectiveness of presidential signaling.

Why Presidents Signal

The logical place to begin developing a theory of presidential signaling is with presidents themselves. Unlike other studies that merely assume speech making is a rational strategy for presidents to influence legislation (Barrett 2004; Canes-Wrone 2001), this chapter puts forth several reasons why presidents should use signals to affect public policy. At base, presidents desire policy success, which requires effective presidential persuasion. Signals may help presidents succeed because they inform, and presidents must inform others of their policy preferences to persuade them. Signals are also an efficient source of communication, given high public expectations, a decentralized Congress, and a thickening federal bureaucracy. Ultimately, presidents must lead to affect policy through signals. Presidents lead by demonstrating commitment to a policy. More commitment to a policy means more leadership, which should contribute to success in achieving their policy goals, all else equal.

Policy Goals

Like all purposive actors, presidents have goals. Presidents ultimately use signals to achieve their goals, whether reelection, good public policy, or a significant place in history (Light 1999). Clearly, different presidents have different motives for supporting one policy position over another. Nixon signed clean air legislation not because he was an ardent environmentalist but because environmental legislation could help his reelection campaign (R. Cohen 1995). Johnson waged war on poverty in part because he was surrounded by it throughout his youth (Barber

1972). Whatever the reason, policy tends to structure other presidential goals. Presidents need a strong policy record to run and be reelected and to have something they can point to as their legacy. If presidential signals are an important tool in the president's policy successes, then they may help presidents secure policy goals, which in turn help them meet their reelection and historical objectives.

Signaling Across Institutions

Scholars have long held that presidents use their public speeches to affect their success in Congress. Yet presidents also use speeches to increase their control over the federal bureaucracy. Given all we know about presidential speeches—that speeches have policy effects, that presidents have organizations within the White House working toward their perfection, and that presidents deliver speeches on a daily basis—it is surprising that few have surmised that presidential speeches may affect bureaucratic behavior. Nonetheless, it follows that the same conditions that have encouraged presidents to use their speeches to affect their success in Congress should also have motivated presidents to use this tool to affect a policy's implementation.

Kernell (1997) argued that institutional changes in Congress spurred presidents to use speeches to increase their success in Congress. As Congress evolved from an institution of individualized pluralism, which favored bargaining between legislators and presidents, to one of institutionalized pluralism, which precluded traditional means of bargaining, it entered an era also of frequent conditions of divided government and increasing instances of legislative gridlock. Such conditions encouraged presidents to rely on a new form of legislative influence—their speeches—to alter the incentives before legislators. Presidents would need their speeches as a way to "expand the scope of conflict" and put additional pressure on legislators to break gridlock or, as I argue, to inform as many legislators as possible of their position in order to increase presidential success in Congress.

It is these same two conditions—divided government and legislative gridlock—that administrative presidency scholars also identify as motivating presidents to shun the legislative and turn toward the bureaucratic arena to achieve policy successes (Nathan 1983). Simply, the cost of achieving success in Congress had increased, whereas the prospects for influencing bureaucratic behavior were relatively new and untapped. As the federal government expanded, the implementation of public policy provided presidents with an additional and vast opportunity to leave a lasting mark on federal policy.

Two conditions—divided government and legislative gridlock—encouraged presidents to both use their speeches to influence legislation before Congress and turn to the bureaucracy to achieve their policy goals. It follows, therefore, that presidents would also use their speeches to influence their policy success in the bureaucracy. At the very least, an increase in presidential speeches on policy also increases the likelihood (as I will argue) that bureaucrats will hear the president's preferences on policy and respond to them (according to cue theory, developed below). Again, for similar reasons, presidents will use speeches to affect policy in both Congress and the bureaucracy, and legislators and bureaucrats will be more likely to respond to presidential signals as public attention to policies increases.

Signals Are Informative and Persuasive

If presidents are to affect the policy process and achieve their policy goals, they must inform others of their policy preferences. Effective communication is particularly important in the US system of separate institutions that share power. Presidents cannot command or dictate policy changes but must rely on others to secure their policy goals. Presidents must employ an effective strategy of communication to ensure that others know what they prefer and how they intend to achieve it. They may rely on other tools to influence the policymaking process and secure their policy goals in Congress and the bureaucracy, but presidents must first communicate their preferences to have any influence at all.

Public signals are informative. Presidents regularly use public speeches and written statements to outline their policy priorities, develop their positions, and explain their reasoning. They give State of the Union addresses and special messages to Congress to inform legislators and bureaucrats of their yearly policy inclinations and specific goals. Minor and local speeches on policy also inform legislators and bureaucrats through the media. The president is a central actor in US politics, and his public statements are rarely made without notice or comment. Both bureaucrats and legislators, in particular, have an ear out for presidential attention to policies that interest them.[1] Moreover, public speeches take time and energy to make; they are costly to the president and his communication organization. Because of this, presidents want to maximize the information they send in speeches and use them in a manner in which they are informative and a genuine reflection of the president's intentions.

To encourage responsiveness, nevertheless, signals must also be persuasive. Neustadt (1990: 30) wrote that "the essence of a President's persuasive task is to convince [people of shared authority] that what the White House wants of them is what they ought to do for their sake and on their authority." Presidents use their public signals to make a case for their policy preferences and to try to convince others of the merits of their policy position. Recall Neustadt's (1990) requirements for compliance to presidential leadership: presidential preferences must be clear in meaning and communicate a legitimate course of action by others. Signals are an effective way for presidents to persuade others so long as they need information provided by the president.

Signals Are Efficient Means of Communication

The public presidency shapes much presidential activity and responsibility (Brace and Hinkley 1992; Tulis 1987). Presidents spend significant time, energy, and resources on public relations (Edwards 1983; Grossman and Kumar 1981; Maltese 1994), and they are constrained by public expectations that require them to give public speeches and appear in public often (Edwards 1983; Waterman, Jenkins-Smith, and Silva 1999; Wayne 1982). Presidents, like all political actors, must satisfice. They must act rationally within myriad contextual and mental constraints and responsibilities (Simon 1957; March and Simon 1958). Speeches communicate to even the most casual follower of presidential politics that the president is in charge and that he is governing appropriately.

These same speeches that assure the public also inform elites of the president's policy priorities. News coverage associated with presidential statements, whether on television, on radio, or in newspapers, ensures presidents that if they discuss policy in their public speeches, interested legislators and bureaucrats will be aware of the president's position and his policy intentions. Since presidents are already devoting considerable time and energy to public activities to meet public expectations, using speeches to also help achieve their policy goals is an efficient course of action.

Presidents have several means of communication and influence beyond speeches at their disposal. They can send private memos to legislators or dictate policy to political appointees; they can meet with party leaders or cut an agency's budget. Presidents can also use legislative liaison, direct appeals,[2] or cabinet secretaries to communicate their preferences with legislators. Although presidents undoubtedly communicate their preferences in these ways, public speeches are the president's most efficient means of communication given a decentralized

Congress and vast, thickening federal bureaucracy. Previously, presidents could call on party leaders and committee heads to recruit votes for their policies. As party leaders have lost some of their internal power and influence (but see Bond and Fleisher 2000), committee seniority has waned, and individual members have begun to pursue their own reelection interests, presidents must persuade more legislators to ensure success. In Kernell's (1997) words, the presidential-congressional relationship has evolved from one of institutionalized pluralism, which favors bargaining, to individualized pluralism, which encourages presidents to cultivate public support as an alternative means of influence in the legislative arena. Signals are a means by which presidents can inform the entire legislative body of their preferences without having to spend inordinate amounts of time and resources courting each legislator individually.

In addition, with a larger federal bureaucracy, including four more departments (Education, Energy, Homeland Security, and Veterans Affairs) since 1970 and many more agencies and commissions, presidents cannot call on a few bureaucrats to carry out their policy directives. They must inform many individual bureaucrats of their policy preferences. Presidential signals are a means of communication that should penetrate all levels of the federal hierarchy and might alleviate some difficulties presidents face communicating their policy intentions to the bureaucracy (see Edwards 1980). That is, repeated communication of policy preferences through signals—so long as they are clear and consistent—will penetrate more layers of a thickening federal bureaucracy and increase the president's influence over the implementation of policy.

The President Must Lead

Presidents must lead to ensure that their preferences translate into policy outputs. By definition, the president as leader is more persuasive than the president as follower. Presidents may increase their success in Congress when they lead or set the agenda on a policy (see Bond and Fleisher 1990), and they should be effective in the bureaucratic arena if they devote their office resources to its management (Nathan 1983).

Signals are a clear indication of presidential commitment and concern for a set of policy preferences. They inform interested actors that the president is concerned with an issue, and this attention suggests that presidents will use their authority to work toward the success of that policy. Presidents want to signal their policy preferences to show others that they are in charge and that they intend to use whatever legitimate power they can to make sure that their policy preferences take hold. Without consistent or repeated signals, conversely, Congress and the bureaucracy may be left wondering whether the president is leading at all.

Through signals, a president attempts to lead, to set the tone and direction for a policy, hoping to persuade others to follow. Because leadership is "the capacity to impact and sustain direction" (Rockman 1984: 6) and requires "ideological commitment and assertiveness" (Shull 1993: 8), a president who signals repeatedly and asserts his policy preferences is leading on policy. Moreover, the president's power to lead through signaling is not a one-time, all-persuasive event. Successful signaling requires repeated presidential attention. A president's dedication to an issue, expressed publicly through signals, is a principal indicator of how effective signals may be. Because policy actors will address the president's policy concerns only if they notice signs of presidential commitment (Kingdon 1995: 28), the more a president discusses an area, the more likely it is that legislators or bureaucrats will know the president's preferences and use them to make an informed policy decision. Signals (or presidential public statements) are a clear indication of presidential commitment (see Bohte 1997; Edwards and Wood 1999; Light 1999; Shull 1983). Those preferences to which presidents give priority are likely to influence congressional activity (Covington, Wrighton, and Kinney 1995; Fett 1992) and possibly bureaucratic activity (Agency director interview 2005; Whitford and Yates 2003). Only if presidents repeatedly signal their preferences to a policy area, therefore, will they be an important source of presidential power, leadership, and influence in Congress and the bureaucracy.

Signals Complement Other Sources of Power

Signals are particularly important to the president's policy strategy because other presidential advantages do not consistently aid the president's goal achievement. Presidents may be able to persuade legislators when they have favorable reputations and public support, but these are limited sources of influence (see Bond and Fleisher 1990; Edwards 1989). Although presidents have had more success controlling the bureaucracy through formal powers, a lack of competent leadership may preclude the president's bureaucratic influence (Durant 1992; Wood and Waterman 1994). Thus, presidents signal because they need to, given the limits of other sources of influence. This is not to say that presidents will use signals alone to affect the policy process. Rather, presidents will use many means at their disposal to influence policy, with signals being an important source of the president's power.

The importance of signals relative to other sources of influence becomes clear if argued from a different perspective. Neustadt (1990) identified three primary forms of influence: reputation, skill, and prestige; each of these could influence the president's success over policy. These advantages cannot necessarily aid the president's success unless the president first signals his policy preferences. Let us take a popular president who does little in the way of policy leadership. Even though he is popular, if he does not signal his policy preferences to either institution, why would legislators or bureaucrats respond to him if they did not know what he stood for? What are the president's policy goals that he would use his popularity to achieve? Of course, favorable conditions—such as high approval ratings or a strong reputation—may improve the effectiveness of the president's signals, as signals are more likely to be influential when presidents find themselves in a favorable political environment. But the president must first inform and then demonstrate leadership and commitment through repeated signals to get others to do what they might not otherwise do.

At times, presidential signaling may coincide with other efforts of political control over the bureaucracy. Administrative clearance through the Office of Management and Budget is one way that presidents increase their power and influence over the federal bureaucracy (Cooper and West 1988), often at the expense of congressional influence (Barilleaux 1988). The rise of administrative clearance, being associated with rising bureaucratic discretion and increased presidential power and authority over the executive branch (Cooper and West 1988), has provided presidents since Ronald Reagan with a unique opportunity to improve public communications with the bureaucracy. In short, administrative clearance may increase the likelihood that policy views of the bureaucracy and the presidency coincide so that public signals may be geared specifically to increase agency morale and motivation, thereby increasing the agency's policy activities.[3]

Ultimately, signals may not compel legislators and bureaucrats to respond to the president when he is without skill, reputation, or prestige, but none of those advantages helps the president achieve his policy goals unless the president first informs the institutions of what he finds important. Signaling is a necessary, but perhaps not a sufficient, condition for presidential influence in Congress and the bureaucracy.

The Signaling Strategy

To achieve their policy goals through signaling, presidents may inform legislators and bureaucrats of their policy preferences either generally, by providing broad support for a policy area, or specifically, through support of acts before Congress or the bureaucracy. As a symbolic institution (Hinckley 1990), presidents offer broad policy support and direction to Congress and the bureaucracy on policy. Signals may at least influence the national policy agenda and, in turn, affect the decisions of bureaucrats and legislators and their policy outputs.[4] Even broad policy signals should affect policy outputs—or at least influence the policy agenda—because, as I argue below, legislators and bureaucrats need the president to ensure that they meet their own policy goals.[5]

In addition, presidents often time speeches to affect specific policies. One use of speeches is for presidents to inform Congress of their position and influence a bill that is up for a vote (Barrett 2004). Legislative signals may also take the form of a veto threat, which can lead to concessions by Congress, especially under divided government (Cameron 2000: 193). Through an administrative strategy (Nathan 1983), presidents may use signals to influence the vigor or languor with which bureaucrats implement specific policies, rules, or presidential directives (Carpenter 1996; but see Shull 1989). Whether presidents choose a broad or specific strategy, signaling is a means for presidents to express their preferences and to pressure government actors to favor their policy positions. Again, presidents signal their policy preferences to inform legislators and bureaucrats and to persuade them of the importance of their preferences, which may help presidents, legislators, and bureaucrats achieve their policy goals.[6]

Measuring Signals

Attention should be sufficient to assess presidential leadership through signals and their influence over public policy because two other attributes of signals—clarity and speech type—are subsumed in this research design. Undoubtedly, a clear and consistent message from the president will eliminate confusion that policymakers and implementers may have about the president's position. Presidential signals that are not clear in meaning are unlikely to affect the policy process because legislators and bureaucrats will not respond to presidential preferences if they do not know what the president stands for in the first place (Member of Congress [Texas] interview 2005). More often than not, presidents who contradict themselves in their public signals or who make public statements contradicting private action will undermine the reason for signaling in the first place.[7] Legislators who know that the president opposes a bill privately but calls on its passage publicly will simply discount the president's words, undermining the president's own attempts at public leadership. In a word, it is not rational for presidents to contradict themselves in this manner, so they rarely do so.

Besides, data for this project demonstrate that presidents are clear and consistent on their policy preferences when they speak about civil rights, clean air, or domestic farm policies (see Chapters 4, 5, and 6). In addition, clarity is not a sufficient condition for legislative or bureaucratic responsiveness.[8] Presidents who are crystal clear about their policy preferences but who communicate them infrequently are not leading on policy and, therefore, should not affect policy through signals, according to the theory of presidential signaling. Moreover, a single clear signal is unlikely to penetrate multiple layers of the federal bureaucracy or influence members in a decentralized Congress. Without sustained presidential leadership, legislators and bureaucrats are free to—and will—ignore the president's policy goals.

The type of speech presidents use to communicate their preferences may heighten bureaucratic and legislative responsiveness. Major addresses indicate a high level of presidential importance for an issue. Although rare because presidents have difficulty securing airtime for their national addresses, the nationally televised address is most likely to be heard by the most legislators and bureaucrats and is the clearest signal indicator of presidential commitment and concern to a policy area. The national address is a signal, in and of itself.

Although my models do not isolate the impact of specific national addresses on legislative and bureaucratic responsiveness, my measure of signals, as presidential attention to a policy area, accounts for the magnitude of a national address. Simply, the *Public Papers of the Presidents* will reflect the time and resources dedicated to a policy expressed through a national address. Because a president will devote more attention to a policy through a national address, it will encompass more page space in the *Papers* than a minor speech would. The importance of national addresses to the public notwithstanding, alone they are insufficient for affecting legislative and bureaucratic policy activities. It is important to note that the ratio of nationally televised addresses to total speeches has decreased over time, meaning that as presidents use their speeches more frequently to achieve their administration's goals, they have used the nationally televised addressed relatively less. Besides, presidents are rarely able to translate national speeches into more success in Congress (see Edwards 2003). Although there may be an added benefit to using national addresses to focus myriad policy actors on the president's policy preferences, he still needs a consistent and dedicated signaling strategy beyond a national address to maintain the focus of legislators and bureaucrats on the president's policy priorities. Much like a measure of signal clarity, if presidents give a national address but do not follow up with additional speeches, it is unlikely that legislators or bureaucrats will follow the president's policy preferences.

Informing policy elites of their policy preferences is the first step that presidents must take to affect the adoption and implementation of policy. Presidential signals are an efficient means of presidential communication because they can effectively penetrate multiple layers of a federal bureaucracy and reach the most legislators in a decentralized Congress. Numerous presidential signals also indicate leadership, such that legislators and bureaucrats are most likely to respond to the president when he leads on policy. For these reasons, I assess the effects that signaling attention to a policy area has on the president's influence over Congress and the bureaucracy.

Cue Taking

Cue taking is premised on a theory of cognitive shortcuts. It predicts that individuals with limited information[9] will find cues useful because, as mental shortcuts, they allow individuals to make consistent and effective decisions without having complete, or near complete, information. These mental shortcuts, signals, or cues are any communication—intended or unintended—with which signal users inform their decisions (see Matthews and Stimson 1975: 51).[10] Legislators use cues or signals because they need to process vast amounts of information with limited expertise in myriad areas on which they must vote (Matthews and Stimson 1975). They might use the votes of colleagues or information from relevant interest groups or congressional committees to inform their decisions. They might even use instructions from party leaders or respond to presidential speeches.

Cues or signals will only be helpful to a signal user if several conditions are met. As already alluded to, the signal user must first have a *need for cognitive efficiency*. I assume that individuals are boundedly rational, that they cannot comprehend all possible stimuli, whether helpful or deleterious to their own preferences. Individuals use signals as mental shortcuts to process a wide range of stimuli in an efficient manner while still being able to make a rational and relatively informed decision. Second, a signal must be *accessible* for one to use it in his or her decision. That is, someone must not only have signaled information but also have done so in an issue-specific area to which the signal user refers when making decisions. Third, the signal must be *relevant* to one's decisions (Mondak 1993: 189). If a signal is related to crime policy, but a legislator needs help voting on the environment, then the crime signal is clearly unhelpful. In addition, for the signal to be useful and effective it should originate from an actor known for past *reliability* (see Krehbiel 1991; Matthews and Stimson 1975: 50). Finally, the *nature of the relationship* between the signaler and the signal user conditions the signal's impact on a decision. If the signaler and signal user share a positive relationship, then the signal user is more likely to rely on a signal than if they have an unfriendly or untrustworthy relationship.

In their study of decisionmaking in the House of Representatives, Matthews and Stimson (1975: 80) identified several reasons why legislators will take cues or use signals. First, signals are legitimate if the signal user thinks that the signaler has a right to send signals in the first place. Only if a signaler is legitimate can he or she hope for responsiveness. Second, rewards are important. If the signaler is able to assist in the signal user's achieving her goals, then the signal user might respond to the signaler's preferences. Indeed, one is inclined to respond to cues when a signaler "is able to provide tangible assistance in the achievement of [the signal user's] goals" (Matthews and Stimson 1975: 80). A similar point of reference or perspective improves both of these prospects and increases the likelihood that she will respond to the signal. Cue theory frames why signaling is a useful strategy for presidents to influence policy in Congress and the bureaucracy. Detailed below are reasons why legislators and bureaucrats may respond to presidential signals.

Presidential Signals in Congress

Political scientists have long explored presidential-congressional relations. Although research highlights some conditions under which the president might be successful, more research demonstrates the limitations of presidential influence in Congress. Nevertheless, studies show empirically that public statements increase the president's success in Congress (see, among others, Barrett 2004; Canes-Wrone 2001; Fett 1994). The literature does not rely on a theory that has been tested or explicitly supported, however, nor does it examine in depth how speech effects might vary by policy type. Cue theory and the congressional decisionmaking literature provide a theoretical frame of reference by noting why legislators might respond to presidential signals.

Legislators Need Cues

Members of Congress have a difficult and complex job to do, with numerous decisions to make (Kingdon 1981; Matthews and Stimson

1975). The number of roll-call votes in either house of Congress might reach several hundred in a year. Legislators must also voice decisions and cast committee votes. These decisions are varied and complex. Legislators vote on a range of matters from agriculture subsidies to civil rights legislation, from the war on drugs to the regulation of air travel. Complex decisions on banking deregulation, space travel, and nuclear power are also part of legislators' voting résumés. The number, scope, and complexity of legislators' decisions dictate that, although they may be experts in a few areas, they cannot possibly know everything about all policies. Legislators need informative shortcuts to make their difficult jobs more manageable. Indeed, "when a member is confronted with the necessity of casting a roll-call vote on a complex issue about which he knows very little, he searches for cues provided by trusted colleagues who—because of their formal position in the legislature or policy specialization—have more information . . . to make an independent decision" (Matthews and Stimson 1970: 22–23). Once more, legislators need signals or cues to process an overwhelming amount of information amid myriad constraints, especially when they "possess low levels of issue-specific information" (Mondak 1993: 188).

Legislators frequently take cues from a variety of sources (Matthews and Stimson 1975: 60). Legislators will listen for signals from their districts and use them when clearly expressed by constituents (McCrone and Kuklinski 1979). Responding to constituency cues not only increases legislators' reelection chances but also ensures that legislators represent their constituents in accordance with democratic values. Legislators also use cues from congressional colleagues. Colleagues who are experts in complex policy areas or who are members of relevant committees can inform a complicated vote decision. Legislators who share a similar ideology also use each other's votes as cues. In addition, legislators who have used cues from trusted colleagues on past votes will look to them on future votes when constrained by time and limited information (Kingdon 1977: 576; Matthews and Stimson 1975: 84).

Presidential signals may also contribute to the efficient vote decisions of legislators (Matthews and Stimson 1975: 104) because they inform legislators of the president's position. Often legislators use the president's position to "define the nature of the issue" (Matthews and Stimson 1975: 104), especially in situations where the legislator is particularly ignorant about the policy issue and its potential consequences. Some legislators then use the president's preferences to mold their own vote decisions (Matthews and Stimson 1975: 106) and even vote with the president's position when the president places a high priority on the policy (Kingdon 1977: 578).

Legislators may even respond to presidential signals because of the president's access to expertise. Presidents have numerous experts on which to rely upon in the vast federal bureaucracy, in their own Executive Office of the President (where they can call upon economic and national security experts at a whim), and on commissions that they themselves create to address pressing concerns.[11] Certainly, if presidents are concerned with an issue, if they lead on an issue and try to persuade others of the merits of their positions, then presidents will likely use executive branch expertise to inform legislators and persuade them to support their policy priorities. As cue theory indicates, after all, expertise is one reason why legislators may use a cue or signal in the first place (Matthews and Stimson 1975), as they conserve their resources to make efficient, yet informed, decisions (Matthews and Stimson 1975; Mondak 1993; see Kingdon 1981).

Why Legislators Might Respond to Signals

In addition to needing signals from presidents to make efficient, yet informed, decisions, Congress may also respond to these signals for two primary reasons. First, the president's legitimacy, as legislative leader, encourages congressional responsiveness to signals (Matthews and Stimson 1975: 80). Constitutionally, presidents are required, from time to time, to deliver information on the state of the union. Legislators recognize modern presidents as legislative leaders because they need priorities from the president (Light 1999; Neustadt 1990: 155; Peterson 1990). Congress is composed of hundreds of members with varied interests and goals, and congressional collective action problems may be alleviated when presidents lead the policy process (see Moe 1989). Without policy leadership from the president, however, activity and legislation can easily stalemate.[12] Through signals, presidents denote their priorities and present legislators with an opportunity to focus their limited time and resources on legislation that stands a solid chance of becoming law. Kingdon (1981: 186) found, indeed, that a high-priority request from the president, on a bill that would otherwise fail without a legislator's support, can encourage responsiveness to presidential signals, especially if the legislator is of the president's party. In short, the president's legitimacy in the legislative process makes him a potential information source for legislators.

Second, signals may help legislators achieve their own policy goals. Absent an overwhelming majority in Congress, legislators need presidential support to achieve their policy goals. If legislators know the president will support their actions—as indicated through signals—they are more likely to devote their limited time and resources to a bill's passage.[13] Presidential support also aids legislators in their reelection chances. To enhance their reelection chances, legislators advertise, take positions, and claim credit (Mayhew 1974). Legislators need the president to sign legislation for which they can claim credit and increase their reelection chances. Without presidential support and a two-thirds majority, legislators are unlikely to achieve their policy goals. They may be better off crafting legislation acceptable to the president or using their limited time and resources for other projects. Signals help legislators anticipate the fruitfulness of their actions and whether the president will support legislators' own policy goals and reward their response with signed legislation.

How Signals Might Influence Congress

There are two ways in which signals may influence the activities of legislators. First, presidential signals may affect the legislative agenda. Because signals provide mental shortcuts to legislators and help set priorities for legislative action, signals should, at the very least, influence which policies Congress votes on in any given legislative session. Again, legislators need presidential priorities, and the nature of setting priorities is equivalent to setting the legislative agenda. Second, presidential signals may affect legislative outputs. Legislators will listen for and use signals from the president when those signals may help legislators decide how to vote on myriad roll-call votes (Kingdon 1981). In turn, presidential signals may influence whether a bill passes or fails to pass Congress.

Impediments to Influencing Congress with Signals

Despite the theoretical expectation that presidential signals can be an effective means of persuasion in Congress, presidential signals do not guarantee presidential influence in Congress. Past research underscores that the president's legislative skills, public approval, and agenda-setting powers are not assurances of presidential influence in Congress. Even those scholars who maintain that the president is a legitimate signaler for legislators' vote decisions suggest that presidential cues may have only a framing impact on the legislative process (Matthews and Stimson 1975). The president's signals help define the issue before Congress, but they do not ordinarily determine the legislator's vote decision. Kingdon (1981: chap. 6) argued that legislators rarely use presidential cues.[14] After all if legislators have colleagues, constituents, and interest groups to listen to, then they may not respond to presidential signals regularly. Political circumstances and possibly the issue area under debate—something that cue theorists do not consider in their work—will increase or decrease the likelihood that members of Congress will respond to the president's signals.

Some argue that members of Congress do not need the president at all to achieve their own policy goals. Jones (1994: 165) stated this point quite bluntly: "Although the government cannot do without a president, most of what the government does requires little or no involvement by the White House. There is a momentum to a working government that cannot be stopped or easily directed." In other words, most of what goes on in Congress and most of the president's success may be a product of factors outside of the president's control (see also Rockman 1984; Skowronek 1993).

Most important, legislators' primary motivation comes from their constituency (see, among others, Arnold 1990; Bond and Fleisher 1990; Fenno 1978; Kingdon 1981; Mayhew 1974). As single-minded seekers of reelection (Mayhew 1974), legislators value their constituents' preferences over any politician's. Legislators may ignore presidential overtures and vote in accordance with their constituency, particularly if constituent and presidential preferences conflict (Kingdon 1977: 578) or when constituents send clear cues to legislators on salient issues (see Miller and Stokes 1963). The reelection connection also renders fear of presidential retaliation a rare means of eliciting a signaling response. If the president is to coerce a legislator into responding to signals, he must convince the legislator's constituents to defeat him on Election Day. But of course, a president may be unlikely to factor into a legislator's reelection chances when incumbents are invariably reelected (Jacobson 1997), members of the president's party may lose their congressional seats at midterm, and the president has difficulty moving public opinion (Edwards and Eshbaugh-Soha 2001) or increasing an issue's public salience (Peake and Eshbaugh-Soha 2002). Furthermore, if other sources of presidential power, such as the president's job approval ratings, do not coerce legislators into supporting the president (Bond and Fleisher 1990), then it is highly unlikely that presidents can persuade a disinterested public into rejecting their own members of Congress.

Explaining the President's Success in Congress

Presidential success in Congress is a function of several variables. The primary independent variable for this study—presidential signals—may affect congressional voting for reasons underscored above: legislators need cues to process vast amounts of information in a complex and time-constraining environment. Yet the potential influence signals have over legislative decisions is a product of the interest and concern presidents dedicate publicly to public policy.

Presidential concern means that presidents have greater personal and political incentive to push for a policy's success. Presidents who are attentive to an issue, therefore, are likely to inform many legislators of their policy priorities. This attention should also communicate to legislators that presidents will use their advantages to achieve their policy goals. If presidents signal policy preferences, but do not follow up with additional signals, however, those signals will be ignored on balance. Legislators have their own interests; without presidential attention to encourage congressional responsiveness, legislators will naturally follow their own goals.[15]

Past research supports the claim that presidential attention through public statements can influence Congress (see, among others, Barrett 2004; Canes-Wrone 2001). Indeed, "the place an issue holds in the president's publicly revealed legislative agenda can affect legislators' voting decisions" (Fett 1992: 510). If presidents are attentive to an issue area, if they signal their policy preferences in a consistent and coherent manner, then Congress should respond to signals. Therefore, *more presidential attention to an issue, in the form of more signals, will increase the president's success in Congress.*

Attention also suggests the potential for presidential agenda setting. Presidents are adept agenda setters because they are the focal point of US politics (Kingdon 1995), and their policy requests typically receive space on the congressional agenda (Edwards and Barrett 2000). Moreover, policy actors will entertain the president's agenda only if they notice signs of presidential commitment (Kingdon 1995: 28). As a result, signals may influence the congressional policy agenda. Signaling is a means for presidents to express their preferences and set priorities for Congress. Legislators need priorities, after all, and presidential attention could be a source for them. Therefore, *more presidential attention to an issue, in the form of more signals, should influence the congressional policy agenda.* Furthermore, because presidents are more successful on policies to which they give priority than those on which they expend fewer resources (Covington, Wrighton, and Kinney 1995; Edwards 1989), *it is likely that presidents who do not affect the congressional agenda through signals will not increase their success on that policy through their signals.*

Although the president is a legitimate participant in the legislative process, he does not always lead it. To be sure, signals indicate whether a president will use his authority and advantages to influence legislation, yet the effectiveness of signals in Congress will fluctuate according to his standing in Congress. As developed in Chapter 2, other factors besides signals aid or limit the president in his quest for legislative success.

One factor that increases the president's success in Congress is his previous success. A president who has been successful in Congress should continue to be influential in Congress. Simply put, success breeds success, and failure leads to more failure. As Neustadt (1990: 53) explained, "the greatest danger to a President's potential influence with [legislators] is not the show of incapacity he makes today, but its apparent kinship to what happened yesterday, last month, last year. For if his failures seem to form a pattern, the consequence is bound to be a loss of faith in his effectiveness next time." An affirmative way to write this hypothesis is that *a president who has been successful will continue to be successful in Congress.*

Prestige, as Neustadt (1990) explained, is important to presidential influence in Congress. High levels of public opposition clearly limit presidential influence (Neustadt 1990: 76; Ostrom and Simon 1985), so lower public approval ratings could diminish the president's effectiveness in Congress. Although public support does not determine legislative success, approval ratings correlate strongly with it (Edwards 1989). Popular presidents are more successful than unpopular ones, controlling for party control of Congress (Bond and Fleisher 1990). Hence, *higher approval ratings should increase the president's success in Congress.* This hypothesis should vary by policy type. Legislators will be more cognizant of the president's popularity on issues about which their constituents are concerned. Hence, *the president's approval ratings should have a larger impact on his success on policies that have salient qualities than on policies that are complex or otherwise not salient* (see Canes-Wrone and de Marchi 2002).

Points of reference also matter to cue takers (Matthews and Stimson 1975: 80). The most obvious point of reference in presidential-congressional relations is political party. Legislators of the president's party are most likely to respond to signals because they identify with the president and share similar concerns (Clausen 1973; Jackson 1971; Kingdon 1981: 183). Same-party members are also more likely than opposition-party members to be loyal to the president's agenda and "prosecute" it on the floor of Congress (Hall 1996). The more seats the president's party controls in Congress, the greater the probability of presidential success (Bond and Fleisher 1990). Therefore, *a larger cohort of presi-*

dential party seats in Congress will increase the president's success in Congress.

Presidents who "hit the ground running" are often more successful than presidents who are not prepared with a legislative agenda when they arrive in Washington (Pfiffner 1988). Because of this, the president's honeymoon is important to the president's success in Congress. All presidents experience a limited honeymoon when they are more popular with the public, media, and Congress. The literature is clear that presidents have the greatest opportunity for legislative success during their first year in office (Light 1999; Pfiffner 1988), so *presidents will be more successful in Congress during their first-year honeymoons than during other years.*

A veto threat, a specific type of signal, may affect the president's success in Congress. One of the most powerful constitutional tools available to the president is his veto authority. If the president does not approve of a passed statute, he can veto it. Yet, vetoing a bill is costly to presidents and legislators, as both legislators and presidents desire good public policy. Because a compromise bill may be better than no bill at all, presidents can wield the threat of a veto to extract concessions from Congress instead of vetoing legislation outright. Veto threats lead to some concessions by legislators (Cameron 2000: 188), so *the president's success should increase with a veto threat.*

Attention devoted by the media to a policy is also relevant to a legislator's vote decisions. On some issues, especially civil rights and other policies with salient characteristics, legislators will listen and respond to their constituency's preferences (Miller and Stokes 1963). Media affect what the public thinks about, so media attention influences whether the public cares about an issue and whether legislators care about their constituents' concerns. Media attention, therefore, is a mitigating factor on the president's success and should have an independent effect on the president's success rate. The more measurably salient an issue is, the less likely legislators are to respond to the president's signals. Hence, *more media attention will limit the impact of presidential signals on his success in Congress.* This hypothesis, more than any other, will vary by policy type. The president's success on policies that have salient characteristics, such as civil rights, is more likely to be affected by media attention than other policy areas.

Combining all of these independent variables into an explanation of presidential success in Congress produces the basic linear model shown as Equation 3.1.[16]

$$\text{Success} = B_0 + B_1\text{Signals}_{t-1} + B_2\text{Congressional Makeup} + \qquad \textbf{3.1}$$
$$B_3\text{Past Success} + B_4\text{Approval} + B_5\text{Media Attention} +$$
$$B_6\text{Honeymoon} + B_7\text{Veto Threats} + \varepsilon$$

Presidential Signals in the Bureaucracy

Like legislators, bureaucrats also need mental shortcuts to make policy decisions. If presidential signals are accessible and relevant, cue theory suggests that bureaucrats will find signals helpful as they implement their policy mission. Bureaucrats are likely to respond to signals because presidents' have a hierarchical and constitutional legitimacy over the bureaucracy, and presidential signals facilitate policy implementation. Of course, bureaucrats have significant discretion over their own activity, and a lack of presidential leadership over a policy area means that bureaucrats will implement a policy consistent with their own mission, regardless of presidential preferences.

Bureaucrats Need Cues

Bureaucrats, like legislators and other individuals, are rational actors who operate under conditions of incomplete information. They are boundedly rational and look for mental shortcuts, cues, or signals as a way to process vast amounts of information in a complex environment. Clearly, bureaucrats are trained in their area of expertise. As "technocrats," they do not look to presidents for specifics about how to argue a criminal case in US district court, read air pollution monitors, or respond to a domestic farm emergency. Nevertheless, bureaucrats will take cues from presidents because they need mental shortcuts from the president, who happens to be the chief executive, the head of the vast federal bureaucracy.

Limited time and resources constrain an agency's propensity to achieve its policy goals, and few agencies are sufficiently large and resourceful enough to implement policy without leadership and priorities. If they act without proper guidance, agencies might be so unfocused as to be ineffective at implementing any aspect of their mission (see Landsberg 1997: 77). Presidential leadership may guide bureaucrats and focus their limited time and resources on the implementation of a handful of policy issues. Bureaucrats need not spend extra time and resources weighing alternatives and calculating the most effective way to implement different aspects to their mission. Presidential priorities, communicated by presidential signals, allow bureaucrats to focus their activity and maximize their time and resources in the implementation of their policy mission. Bureaucrats are likely to listen for signals for these reasons.

Why Bureaucrats May Respond to Signals

Bureaucrats have several reasons to respond to presidential signals. Although bureaucrats have considerable expertise in their policy area and do not need technical information about a policy to implement it, they need to know the president's position, given his legitimate authority over the executive branch. Signals are the most efficient and penetrating way for bureaucrats to know the president's position. Certainly, presidents inform the bureaucracy of their policy preferences, whether through executive orders, proclamations, memorandums, or messages through political appointees. But signaling occurs more frequently than these other sources of information. Moreover, signals may be more effective than these formal means of communication because signals have a greater potential to penetrate the bureaucracy and to be heard by bureaucrats given an ever-thickening federal hierarchy (Light 1995). After all, members of the bureaucracy often have an ear out for presidential statements on policies that interest them (Agency director interview 2005); they will hear the president's speeches, as delivered through the media, on policies that interest them.

Bureaucrats, much like legislators, should respond to presidential signals for two reasons. First, presidential signals are important to bureaucratic behavior precisely because the president has the constitutional authority to lead the bureaucracy. As chief executive, the president has influence over the bureaucracy, and he legitimizes bureaucratic behavior. Indeed, "choice by the executive branch is legitimized insofar as it can be plausibly seen to have radiated down from a presidential choice or preference" (Polsby 1978: 10). Bureaucrats are also rational to respond to signals because support from the chief executive is important to a bureaucrat's primary goal, to fulfill his agency's mission (Friedrich 1940; Long 1949; Meier 1993; Rourke 1969). The president's authority over the executive branch does not differ according to a bureaucrat's status. Both appointees and career bureaucrats ultimately tend to be loyal to presidents (Edwards 2000), suggesting that presidential signals should influence both appointees and career members of the bureaucracy. Presidential influence over an agency's policy outputs is therefore likely, because members of the bureaucracy are loyal and will consider the president's policy aspirations (Edwards 2000).

Second, bureaucrats may respond to presidential signals because presidents can help bureaucrats achieve their own policy goals. Presidential support for the bureaucrats' mission and policy goals facilitates bureaucrats' being able to achieve their policy goals. That is, supportive signals *motivate* the bureaucracy to implement policy; supportive signals enhance agency commitment and morale, leading to an increase in bureaucratic outputs. Organization theory teaches us, after all, that executive leadership succeeds according to the distribution of an economy of incentives (Barnard 1938). The executive is responsible for creating and maintaining a sense of purpose and moral code for organization, establishing a communications system, and "ensur[ing] the willingness of people to cooperate." An executive employs the method of incentives (specific inducements and the "method of persuasion") to promote organizational satisfaction and therefore effectiveness (Barnard 1938: 175–181). If a president mentions an agency's policy interests in his public statements, that is, if he signals support for the agency's policy goals frequently, bureaucrats may be motivated to implement the president's preferences.[17]

High-ranking officials in the federal bureaucracy concur. Presidential leadership through public speeches "seems to make a difference in agency morale and motivation." Although the "White House has leverage over what an agency does by what it says publicly," the president must sustain attention to an issue area through repeated addresses, not give a speech on a policy in what appears to be a response to political or media pressure (Agency director interview 2005). A director at a large federal department conceded, indeed, that presidents must respond to events in the news and dictate and attend to their own policy priorities. If an agency's policy concerns are not administration priorities—if they are not salient—the president is unlikely to discuss the issue frequently or have any real impact on the bureaucracy. In short, presidential attention through public statements should increase agency morale and lead to an increase in the conviction and activities of those bureaucrats, so long as the president makes the issue his own priority.

A speech from the George W. Bush administration and its impact are worth mentioning. On April 27, 2004, President Bush visited the Veterans Affairs (VA) hospital in Baltimore, Maryland. After his tour, the president delivered a lengthy speech about the cutting-edge technology that he saw at the hospital. Instead of appealing to the stereotype of the VA as a bloated, overstaffed, and inefficient federal bureaucracy, the president praised its efficiency in providing health care and promoting patient safety. Among other things, the president noted:

> You're about to hear an example from our Secretary and the administrator of this hospital and the assets here in Baltimore about forward thinking by people who care about the patients they serve. I know the veterans who are here are going to be proud to hear that the Veterans Administration is on the leading edge of change. That's what we expect. The taxpayers' money is being well spent . . . this system, when it gets advanced beyond the VA, will save American consumers a lot of money. If we're wise about how we use technology, we can save money.

According to an official in the Department of Veterans Affairs, this is one instance where the president's positive comments about the VA increased agency morale (Agency director interview 2005). It was so central to agency productivity that the agency reprinted and circulated the president's positive signals in internal memos and reports. People felt good about national recognition from the president, and the Department of Veterans Affairs organization took advantage of this by reminding its workers of the president's support. Although this anecdote does not demonstrate an actual increase in bureaucratic productivity, it provides suggestive evidence that positive signals can do so.

When Bureaucrats May Not Respond to Signals

Although bureaucrats are likely to respond to particularly positive presidential signals, the use of negative signals by presidents is unlikely to influence bureaucratic activity. When presidential and bureaucratic goals conflict, bureaucrats may use their discretion, their ability to implement their own goals and preferences, to ignore or at least not to respond to presidential signals. A bureaucrat's primary goal is to implement his or her mission. Unless a congressional statute or executive order clearly changes that mission, a bureaucrat will proceed as he or she has been doing with the inertial qualities of the federal bureaucracy, implementing his or her policy mission.

Disagreement and conflict also produce shirking, requiring intensive follow-up and review on the part of the president and his administration. The organizational relationship is cooperative, not one of command or fiat. Subordinates have a "zone of acceptance" outside of which they will not allow superiors to alter their behavior voluntarily (Simon 1957). Coercive signaling increases the costs to the president. A negative signal might communicate the president's policy preferences, but again, a bureaucrat is free to ignore these signals if they conflict with his or her mission.

At times, the bureaucracy may simply be unable to respond to presidential criticisms. As Durant (1992) has shown, agencies that are crippled by budget cuts or otherwise doing all that they can to implement the president's priorities have little room to respond to a presidential criticism or change their mission. Although bureaucrats want to be responsive (Agency director interview 2005), an agency that is doing all that it can do might only be able to fine-tune its actions; responsiveness, if it does occur, will likely occur only at the margins.

The president cannot expect bureaucrats to alter their mission simply because he disagrees with it and happens to say so publicly. When the president's goals conflict with an agency's, presidents are only likely to alter the direction of any agency's outputs by using their formal tools of influence—budgets and appointments (Wood 1988). In other words, only when the president severely undercuts the agency's ability to do what it was designed to do, may the president consistently alter the direction of an agency's policy outputs.

Explaining Presidential Influence in the Bureaucracy

The key to successful signaling in the bureaucracy is presidential attention to a policy area. To influence the bureaucracy through signals, presidents must first convey their preferences to the bureaucracy. Then, to increase agency responsiveness, presidents must show commitment, concern, and leadership in support of a policy area. If a president does not communicate a consistent theme, is not attentive to an area, or attempts to alter an agency's mission through signals, bureaucrats have discretion to ignore the president's preferences.

Constitutional authority alone does not mandate responsiveness to presidential signals. Presidents cannot simply command a bureaucrat or an appointee to implement policy in a certain way. They must follow up and publicize their policy preferences to increase the likelihood of influence (Neustadt 1990). Although Moe (1985: 1101; see Moe 1982) argued that the president can lead the bureaucracy "because he occupies the office of the president," presidents need to communicate their preferences so that bureaucrats know how to follow presidential preferences on specific policies. To influence the bureaucracy, after all, "the president must set and communicate a consistent theme and then motivate bureaucracies to respond" (Meier 1993: 178). With sufficient leadership and their constitutional prerogative, presidents can expect career bureaucrats to be responsive and to follow administration requests (Pfiffner 1988: 100–102). Therefore, the president's policy statements should affect bureaucratic outputs, so long as the president is attentive to and regularly discusses the agency's policy concerns.[18] More presidential signals will increase presidential influence over bureaucratic implementation.

Presidents might be able to control the bureaucracy through positive and motivational signals or through negative and coercive ones.[19] Positive signals build public support and agency morale, both of which motivate bureaucrats to do a better job. Presidents who agree with an agency's mission will use positive signals and incentives to motivate bureaucrats to do more. Negative signals encourage an agency to stop what it is doing or at least alter its policy focus. Presidents who disagree with the agency's policy mission will use coercion (budget cuts or unfavorable appointments) to decrease an agency's outputs or alter its policy focus.

As already discussed above, presidents should find it much easier to push an agency to do more in accordance with its mission than to prevent it from acting out its task demands; honey catches more flies. Moreover, signals that elicit fear of retribution must rely on intensive follow-up and review, which makes presidential control difficult or at least successful only with drastic and direct measures, such as substantial budget cuts (Wood 1988). Positive signals do not force the alteration of an agency's policy mission; they simply push it to work harder in the same policy direction. Therefore, *positive signals will increase an agency's output, whereas negative signals will have little impact on decreasing an agency's activity.*

The measurable salience of issues may also affect the extent to which presidents influence the bureaucracy. When the news media cover a policy area, bureaucrats are more likely to respond to political actors; they are more likely to "look over their shoulders" (Gormley 1986) and follow political leadership than on issues that are not on the national agenda. Media coverage (or measurable salience) provides incentives for bureaucratic responsiveness to elected officials and should therefore increase the likelihood that bureaucrats will respond to political actors. In other words, *more media attention to a policy area will increase the likelihood that bureaucrats will respond to the president.*

It is also possible that a president's standing with the public may encourage bureaucratic responsiveness. Just as higher approval ratings provide presidents will more political capital in dealing with Congress, it is likely that high approval ratings also supply presidents with more political capital in dealing with the bureaucracy. A popular president is insulated from public backlash and may be more likely to use his formal tools to control the bureaucracy, even when doing so may be controversial.[20] Hence, *the more popular a president is, the more likely bureaucrats are to respond to him.* The effects of media attention and presidential approval ratings will vary by policy type: bureaucrats who implement those policies that have salient aspects are more likely to respond to these variables than bureaucrats who implement nonsalient or complex policies.

The president's constitutional powers will likely affect the president's control of the federal bureaucracy. Indeed, three of these factors should have independent effects on bureaucratic implementation beyond presidential signals. First, political appointees have a good deal of influence over their rank-and-file bureaucrats, whether by directing the everyday activities of bureaucrats or acting as a conduit between presidential directives and bureaucratic outputs. Appointees can act on behalf of the president, augmenting his signals and providing additional leadership. Presidential appointment authority is an important tool available to presidents in their attempts to control the bureaucracy (Wood and Waterman 1994).

Second, budgets can influence the bureaucracy (Carpenter 1996; Wood and Waterman 1994). The bureaucracy needs an adequate budget to function and survive, and without sufficient resources, federal agencies have difficulty implementing policy effectively (Wood 1988). Therefore, an agency's budgetary resources might really drive bureaucratic outputs, whether or not presidents signal their policy preferences to the bureaucracy. Given slack resources (Wood 1988), inertial aspects to the budget process (Wildavsky 1984), and the ability of bureaucrats to implement their policy mission without typically having adequate staff and resources, budget cuts have to be significant to have an impact on bureaucratic outputs. Moreover, they need to be clear from both the president and Congress (Krause 1996). Hence, *significant budget cuts will decrease an agency's implementation activity.*

Finally, the president is not the bureaucracy's sole principal (Aberbach 1990; Arnold 1979; Ogul 1976; Weingast and Moran 1983). Congress has both oversight and budgetary powers to monitor bureaucratic activity. In particular, Congress may send its own signals to the bureaucracy, whether in support of or opposition to its activity, and influence bureaucratic outputs. The courts may also affect the bureaucracy (West 1995). Court decisions may constrain or expand opportunities for bureaucratic action. Clearly, if Congress and the president tell the bureaucracy to implement a law, and the courts later declare it unconstitutional, then bureaucrats are bound to this final arbitration, not the former principals' decisions. Interest groups also play an important role in bureaucratic implementation. Groups tend to dominate access points to the implementation phase of public policy (Lowi 1979). For some areas, such as farm policy, interest groups are prominent players in ensuring that public policy meets the demands and concerns of their members.

This model of presidential influence in the bureaucracy is expressed linearly in Equation 3.2.

$$\text{Policy Implementation} = B_0 + B_1 \text{Signals}_{t-1} + B_2 \text{Congress} + B_3 \text{Courts} + B_4 \text{Approval} + B_5 \text{Media Attention} + B_6 \text{Appointments} + B_7 \text{Budget} + B_8 \text{Interest Groups} + \varepsilon \qquad \textbf{3.2}$$

Once more, presidential control of the bureaucracy is a function of many variables. The president's formal tools of control, such as budgetary and appointment or removal powers, are of vital importance to presidential leadership of the bureaucratic agencies. Although previously ignored by political scientists, signals should also be influential. Signals that support an agency's mission will be most effective because they help bureaucrats achieve their own policy mission.

Why Signals?

The theoretical argument for this book centers on why presidents will use their speeches to affect the policy process and why legislators and bureaucrats will respond to them. But why might signals be influential when the president has numerous advantages (as Neustadt [1990] called them) in Congress or formal tools of influence in the bureaucracy?

Signaling theory relies on cue theory, a theory of mental shortcuts. Presidential signals communicate to legislators and bureaucrats the president's intent to lead on which policies. Moreover, signaling theory assumes that legislators and bureaucrats know that the president has formal and informal tools that influence the policy process and play a legitimate role in the adoption and implementation of public policy. Legislators know whether the president is popular, reputable, or trustworthy; they know he is a legitimate actor in the policy process and that he can provide support for their policy goals. Bureaucrats know that the president has the power to request budget cuts or increases for an agency and appoint or remove subordinates. What they need to know, again from a standpoint of cognitive efficiency, is where the president stands on policies that concern them, whether the president intends to lead, and how he intends to do so.

Surely, legislators and bureaucrats realize that the president's power varies by his political standing. Because of this, they will look for and respond to signals from a president in a favorable political environment. The tenuous nature of the president's political environment is why signaling effectiveness is likely mixed. Signals are not a guarantee of presidential power, nor do I argue that they are. Signals complement presidential powers and are one among several arrows in a quiver of presidential influence. Legislators and bureaucrats need to know the president's preferences, and as long as he is politically viable—so long as he can act on his signals—they will respond to signals to meet their need for cognitive efficiency. They will anticipate that the president can act on his signals and will therefore respond to the signals, not his actions.

In short, legislators and bureaucrats need and look for mental short-cuts. They respond to signals because signals satisfy this need. Legislators and bureaucrats know that the president is a legitimate actor in the policy process and that he can support or ignore their policy goals. Given a favorable political environment, one that allows the president to act on his signals, legislators and bureaucrats should respond to the president's signals. As developed in the next section, the effectiveness of signals varies more than just by the political environment in which presidents find themselves. The type of policies on which the president signals also explains why legislators and bureaucrats may respond to them and whether presidents will signal at all.

The Conditioning Effects of Policy

Policy has an enormous impact on political processes (Lowi 1972). Members of Congress tend to represent their constituents differently on distinct issues (Erikson 1978; Hill and Hurley 1999; Miller and Stokes 1963; see MacRae 1970). Presidential leadership of the public, media, and Congress also varies by policy type. Presidents lead public opinion on civil rights issues, but only in the short term, and they have affected the public's attitude on foreign affairs (J. Cohen 1995; Hill 1998). Presidential agenda-setting skills and their impact on congressional and media agendas also vary by policy issue (Edwards and Wood 1999; Peake 2001).

Conditioning effects of policy are likely for not only the adoption (see Clausen 1973) but also the implementation of public policy (Wood and Waterman 1994). Because of this, policy type should more finely differentiate the degree to which presidential signals affect policy out-puts. But what is it *about* different policies that is important to signals? Gormley (1986) argued that political processes surrounding regulatory policies differ according to the salience and technical complexity of a policy issue. I apply his insight to all public policies and use his typology to select three policy areas with which to test my theory of presidential signaling.

Different levels of complexity and salience affect the dynamics of the policy process and offer different incentives for actors to participate in the policy debate. Salience pushes elected leaders to deal with an issue. A salient policy affects a sizable portion of the general population (Gormley 1986: 598), and salience demands that elected representatives respond to the public or face electoral consequences and a decline in public support. When a policy is salient, bureaucrats are particularly wise to listen to elected politicians. Indeed, "bureaucrats are not free to do as they please. They must constantly look over their shoulders at politicians who refuse to relinquish control over [these] vital decisions" (Gormley 1986: 610). Bureaucrats might respond to either Congress or the presidency when a policy is salient, depending on other factors specific to the creation and development of the implementing agency. Salience might also change over time as a problem worsens, demographics change, or the issue is redefined (Gormley 1986: 599).[21]

Complexity encourages policy adoption and implementation outside of the public eye. If a policy is technically complex, politicians are unlikely to look to the public for guidance. They are not motivated by electoral or other democratic concerns to adopt complex policies. Instead, politicians will look for expert opinion to inform their decisions on complex policies or defer to experts to make policy decisions. Deciding complex policies requires expertise, and cues from experts provide sufficient information to make a complex policy decision. Because they are experts, bureaucrats are likely to dominate the implementation of complex policies without much political oversight. Complexity refers to technical issues that cannot be addressed or answered by the average person. Technically complex policy requires "specialized knowledge and training" (Gormley 1986: 598). Complexity is less malleable than salience, and for the policies under investigation for this study, remains constant.

Presidential signals may influence Congress and the bureaucracy when a policy is not complex. Expertise is a common reason why people rely on cues from others (Matthews and Stimson 1975). Presidents are typically not experts in many policy areas, so legislators and bureaucrats may be more likely to look for presidential signals when expertise is not an important reason for using signals.[22] Many presidential signals will indicate support or opposition for a policy, but few will be laden with policy specifics and technically complex explanations (see Hinckley 1990). When a policy is not complex, furthermore, bureaucrats will look to elected officials for guidance, according to Gormley (1986), because they cannot hide behind their expertise. Rather, they must be cognizant of and responsive to democratic values. Even though legislators are free to use other cues in their vote decisions, they may be more likely to respond to presidential signals on uncomplicated than on complex policy areas.

Complex issues typically preclude responsiveness to presidential signals. Legislators will look for signals from experts on complex issues. Presidential signals are unlikely to be effective over complex policies because legislators and bureaucrats will not look to the president—a policy generalist—on complex issues. Experts in the policy area might look to the president for his position, but even if these legislators respond to the president's signals on complex policies, they will be few in number (given the decentralized specialization of Congress) and unlikely to influence the president's overall influence in Congress. When a policy is complex, bureaucrats have a monopoly on expertise and provide it to others through their own cues, letters, and memorandums. Bureaucrats, who are experts in their policy areas, are unlikely to respond to presidential signals when they have already researched the best ways to implement a policy.

Salient issues are most amenable to presidential leadership through signals. Presidents have an incentive to discuss a policy area that is relevant to the public. Salience demands that presidents and other public leaders deal with an issue or face public retaliation, such as a loss of support or election defeat. Indeed, sometimes presidents are forced to deal with an issue that they would not have otherwise because media and public attention mandate that they do (Edwards and Wayne 1999: 175). Although presidents cannot typically increase an issue's salience, they must be able to take advantage of favorable situations—in this case, a salient policy area—to influence policy through their signals. If a policy area is not salient, however, presidents have little incentive to dedicate limited time and public resources to that policy. Presidents may direct cabinet secretaries to implement policies that most of the public is unaware of, but they are not likely to use public statements to signal those ends.

Salience and complexity dimensions of public policy should condition the effectiveness of presidential signals because they offer different incentives to politicians and bureaucrats to participate in the policy process. When incentives encourage presidential leadership, presidential signals should affect the policy activities of legislators and bureaucrats. When policies constrain or restrict incentives for presidential leadership, signals should not be effective. In other words, those policies that are salient yet not complex—such as civil rights—should encourage responsiveness to presidential signals. Those policies that are complex yet not salient should preclude the effectiveness of signals as a tool in the adoption or implementation of public policy. Hypothetically speaking, *signals on salient policies will increase the president's influence over congressional and bureaucratic activity; signals on complex policy will not increase presidential influence in Congress and the bureaucracy.*

Of course, just as salience increases presidential signaling effectiveness, it also encourages legislative responsiveness to constituency cues. A legislator's constituency is his primary motivation. If a policy is salient, then constituents should be more active in expressing their preferences, encouraging legislators to respond to constituents. When an issue is salient, legislators will consider their constituency first (Kingdon 1977: 578). Hence, salience may dissuade legislators from responding to presidential signaling and instead encourage them to take cues from constituents. Despite its usefulness, therefore, Gormley's typology cannot by itself differentiate between which elected officials will have greater influence over civil rights policy in the bureaucracy. Both presidents and legislators have incentives to prefer salient and not complex policies.

Because salience may be a mitigating factor in the process of presidential signaling, the independent effects of media attention (a measure of salience, or a policy's measurable salience) must be modeled to accurately assess to whom legislators and bureaucrats, as the case may be, are responding. After all, salience may independently impact the signaling process, meaning that legislators and bureaucrats may respond to an issue's salience, not to the president's signals. Media attention to an issue, in other words, could affect policy outputs independent of the president's signals. Hypothetically speaking, *the more attention media devote to a policy issue, the more congressional and bureaucratic activity will increase.*

Three distinct policy types, based on the salience-complexity dimensions of Gormley's (1986) policy typology and the expectations therein, provide an opportunity to test policy variations in presidential signaling. Civil rights policy is salient and not complex; clean air regulation is salient, yet complex; and farm policy is not salient, yet complex. This range of policies assures variance across dependent variables and leads to different expectations for presidential signaling in Congress and the bureaucracy. Legislators and bureaucrats are most likely to respond to signals on civil rights policy yet least likely to respond to signals on farm policy. Clean air policy, detailed in Chapter 5, is a special case, as it provides conflicting incentives for bureaucratic responsiveness.

Summary

This chapter builds a theoretical foundation for explaining the direct linkage between presidential speeches and the president's influence in Congress and the bureaucracy. According to the theory of presidential signaling, the president's policy statements should have a direct, informative effect on the policy decisions of legislators and bureaucrats.

Presidential signals set priorities that help legislators and bureaucrats make policy decisions despite their limited time and resources. Legislators and bureaucrats should respond to presidential signals, in addition, because they need the president's support to achieve their own policy goals. Bureaucrats, in particular, should respond solely to positive signals, as these signals may motivate bureaucrats to implement their policy missions more vigorously. In the face of goal conflict, bureaucrats are free to ignore presidential preferences and act on their mission.

Of course, presidents signal because doing so is an efficient way for them to influence congressional and bureaucratic policy outputs and achieve their policy goals. Presidents are rational to use speeches to affect policy, speeches they already have to make to meet public expectations. Moreover, presidents need signals to augment other limited sources of influence. Given sufficient attention and leadership, presidents will inform and possibly persuade legislators and bureaucrats that they should adopt or implement the president's policy preferences. The guiding proposition of this theoretical argument is therefore quite simple: the more attentive presidents are, the more influence they will have over congressional and bureaucratic outputs.

Because policy affects politics, the signaling relationship hinges on the policy area in which the president sends signals. Three policy areas that vary by salience and complexity—civil rights, clean air, and domestic farm policy—help illuminate the conditional impact of policy that presidential signals have on Congress and the bureaucracy. In Chapter 4, I begin my discussion of the success presidents have had in influencing the policy activities of legislators and bureaucrats through signals with a policy area that is primarily salient: civil rights policy.

Notes

1. This seems like common sense, that we are more likely to be drawn to topics in the news that interest us. Indeed, in a personal interview, I confirmed with my source that bureaucrats pay attention to presidential news, with an ear toward presidential speeches on their agency or policy area (Agency director interview 2005).

2. A former member of Congress stated that he was predisposed to support the president if the president made a personal appeal (Member of Congress [Texas] interview 2005).

3. I thank a reviewer for raising this point. Although I do not explore this claim further, perhaps future research can do so through hypothesis testing.

4. We see this, in part, during the early stages of President George W. Bush's intention to reform Social Security. Although he did not announce a spe-

cific and detailed plan nor comment specifically on legislation before Congress, his general, public attention to Social Security encouraged Congress to at least discuss the issue of Social Security reform. Whether or not the president's signals affect his eventual success in reforming Social Security is a topic for future inquiry.

5. My work differs from Bose's (1998) work on signaling. Whereas I examine public signals, she explored the impact of private signals on presidential decisionmaking.

6. An interesting and supportive anecdote: As many legislators do, Senator John McCain of Arizona discussed his policy interests with Tim Russert on *Meet the Press* on March 18, 2001. McCain answered questions ranging from campaign finance reform to his relationship with newly elected President George Bush. McCain indicated that he used the president's public statements, expressed through the media, to learn about the president's position on tax cuts. Indeed, "I think that it's from the media that the president is willing to negotiate on those, including perhaps some cap on the real estate taxes." In other words, the president signaled his preferences, and Senator McCain used these to inform his own vote decision. What is important, of course, is whether Bush's signals were persuasive enough to convince McCain to support the president's tax package. Bush's repeated emphasis on taxes could have persuaded McCain and other senators' votes. A modified version of Bush's tax plan did pass, without the support of the senator from Arizona.

7. President George W. Bush did just this in 2001, taking a position against the farm bill but urging its passage in his public statements.

8. Alternative model specifications in the empirical chapters indicate that clarity has no impact on bureaucratic implementation of congressional voting. Measured as the proportion of supportive to total signals, clarity does not significantly affect the dependent variables.

9. Technically, we could call these individuals "boundedly rational."

10. A reader may ask: If presidential signals do not specifically target either the Congress or the bureaucracy, does this mean that presidents are unaware of the power of their signals or that we should not count an effect of signals unless the president makes explicit reference to a bill, an agency, or an implementation strategy? The answer, as the reader may have already gathered, is no. Presidents make statements on public policy when they have a preference for that policy, but it is up to a legislator or bureaucrat to use or respond to the president's policy signals, whether or not the president intends for them to use them. In other words, it is not the specific intent of the president to speak specifically to Congress or a federal agency that matters to the success of a presidential signal. The key is whether a legislator or bureaucrat sees a signal as relevant to his or her decision and whether he or she then responds to it. Of course, as a strategic actor (see Eshbaugh-Soha 2005), the president acts purposively and it would be unlikely that he would deliver a policy-specific statement without knowing that Congress or the bureaucracy would pay attention. At the same time, the president's intent to move public opinion, increase media attention, or affect the legislative process through any number of means is not always successful. So, once again, even if presidents mean to affect policy, they may not; it is up to the actor, the legislator or bureaucrat, to accept, use, and respond to the president's signals.

11. In January 2005, President George W. Bush commissioned a panel of

experts to address the Social Security crisis. Ronald Reagan did this in 1983, and President Clinton suggested a similar commission during his presidency.

12. George H. W. Bush offered his own clean air legislation that contributed to congressional action on major air pollution regulations. Many of the publicly accessible letters and memos (available at the George Bush Presidential Library) on clean air legislation support the point that presidential leadership can make the difference between passed and stalemated legislation. Members of Congress, in particular, were adamant about Bush's providing an aggressive and comprehensive proposal to guide legislators' clean air policy decisions (see also at the George Bush Presidential Library, HE007-01, Boxes 59–64). Without presidential leadership, it is unclear that clean air regulations would have been strengthened in 1990.

13. Clean air legislation was not debated heavily during the 1980s because Ronald Reagan preferred not to support major clean air regulations. George H. W. Bush, on the other hand, signaled to Congress that he was willing to support a new Clean Air Act. Legislators had a clear incentive—from the president's signals—to pursue clean air policy because they had a reasonable chance of securing those policy goals.

14. This claim should be placed in its proper context: legislators cast several hundred roll-call votes per year; presidents take positions on only a handful of these votes. Thus, most of the time, the president is not even part of the legislative process, discouraging legislators from looking for presidential cues on most issues.

15. Legislators can always follow their own goals, irrespective of presidential preferences. They are more likely, however, to consider presidential policy goals if they know what the president's positions are and that the president is concerned and interested in a policy area. Attention through signals conveys this to legislators.

16. Equation 3.1 presents a parsimonious and unidirectional model of signals. A more accurate reflection of empirical reality may be that presidents also respond to activity in Congress or the news media. My model explains congressional voting, even though it and other explanatory variables may also have a reciprocal or independent impact on the president's own tools of influence. Equation 3.1 ensures some definitive impacts of presidential signals, despite the possibility for reciprocal influences on the president's signaling powers. As I clarify in the subsequent policy chapters, I lag presidential signals in my models to satisfy the time-order criterion for causality. Even though presidents may signal in response to the political environments in Congress, the time lags are a simple and parsimonious way to test clearly that the relationship that I have hypothesized exists: presidents affect congressional voting with their signals. I address these issues of complex causality and other pitfalls of parsimony further in the concluding chapter of this volume.

17. Numerous anecdotes support the basic tenor of this argument. Upon his visit to Iraq on Thanksgiving Day 2003, President George W. Bush undoubtedly increased troop morale, increasing the motivation and conviction of the troops as they attempted to achieve their goals and mission.

18. A director in the Department of Veterans Affairs reiterated this point several times (Agency director interview 2005).

19. A good deal of the research on political control of the bureaucracy employs a principal-agent model (see, among others, Moe 1985; Wood 1988).

Because principal-agent models assume goal conflict, however, and because my theory leaves open the strong possibility that presidents and bureaucrats will agree on public policy, a principal-agent model is not appropriate across all presidents. I do not make use of principal-agent models in my theory, even though they could help explain the effectiveness of presidential signals amid goal conflict with an agency.

20. Lacking any scholarly evidence to support this point, I refer to Reagan's efforts early in his tenure to limit environmental protections. When he was relatively popular in early 1981, he used budget cuts and appointments to affect EPA clean air enforcement activity. When the public became dissatisfied with the Reagan administration, President Reagan removed his controversial EPA director, appointed a more EPA-friendly director, and refrained from cutting the EPA's budget further.

21. Because of this, I refer to salience in terms of a broad characteristic of public policy and whether a policy is "measurably salient" at a given time. Two of my three policy types, civil rights and clean air, have broad salient characteristics. When media attention to these policies is high, they are also measurably salient.

22. Presidents may be "experts" in the eyes of legislators on some issues. But this expertise comes from the president's institutional expertise. A generalizable theory across institutions must make claims about how a president will interact with both institutions. Moreover, although legislators may look to presidents for the expertise that presidents receive from key actors in the Executive Office of the President or the larger federal bureaucracy, legislators are still likely to respond to their expert colleagues first, even on complex issues (Matthews and Stimson 1975).

4

WHEN SIGNALING WORKS

LYNDON JOHNSON WAS NEVER A GREAT ORATOR. DELIVERING ALL speeches from behind a monstrous podium nicknamed "mother," Johnson read stiffly from prepared text. He was terrified of making the slightest grammatical mistake or ad-libbing overly "colorful" language. Accordingly, "he projected an image of feigned propriety, dullness, and dishonesty" (Kearns 1976: 303). Most people would maintain that clearly it was not President Johnson's speaking style that contributed to his early legislative victories. That Johnson cajoled and prodded committee chairs over the phone, that he towered over senators of much shorter stature, and that he would persist until a representative's nay became a yea is the foundation for Johnson's legendary success as a legislative president. Johnson spent years in Congress, after all, and he knew how the institution worked. He knew who to call, where to introduce a bill, and when to push for a vote. The American people, historians teach us, had to wait for more than ten years for another orator with the skill and charisma necessary to lead the US public.

This depiction of Lyndon Johnson ignores a central aspect of the Johnson presidency and all other presidencies that followed: despite their speaking inadequacies (see Edwards 1989: 128–131 for a synopsis of several presidents' speaking shortcomings), all modern presidents have used speeches to motivate, cajole, and inform. The bully pulpit coupled with the expanding use of television in US politics provided opportunities for presidents to use their public speeches to affect public policy. Johnson's appeals not only forced legislators to consider the importance of historic civil and voting rights measures but also arguably increased morale at the Department of Justice. It is arguably through Johnson's public speeches, not only his powers of personal persuasion,

63

that he was able to champion the success of a salient, however contro-versial, set of policies.

Presidential signals, like those Johnson delivered on civil rights pol-icy, are a potential source of influence over the policy activities of legis-lators and bureaucrats for reasons developed in Chapter 3. An analysis of archival resources from the presidential libraries and quantitative data of civil and criminal civil rights cases filed in US district court and civil rights roll-call votes on which presidents took positions shows that pres-idents have successfully used their signals to influence the adoption and implementation of civil rights policy. It is the nature of civil rights poli-cy, that it is salient yet uncomplicated, that conditions this expectation.

Conditions for Success:
Salience and a Lack of Complexity

Public policy type should affect the propensity of presidents to signal their policy preferences and of legislators and bureaucrats to respond to them. Although political scientists have long understood the variation across public policies (Lowi 1972), few scholars of presidential-con-gressional and presidential-bureaucratic relationships have systematical-ly explored variation across broad policy characteristics. Gormley's (1986) salience-complexity policy typology allows an examination of systematic variation by public policy in the context of presidential sig-naling in Congress and the bureaucracy.

Two characteristics of public policy—salience and a lack of com-plexity—provide the best opportunity for presidential leadership and, therefore, legislative and bureaucratic responsiveness. Presidential lead-ership takes place in the public eye. Hence, presidents have an incentive to discuss those policies that the public is most likely to understand (or form an opinion about) and be affected by. The theory of direct signal-ing predicts that with more attention devoted to a policy area, legislators and bureaucrats will respond to presidential attention to a policy area and will therefore respond to presidential signals.

These characteristics of civil rights policy encourage action from presidents, legislators, and bureaucracy. Civil rights policy is not com-plex. Even a civil rights policy that is complicated from a tactical stand-point, such as busing, does not require a technical understanding. Parents will find out how busing affects their children and in what way and will form an opinion without necessarily understanding the com-plexity behind busing as a solution for years of segregation. Civil rights policy is easy to understand, and citizens usually have an opinion about it, whether voting rights, busing, or affirmative action (Page and Shapiro 1992: 70).

Moreover, civil rights policy concerns a sizable portion of the population and is therefore salient (Gormley 1986). A government's decision to remedy segregation through busing, for example, affects numerous groups and individuals. It affects those who ride buses across town to attend school. The bus ride across town lengthens their days, possibly affecting their performance in schools. It affects those students originally enrolled in the school, whether by losing friends to busing or having to make new ones. It also affects commuters, who have to contend with cross-town buses, their frequent stops, and bursts of diesel emissions.

A History of Civil Rights for African Americans

Race and civil rights have been prominent issues in US politics since the ratification of the Constitution in 1789. Systematic denial of civil rights to African Americans, other minorities, and women characterized the first seventy years of the Republic. Congress and the states ratified several amendments to alleviate the burden of race, yet legal roadblocks limited the suffrage of African Americans. The modern civil rights movement, which began with the creation of the Civil Rights Section of the Department of Justice at the behest of President Franklin D. Roosevelt in 1939 (McMahon 2004) and continued with the desegregation of the armed forces following World War II,[1] led to voting rights, equal employment opportunities, and higher standards of living for African Americans.

Presidents have played a central role throughout the modern civil rights movement. Civil rights leaders often implored the president to champion legislation or speak out against egregious and public violations of minorities' civil rights (Graham 1990). In one striking act of leadership, President John F. Kennedy delivered a national address on civil rights. Not only did he please his liberal constituency who demanded presidential leadership on civil rights, but also he focused the attention of the US public on civil rights (Bohte 1997). His rhetoric stimulated debate on comprehensive civil rights legislation and provided momentum for the Civil Rights Act (CRA) of 1964.

Other examples of presidential leadership on civil rights pepper the latter half of the twentieth century. President Carter, however lacking his administration was in legislative civil rights accomplishments, appointed more minorities to federal judicial positions and visible cabinet positions than any of his counterparts (Goldman 1995). Presidents have also used their power of executive action to further civil rights. Harry Truman issued an executive order to desegregate the armed forces; Eisenhower called upon the National Guard to enforce court-ordered desegregation in Little Rock, Arkansas. The president's position as leader of the US public can also benefit civil rights awareness. Clinton's "national conversation on race" increased the public's and media's attention to race,[2] even though it did not lead to new civil rights legislation or administrative directives.

In the legislative arena, some presidents have championed civil rights legislation while others have resisted the expansion of those rights. President Truman sent the first comprehensive civil rights legislation to Congress since the nineteenth century. Owing to southern Democratic resistance, however, the legislation failed to pass Congress. Nevertheless, a string of civil rights bills managed enough support to become law during the late 1950s and 1960s. Eisenhower signed the Civil Rights Act of 1957, which granted the US attorney general broad powers to litigate civil and criminal civil rights violations. It also established the Civil Rights Division of the Department of Justice as the enforcement body of federal civil rights laws. Continued resistance by southerners and the reluctance of the Kennedy administration to submit civil rights legislation to Congress stalled comprehensive civil rights protections until the early years of the Johnson administration. Since his days as Senate majority leader when he had helped pass the 1957 Civil Rights Act, Lyndon Johnson had been a leader on civil rights policy. He made passage of the Civil Rights Act of 1964 his top legislative priority and later signed the Voting Rights Act of 1965. Indeed, President Johnson translated Kennedy's legacy and a somber national mood following his assassination into sufficient political capital to bolster protections for the rights of African Americans and other minorities.[3]

Following the civil rights advances of the 1960s, subsequent administrations offered little in the way of civil rights legislation. Finding Congress to be an unfriendly institution for some of his programs, Nixon followed an administrative strategy on civil rights. He sought to restrict federal control over local elections by eliminating the "preclearance" provision of the Voting Rights Act of 1965.[4] Nixon was unsuccessful, however, and the Civil Rights Division has continued to use preclearance to effectively veto any change in local and state election operations (Edsall and Edsall 1992: 84–94). Although Presidents Reagan and George H. W. Bush both signed major civil rights legislation in the form of a Voting Rights Act of 1965 extension and the Civil Rights Act of 1991, their civil rights preferences were often at odds with those of the African American community. They also vetoed two key pieces of civil rights legislation. Congress overrode Reagan's veto of the Civil Rights Act of 1987; Bush compromised and signed the Civil Rights Act of 1991 despite his public opposition to quotas.

The later half of the twentieth century exemplifies the president's potential influence over civil rights policy. Johnson championed civil rights legislation that guaranteed rights to African Americans that had been "constitutional" for 100 years prior. Reagan and Bush sought to limit the role of the federal government over civil rights policy. Although it remains to be seen whether presidents have encouraged legislators and bureaucrats to respond to their civil rights preferences, this brief history insinuates that presidents are in a unique position to affect civil rights policy through their public speeches.

Civil Rights Policy in Congress

Congress has passed numerous civil rights laws in recent years, despite being resistant to civil rights legislation during the late nineteenth and early twentieth centuries. With the help of southern states purged for a time of Confederate influence, the Reconstruction Congress ratified the civil rights amendments (the thirteenth, fourteenth, and fifteenth) and passed the overly ambitious Civil Rights Act of 1866. Despite congressional intent, these safeguards were not enforced throughout much of the Union. The Supreme Court chipped away at these protections in a series of decisions from the *Civil Rights Cases* (109 US 3 1883) to *Plessy v. Ferguson* (163 US 537 1896). Post–World War II Congresses were initially reluctant to pass real civil rights protections for minorities.

Since World War II, Congress has looked to the White House for leadership on civil rights policy. Naturally, presidents can provide guidance to an institution such as Congress that has collective action problems that prevent it from organizing and passing legislation to address social problems (Moe 1989). Whereas the courts had whittled away at segregation laws in higher education throughout the 1930s and 1940s[5] and presidents had issued executive orders to desegregate the armed forces, it was not until 1957 that Congress legislated moderate civil rights protections. Parochial, primarily southern resistance to desegregation and voting rights protection laws prevented consistent congressional commitment to civil rights policy. Because of a lack of congressional leadership on civil rights policy, modern presidents have led most statutory fights for equal opportunity and have backed important civil rights laws (see discussion above). Since the 1960s, moreover, presidents have been a dominant force in setting the civil rights agenda. Kennedy's and

Johnson's support of strong civil rights legislation, George H. W. Bush's opposition to quotas, and Clinton's attention to civil rights through his "national conversation on race"[6] affected congressional and public civil rights agendas (see Bohte 1997).

The nature of civil rights policy encourages action from politicians. Civil rights policy is not complex. Even a civil rights policy that is complicated from a tactical standpoint does not require a technical understanding. Citizens may not comprehend the long-term collective and societal consequences of segregation, but being in favor of or against it only requires an opinion, an opinion that may be used to hold politicians accountable for their actions. Because civil rights policy concerns a sizable portion of the population (Gormley 1986), it is also salient.

Although the historical evidence demonstrates substantial presidential leadership of civil rights policy absent congressional initiative, the nature of civil rights policy does not offer a clear expectation for *only* presidential leadership. Being uncomplicated yet salient, civil rights policy encourages action by presidents *and* legislators. Presidents desire national support and approval, so they wish to lead on salient issues. But salience alone does not guarantee responsiveness from legislators. Members of Congress are responsive to their constituents on salient issues in general and civil rights policy in particular (Clausen 1973; Miller and Stokes 1963). The responsiveness of legislators to their constituents on civil rights policy poses a problem for presidents: legislators may respond not to presidential signals but to cues sent by their constituents. Especially if the president's and a constituency's preferences conflict, legislators are rational to respond to those whom they represent and by whom they must be reelected. Even though the recent history of civil rights policy shows significant presidential leadership on civil rights policy, presidents will not always dictate legislators' decisions on civil rights.

One way to account for the dual nature of legislative responsiveness to civil rights policy signals is to control for the mitigating and independent effects that the measurable salience of civil rights may have on legislators' own vote decisions. A quantitative model that controls for salience (or media attention, the operationalization of salience for this book) ensures that if signals have a statistically significant impact on the president's legislative success, it is not caused by another factor not controlled for in the model. In other words, controlling for salience alleviates a possible spurious relationship between presidential signals and a president's civil rights policy success rate in Congress.

Ultimately, legislators will respond to presidential signals on civil rights only if presidents provide adequate leadership and policy direction to legislators. Significant presidential leadership on civil rights policy sets priorities for legislators and simplifies legislators' difficult jobs by presenting a clear choice for legislators: follow or ignore the president's priorities on civil rights. Legislators may also respond to the president's civil rights policy signals because they need the president's signature to achieve their policy goals. After all, a noteworthy policy record, on which a legislator may run and garner electoral support, may improve a legislator's reelection chances. In short, responding to presidential priorities provides legislators with an efficient course of action—amid time and resource constraints—that might also lead to attainment of their own policy goals. The historical evidence and the nature of the policy area suggest that legislators may respond to presidential signals on civil rights policy given a favorable political environment. As explained in Chapter 3, several other variables, such as presidential approval and congressional makeup, may limit the influence of signals in Congress and will be controlled for.

Civil Rights Policy in the Bureaucracy

Activists in the civil rights movement used many venues for affecting change in government and society. Protesters relied on boycotts, sit-ins, voter registration drives, and marches during desegregation and voting rights movements of the 1950s and 1960s. Although these events were helpful in bringing national attention to civil rights issues (Rosenberg 1991: 134–137), these efforts could do little to guarantee civil rights for minorities without government enforcement.

To affect real and lasting change, civil rights supporters trusted the federal government, litigation, and the judicial system. Litigation is a powerful means to affect change, and it has been a critical weapon in the enforcement of civil rights and insurance against future violations of those rights. The Department of Justice (DOJ) is responsible for protecting federal civil rights. The Civil Rights Division (CRD) within the DOJ litigates both civil and criminal civil rights cases in US district courts (see Eshbaugh-Soha 1999; Shull 1989: 160).

The Civil Rights Division

Since 1939 and the creation of the Civil Rights Section (CRS) of the Criminal Division, the DOJ has had the authority to pursue noncriminal (or civil) civil rights cases (Landsberg 1997: 9). This act by the Roosevelt administration is one of the earliest examples of presidential leadership of and commitment to changes in civil rights policy. Although Attorney General Frank Murphy formed the CRS, he did so at the specific request and urging of President Franklin Roosevelt (McMahon 2004: 145). The creation of the Civil Rights Section, and the judicial and enforcement strategies of the Roosevelt administration, laid the foundation for later progress in civil rights policy (McMahon 2004). Inevitably, the CRS proved insufficient to prosecute civil rights policy, and a new, more forceful office became necessary.

Modern civil rights enforcement began after Eisenhower signed the Civil Rights Act of 1957, which created the CRD of the DOJ (Graham 1990: 363). Prior to 1957, "civil rights enforcement was relegated primarily to suits by private individuals and to very limited authority of the Attorney General to prosecute those who criminally deprived individuals of civil rights" (Landsberg 1997: 174). With the Civil Rights Act of 1957, however, the CRD became responsible for enforcing criminal civil rights laws in US district court.[7] The legislation also gave presidents the potential to influence CRD activity.

Notwithstanding its importance, the Civil Rights Act of 1957 did not substantially expand the Civil Rights Division's influence over civil rights litigation. Suits filed after 1957 were directed mostly by citizens' complaints (Landsberg 1997: 84), which were not vigorously pursued by CRD "desk lawyers" (Landsberg 1997: 104). After several years of rhetoric and heated debate, Congress broadened the authority of the CRD through the Civil Rights Act of 1964. Specifically, the DOJ was authorized to "intervene in race-based equal protection cases initiated by other parties" and had its jurisdiction extended to "suits against discrimination in public accommodations, facilities, and education as well as in employment" (Landsberg 1997: 14). Although efforts have been made to limit the division's litigatory power since 1964 (see Edsall and Edsall 1992), its authority has remained virtually constant.

Presidential Influence in the CRD

There are several reasons why the CRD should respond to presidential signals. First, the CRD is not an isolated agency free from political influence. It is amenable to political persuasion given its relationship to its external political environment. The division's policies and priorities "are shaped by the external checks that characterize the allocation of responsibilities among the three branches of government" (Landsberg 1997: 4). Because the CRD is susceptible to political control generally and the president's policy priorities in particular (Landsberg 1997: 81), it may respond to presidential signals.

Second, the Civil Rights Division is subordinate to the presidency. The president is its chief executive and his constitutional authority requires the CRD to at least listen to presidential preferences and follow the president's leadership on civil rights policy if he offers it. Bureaucrats should respond to signals from the president because he is the constitutional leader of the Civil Rights Division, and legitimacy is one reason why bureaucrats will rely on signals for policymaking. Indeed, the president's constitutional legitimacy over the Civil Rights Division encourages division lawyers to believe that the president "has a right to offer evaluations and to have them heeded in the absence of contrary inclinations" (Matthews and Stimson 1975: 80). Because the president is the constitutional leader of the CRD, in other words, division bureaucrats will respond to presidential signals so long as they are clear and do not contradict something more fundamental to an agency, such as its mission.

The importance of signals to presidential influence in the CRD is furthered in part because constitutional authority alone is not sufficient for presidents to influence the bureaucracy; the president must make the bureaucracy work for him (Landsberg 1997: 168–169). Presidents may influence the division if they use their formal authority effectively (see Wood and Waterman 1994), but they must also "bargain and compromise in order to increase their influence over the bureaucracy" (Waterman 1989: 170). Signals are a way for presidents to lead and continually inform the Civil Rights Division of their civil rights preferences. Again, the president's legitimate authority over the Civil Rights Division gives this agency a reason to respond to presidential signals.

Third, the division needs power to function effectively, and the presidency is uniquely situated to either withhold or provide support for the division's activities, thereby affecting the division's power. Signals may be particularly effective in the CRD because they can help it set priorities. The division has limited time and resources to devote to litigation, its most common, yet costly endeavor (Landsberg 1997: 113). Policy leadership from the president may guide the division's decision to use time and resources to prosecute cases. Presidents can motivate lawyers to enforce their mission vigorously by providing leadership and facilitating cohesion among bureaucrats.[8] Presidents can facilitate the CRD's policy goals by supporting its mission. If the president supports civil rights through signals, the CRD has an incentive to prioritize litigation because the president provides power, legitimacy, and motivation to the division. As a result, presidential signals in support of civil rights policy may motivate the CRD to do more of what it does: litigate civil rights cases.

Despite reasons to expect presidential signals to influence the CRD, bureaucratic discretion over policy activities can hinder presidential influence. Discretion means that CRD lawyers can ignore policy directives that contradict an agency's core beliefs. If a president does not support civil rights, if he is against the CRD's mission to litigate civil rights violations, he is less likely to have influence over the division because lawyers can use their discretion to ignore the president's preferences and proceed with their own docket of cases. Especially when goals conflict, presidents may attempt to coerce the agency into compliance through the threat of a loss of bureaucratic power. A negative signaling strategy is unlikely to be effective because discretion and an informational advantage allow bureaucrats to ignore presidential signals and force presidents to use administrative strategies of control, such as budget cuts or appointments when goals conflict. Discretion is especially pronounced in the Civil Rights Division, as CRD lawyers have significant prosecutorial discretion (Landsberg 1997: 79).[9] Although presidential signals opposed to civil rights may encourage CRD lawyers to cut back on their prosecution of civil rights cases and a lack of presidential support may push lawyers to deemphasize the litigation of cases, implement civil rights policy with a nonlitigation strategy (Landsberg 1997: 114), or prosecute areas of the law to which the president is not opposed, presidential signals that oppose civil rights policy are unlikely to have much impact on CRD activities. Bureaucratic discretion should preclude the impact of negative signals on CRD activities.

Finally, civil rights are salient and not complex (Gormley 1986), which facilitates presidential influence over the Civil Rights Division. On primarily salient policy areas, bureaucrats are encouraged to "look over their shoulders" and respond to presidential or political leadership. Salient policies also provide presidents with a clear incentive to lead and signal their preferences. Presidents are expected to lead, especially when the public demands government attention to an issue. Moreover, bureaucrats need to respond to elected officials on salient issues to ensure their own democratic legitimacy. Because civil rights policy is not complex, bureaucrats will not rely solely on their own expertise when they decide how to implement civil rights policy; because civil rights policy is also salient, bureaucrats should defer to presidential leadership.

Other Influential Institutions and Events

Signals from the bureaucracy's other principals may influence policy implementation as well. Indeed, Congress and the Supreme Court have their own reasons for trying to influence the Civil Rights Division.

Salient issues encourage members of Congress to respond to their constituency's preferences and translate them into government policy (Miller and Stokes 1963). Legislators may therefore oversee the implementation of civil rights policy, a salient policy area, and affect CRD activity. Congress also has institutional incentives to oversee the implementation of civil rights policy because it created the CRD, granted it the authority to litigate, and provides appropriations for its activities. Congress oversees federal agencies through committee hearings. The more Congress oversees civil rights policy through committee hearings, the more it should influence CRD activity.[10] Congress has also passed several key civil rights statutes. The Civil Rights Acts of 1957, 1964, and 1991 all expanded the litigatory obligations of the Civil Rights Division. Each act, therefore, should have a positive impact on CRD activity.

The Supreme Court affects the CRD by expanding or restricting the legal basis for civil rights litigation. As a law enforcement organization, the Civil Rights Division is clearly subordinate to the Supreme Court and its decisions on civil rights. More cases that uphold civil rights laws should lead to more litigation by the Civil Rights Division in US district court. In other words, more cases that further civil rights expand the scope of civil rights protections and give the division more protections to enforce and to prosecute civil rights law. Early affirmative action cases, for example, clarified the legality of minority recruitment and hiring practices by allowing preferences based on race. These decisions expanded opportunities for the CRD to find violators of federal affirmative action laws and therefore prosecute such cases. Decisions by the Rehnquist Court have curtailed the use of race in remedying past discrimination or promoting diversity as a value in public education and employment. These cases may have had a negative impact by restricting the litigation of civil rights violations.

Findings

Civil rights policy is an area over which presidents historically have had much influence. It remains to be seen if signals had a role in this influence. Descriptive counts of presidential signals assess whether presidents meet the first requirement of signaling influence: only if presidents pay attention to civil rights policy can signaling be an effective tool to influence legislative and bureaucratic outputs. Quantitative models provide evidence to determine whether or not legislators and bureaucrats have responded to the president's signals on civil rights policy.

Descriptive Evidence

The data in Table 4.1 show that presidents have often used their public statements to express their civil rights policy preferences. From a high of nearly seventy pages per year devoted to civil rights policy by Johnson, to a low of about five pages by G. W. Bush, presidents have varied their attention to civil rights. Predictably, signals were most frequent during the civil rights struggles of the 1960s. Signals also follow individual presidential preferences. Although Eisenhower signed the Civil Rights Act of 1957, he was not enthusiastic about reprimanding segregationists, as his lack of attention to civil rights affirms. Most presidents after Nixon have averaged fewer than fifteen civil rights signals per year, even though President Clinton averaged more than twenty, in part owing to his devotion to a "national conversation on race."

Table 4.1 also presents the yearly averages for the number of positive, negative, or neutral signals for each administration. The

Table 4.1 **Yearly Average Signals on Civil Rights Policy by Presidential Administration**

President	Total Average	Positive	Neutral	Negative
Truman	17.4	6.8	10.4	0.2
		(39.1 %)[a]	(59.8 %)	(1.1 %)
Eisenhower	15.5	7.8	6.3	1.5
		(50.8)	(40.6)	(9.7)
Kennedy	41.0	32.7	8.0	0.3
		(79.7)	(19.5)	(0.7)
Johnson	66.8	54.0	12.8	0.2
		(80.6)	(19.2)	(0.2)
Nixon	24.5	12.7	4.7	7.2
		(51.8)	(19.1)	(29.3)
Ford	14.0	2.0	1.0	11.0
		(14.3)	(7.1)	(78.6)
Carter	12.0	10.0	2.0	0.0
		(83.3)	(1.7)	(0.0)
Reagan	11.3	4.8	3.5	3.0
		(42.5)	(31.0)	(26.5)
G. H. W. Bush	16.0	4.8	6.0	5.3
		(29.7)	(37.5)	(33.1)
Clinton	24.0	10.6	13.1	0.3
		(44.2)	(54.6)	(0.01)
G. W. Bush[b]	4.5	2.0	2.0	0.5
		(44.4)	(44.4)	(11.1)

Notes: Numbers are administration averages of the number of pages in the *Public Papers of the Presidents* on which presidents mention civil rights policy.

a. Numbers in parentheses are the average percentage of all positive, neutral, or negative civil rights policy signals.

b. Numbers for G. W. Bush are through 2004.

Democratic presidents of the 1960s were most supportive of civil rights. Both Kennedy and Johnson supported federal civil rights legislation and were not shy about publicly admonishing egregious acts of civil rights abuses. On the other hand, Presidents Gerald Ford and Nixon opposed busing as a governmental remedy for school desegregation; they spoke most often in opposition to civil rights policy.

The rhetoric behind the president's signals reveals why he spoke favorably or negatively about civil rights. Early presidents mixed a general message of support with mentions that neither supported nor opposed governmental intervention in civil rights policy. Truman made important speeches on civil rights that helped direct the civil rights agenda, even though he signed no legislation (see Pauley 1999). Nevertheless, many of his signals were curt remarks to reporters during press conferences that did not suggest support for or opposition to any civil rights policy. Although Eisenhower signed the Civil Rights Act of 1957, he proved passive on civil rights. He frequently dodged questions in press conferences about his civil rights position, claimed repeatedly that "you can't change men's hearts with laws," and refused to chastise southern governors for resisting the Supreme Court's desegregation orders. He rarely lent explicit and unwavering support for the Court's decisions, only recognizing that it was his duty to uphold the Constitution.

Kennedy and Johnson were almost exclusively positive in their civil rights rhetoric. John Kennedy vigorously supported the civil rights movement through his speeches, even though his legislative record is less robust than Eisenhower's record. Although he did not move on legislation as fast as civil rights leaders would have preferred (he claimed that legislation would be submitted when the time was right), Kennedy was able to shape the civil rights agenda with a national address urging the passage of comprehensive new civil rights legislation (Bohte 1997). Johnson was particularly supportive of civil rights legislation through his public statements. Some of his speeches had a clear motivational impact on the bureaucracy, as I theorized. Specifically, Johnson's 1964 speech on civil rights dramatically increased morale at the Civil Rights Division (Ramsey Clark Oral History Interview I 1968: 10). Johnson staffers also recognized the importance of presidential statements to the civil rights movement.[11]

With the 1964 presidential election, civil rights developed into a party-defining issue (Carmines and Stimson 1989). Democrats defended civil rights and received overwhelming electoral support from African Americans. Republicans, conversely, increasingly opposed a prominent federal role in civil rights policy. Presidents Nixon and Ford paid less attention to civil rights than had Kennedy and Johnson and proposed virtually no civil rights legislation. They questioned court-ordered busing as a legitimate means for school desegregation, opposed affirmative action programs in employment, and offered only two civil rights executive orders between them (Nixon had both).[12] Ford was particularly not supportive of civil rights policy. Most of Ford's rhetoric opposed court-ordered busing as a solution to lingering segregation in the US public school system. Many of Nixon's supportive statements came early in his term as he discussed his own affirmative action program called the Philadelphia Plan. As his term progressed, however, Nixon opposed court-ordered busing as a remedy for continued school segregation. He also shifted his rhetoric from advocating racial hiring in accordance with his Philadelphia Plan to appealing to the "silent majority" and blue-collar, Caucasian workers concerned for their own jobs (Edsall and Edsall 1992: 97).[13] Although on average Nixon discussed civil rights more than Carter did, Nixon was generally less supportive of civil rights overall than Carter: 83 percent of Carter's statements supported civil rights, whereas only 51 percent of Nixon's did.

For the presidencies of Clinton and George W. Bush, civil rights policy was not a clear legislative priority. President Clinton devoted numerous speeches to highlighting race relations in the United States, including the changing face of affirmative action ("mend it, don't end it," in the words of the Reverend Jesse Jackson). Yet, he advocated no major civil rights legislation and did not push for significant enforcement of existing civil rights legislation through the federal bureaucracy. George W. Bush has virtually ignored civil rights. Save for a handful of symbolic speeches (such as those to honor the Reverend Martin Luther King Jr. or to commemorate the fortieth anniversary of the Civil and Voting Rights Act) and references to the importance of protecting civil rights of Americans amid the war on terrorism, he has not prioritized civil rights policy or discussed it frequently and therefore is unlikely to have had any impact on its adoption or implementation.

Presidents Reagan and George H. W. Bush were ambivalent in their speeches on civil rights policy. Although Reagan and Bush spoke of their own strong and supportive civil rights record, both vetoed key civil rights legislation and authored few executive orders supporting civil rights. The African American community was critical of both Reagan's and Bush's mild support of civil rights legislation. Reagan supported the Senate's extension of the Voting Rights Act, for instance, a weak version that was not preferred by most civil rights leaders. Bush opposed quotas in the 1991 Civil Rights Act, an action that opened him up to criticisms of being soft on civil rights (Shull 1993). Both spent some time defending their civil rights records in their public statements on civil rights, although as the information in Table 4.1 shows, their signals were not clearly against civil rights policy for African Americans.

Reagan was a master of sending mixed signals to Congress and the bureaucracy. He favored equal opportunity for all, but opposed the African American community's version of the Voting Rights Act extension and vetoed civil rights legislation in 1987. Edsall and Edsall wrote:

> In articulating a politics of generalized government restraint, Reagan mastered the excision of the language of race from conservative public discourse. In so doing, Reagan paralleled Nixon's success in constructing a politics and a strategy of governing that attacked policies targeted toward blacks and other minorities without reference to race. . . . [Furthermore,] Reagan had found an ostensibly neutral language that would become a powerful tool with which to advocate stands that polarized voters on race-freighted issues—issues ranging from welfare to busing to affirmative action. He did so without communicating overt bigotry or anti-black affect to whites, while large numbers of blacks perceived his policies as anti-black. (1992: 138–139)

Cameron (2000) observed that there are times when presidents may not want actors to know their precise positions on some of what I believe are usually valence issues. The nature of civil rights policy— that it is a valence issue—helps explain Reagan's rhetorical strategy on civil rights, including the paucity of his opposition signals. In part because freedom from persecution and freedom to do as one pleases is fundamental to US democracy, all presidents in this study claimed to be strong supporters of civil rights because they could claim nothing less. A valence issue, such as civil rights, encourages a strategy called "staying private" (Covington 1987). It is clear from his public statements that President Reagan opposed a more expansive version of the Voting Rights Act of 1965 extension, but he "stayed private" and did not publicly express his true preferences often. Speaking out on this issue may have mobilized many civil rights supporters, possibly encouraging them to use the president's national position against him by forcing Reagan to answer why he did not support the African American community's position on the Voting Rights Act extension. By "staying private" on this valence issue, Reagan was able to "go public" on issues more important and central to his conservative, but activist, first-term policy agenda.[14]

When presidents do not use signals to affect policy, they must rely on other sources of power. Reagan did not speak much on civil rights but depended on his appointment power to sway civil rights policy in his direction. Reagan appointed William Bradford Reynolds to head the CRD; Reynolds, consistent with Reagan administration policy, was against affirmative action, quotas, and racial preferences. He claimed that government should protect individuals only from actual and specific acts of discrimination. This differed greatly from more active remedies supported by previous administrations, which sought to protect minorities before discrimination occurred. Under Reynolds, the CRD filed many suits to limit the scope of affirmative action policies. These efforts were later supported by two important Supreme Court cases that limited the breadth of legal affirmative action at the city, state, and federal levels (*City of Richmond v. JA Croson*, 488 US 469; *Adarand Constructors, Inc. v. Pena*, 115 SCt 2097).

At least cursorily, all presidents must be in favor of civil rights policy. The relative number of signals supportive or neutral toward civil rights policy supports this contention (Table 4.1). Not all presidents were explicitly supportive, however, when their preferences could have been interpreted as contradicting a fundamental ideal of US democracy, equality of opportunity. Hence, presidents who "go against the book" on civil rights are unlikely to have effective signaling influence over either Congress or the bureaucracy. This limitation means that presidents will either send no public message at all or will use other means of influence to affect congressional or bureaucratic behavior. Signaling will only be effective when presidents can publicly express their preferences.

Legislative Activity

Signaling theory predicts that Congress will be responsive to presidential signals on policy areas that are salient and not complex. To test whether this prediction holds for civil rights policy and because signaling effects could vary by house of Congress, I present two models by house of Congress, which include the following independent variables. My measure of signals is the total number of pages in the *Public Papers of the Presidents* that presidents devote per year to civil rights policy, lagged six months for causality purposes (see Appendix A). Other independent variables are necessary controls or factors that could mitigate the president's signaling influence (see Chapter 3). These include media attention to civil rights, the percentage of the president's party coalition in Congress, the president's past success, his approval ratings, his veto threats, and his first-year "honeymoon." Finally, I control for the 1964 Civil Rights Act. This act was atypical in both process and outcome. Congress debated the Civil Rights Act more than any other civil rights legislation before its passage. In the 88th Congress alone, the Senate debated more than 100 civil rights votes on which the president took a public position. Moreover, the act ensured civil rights protections for minorities unheard of during the prior 200 years of the United States.

The first model assesses the president's success on individual civil rights roll-call votes. Pooled data, with the vote as the unit of analysis, are used to test whether presidential signals have a direct impact on the president's success. In this model, I count those signals that presidents make six months prior to the vote and use the president's approval ratings for the month in which the vote takes place. A second model controls for any dynamic effects of signals. There are two dependent variables in this model. The first, for the substantive equation, is the president's average yearly success on civil rights roll-call votes. The second, for the Heckman selection equation, is one or zero for whether or not civil rights policy comes to a roll-call vote in a given year. The dichotomous nature of this variable allows me to control for the selection bias in yearly civil rights roll-call votes over time and assess whether presidents have an agenda-setting impact (whether or not Congress votes on civil rights policy in a given year) on congressional floor activity. The Heckman selection model allows me to test whether presidential signals have an agenda-setting impact in both houses of Congress. It is also useful to account for the selection bias missing years might create (see Appendix B); Congress did not debate civil rights policy in just over one-half of the years under investigation. These models run through 2000 only, as Congress cast no floor votes on civil rights legislation between 2001 and 2004.

The Senate. Significant civil rights legislation has been debated heavily in the Senate, where it experienced substantial opposition in the 1950s and 1960s. Then Senate Majority Leader Johnson pushed the Civil Rights Act of 1957 through the Senate. As president, Johnson also found himself concentrating his efforts in the Senate to secure passage of the Civil Rights Act of 1964. Although the act eventually crossed many important hurdles in the Senate, civil rights opponents tried adamantly to fight the 1964 act through a flurry of amendments. Later Congresses have also extended Voting Rights Acts, passed additional civil rights protections, and extended civil rights protections to other minority groups.

I analyze Senate outputs both dynamically (signaling impacts are bound to differ by administration, and effects should differ over time) and pooled, to assess what impacts signals have on individual roll-call votes. Both models support signals as a source of influence over the president's success on civil rights roll-call votes in the Senate. Correcting for selectivity bias in the yearly signaling model, indicated by the statistically significant sigma, signals have no direct impact on the president's civil rights roll-call vote success in the Senate. Nevertheless, signals do have an agenda-setting impact (Table 4.2). Again, the Heckman estimation model considers several variables that affect whether the Senate votes (coded as one) or does not vote (coded as zero) on the issue during that year. Since the Heckman model estimates a dichotomous dependent variable, the coefficient is correctly interpreted as a probability. In effect, civil rights signals in a given year contribute to a greater likelihood that civil rights will come up for a vote in the Senate. This model does not rule out the possibility that presidents respond to legislation on the floor of the Senate, yet most historical evidence shows that presidents usually lead civil rights policy in Congress. Regardless, this model shows that signals on civil rights policy have an impact on the Senate's yearly civil rights policy agenda.

Several independent variables also significantly explain the president's average yearly roll-call vote success in the Senate (Table 4.2). Media attention positively and significantly affects the president's success. The positive media attention coefficient implies that if the media focus the nation on civil rights, presidents will be successful even if they

Table 4.2   Presidential Success on Senate Civil Rights Roll Calls, 1948–2000

	Parameter Estimate	Standard Error	t-statistic
Total signals	−0.22	0.24	−0.94
CRA 1964 (step)	15.11	9.30	1.62
Past success	0.46*	0.21	2.20
Presidential approval	1.03*	0.42	2.46
Media attention	0.13*	0.07	1.87
Presidential party seats (%)	−0.79*	0.35	−2.30
Presidential honeymoon	0.53	8.51	0.06
Veto threat	−19.90*	8.80	−2.26
Constant	−9.48	40.08	−0.24
Heckman Selection Model			
Total signals	0.02*	0.01	1.83
Presidential approval	0.02	0.02	1.45
Presidential party seats (%)	0.003	0.02	0.10
Past success	−0.01	0.01	−0.41
Constant	−1.75	1.55	−1.13
N (censored N)	53 (32)		
Wald χ^2 (8)	21.26*		
σ (sigma)	11.81*		
Log likelihood	−113.18		

Note: * p < .05 (one-tailed).

cannot themselves motivate the Senate to support the president through signals. In other words, the salience of civil rights policy has had an independent impact on the president's yearly success rate. When civil rights policy is salient, it behooves senators to consider the public in their voting decisions (Clausen 1973; Hill and Hurley 1999; Miller and Stokes 1963), especially senators who should be responsive to the public mood given their greater national visibility and larger constituencies (Stimson, MacKuen, and Erikson 1995).

The president's approval ratings, the percentage of Senate seats that are held by members of the president's party, and veto threats are also statistically significant, although the latter two are in the unexpected direction (see Note 15 and the explanation in the text for some suggestion for this finding). An extra ten seats in the Senate leads to just about an eight-point decline in the president's average success on civil rights roll calls, and presidential veto threats lead to much less success overall. The veto threat's negative coefficient is a function of the limited number of veto threats on civil rights legislation, not the success of threatening a veto across several policy areas and in different situations. Presidents have threatened vetoes on only three pieces of civil rights legislation, all in years of divided government. Ronald Reagan threatened and actually vetoed the Civil Rights Act of 1987 in spite of overwhelming congressional support for the act. Nixon and Bush also threatened vetoes for civil rights acts in 1972 and 1991 with mixed success. The model also performs well overall, according to the significant goodness of fit measure, the Wald statistic. The Wald statistic is similar to an F-statistic, which tests the overall significance of a regression (Kennedy 1998: chap. 4). It is χ^2 distributed, and a significant coefficient supports the overall fit of the regression.

The pooled model is most revealing, as it tests the direct impact that presidential signals have on the president's roll-call vote success (Table 4.3). With the use of robust standard errors to account for heteroskedasticity in the model, I interpret these coefficients cautiously as directional impacts only.[15] The president's signals on civil rights have a direct, positive, and statistically significant impact on his success in the Senate. Indeed, more pages in the *Public Papers* devoted to civil rights policy leads to a percentage increase in the president's success rate on individual roll-call votes. The president's approval also has a positive and significant impact. This suggests, consistent with recent studies (Canes-Wrone and de Marchi 2002), that presidential approval affects the president's success rate in the Senate, but these impacts vary by a policy's salience and complexity. Surprisingly, the Senate seats' variable is in the negative and unexpected direction; this may be a function of the

Table 4.3   Presidential Success on Senate Civil Rights Policy Roll-Call Votes

	Parameter Estimate	Standard Error	t-statistic
Signals	0.36*	0.15	2.32
Honeymoon	−6.01	5.79	−1.04
Veto threat	−16.31*	6.54	−2.49
Presidential party seats (%)	−0.69*	0.24	−2.90
Civil Rights Act 1964	−10.31	6.42	−1.61
Past success	0.25	0.23	1.08
Media attention	−0.02	0.05	−0.38
Presidential approval	0.63*	0.16	3.93
Constant	37.59*	14.27	2.64
R-square	.28		
F-statistic	8.98*		
N	235		

Notes: * $p < .05$.
Robust standard errors to account for heteroskedasticity.

numerous amendments defeated for the Civil Rights Act of 1964. Indeed, the negative coefficient on the 1964 act dummy variable seems to confirm this anomaly, that the president had to deal with substantial opposition from southerners in his own party primarily during the 100-plus votes on the 1964 act.[16] Media effects are also present in this model.

Finding media effects in this model, but not in the previous one, begs the question: Why does media attention to civil rights policy affect the president's average yearly success but not his success on individual roll-call votes? One explanation may lie in the different units of analysis for the models. Media effects may be more likely when attention is sustained. Simply, the compounding effects of media attention to civil rights over the course of a year increases the likelihood that legislators will hear a significant and relevant story (relevant to their constituents perhaps) and therefore respond to the increase in subsequent public concern about civil rights policy. Media attention may not affect legislators' vote decisions on individual roll-call votes because this compounding effect is not necessarily present.

The House. Signals may be less effective in the House of Representatives than in the Senate because of a larger diversity of interests. There is simply a greater likelihood that presidents have to persuade many more legislators in the House of Representatives than in the Senate and that several of those representatives must weigh their constituency's interests heavily in light of their frequent electoral evaluations. Moreover, the congressional decisionmaking literature, which tests House of Representatives data, demonstrates that House members rely more on other cues (party leaders, trusted colleagues, previous votes) than they do on the president's signals (Matthews and Stimson 1975).

I first present a Heckman selection model to assess the dynamics of presidential influence in the House. The information in Table 4.4 reveals selectively bias (according to the significant sigma), so a Heckman selection model is appropriate for this dataset. No independent variables have a statistically significant impact on the president's yearly success rate in the House, even though most variables are in the expected direction: signals, House seats, past success, media attention, and the president's honeymoon positively relate to success. The insignificant Wald statistic shows further that the model does not adequately explain the president's yearly success on civil rights roll-call votes in the House. According to the selection model, signals are nonetheless a potential source of influence over the civil rights policy agenda, as they affect whether or not civil rights policy comes to a vote in the House of Representatives. Presidents can frame the issue before the House, much as Matthews and Stimson (1975) found for all roll-call votes in the

Table 4.4 Presidential Success on House Civil Rights Roll Calls, 1948–2000

	Parameter Estimate	Standard Error	t-statistic
Total signals	0.06	0.23	0.26
CRA 1964 (step)	−5.51	8.66	−0.64
Past success	0.04	0.29	0.15
Presidential approval	−0.09	0.39	−0.22
Media attention	0.07	0.06	1.10
Presidential party seats (%)	0.32	0.47	0.68
Presidential honeymoon	6.14	9.02	0.68
Veto threat	−3.38	10.94	−0.31
Constant	37.88	37.41	1.01
Heckman Selection Model			
Total signals	0.03*	0.01	2.41
Presidential approval	0.01	0.02	0.89
Presidential party seats (%)	−0.02	0.02	−0.94
Past success	0.01	0.01	0.61
Constant	−1.13	1.49	−0.76
N (censored N)	53 (28)		
Wald χ^2 (8)	6.96		
σ (sigma)	15.26*		
Log likelihood	−134.49		

Note: * $p < .05$ (one-tailed).

House. Agenda setting is in itself an important power for presidents, and a first step to influencing success on individual roll-call votes.

I next examine whether presidential signals directly increase the president's success on civil rights roll-call votes in the House (Table 4.5). The pooled model is not convincing. Signals do not have a significant direct impact on the president's success on individual roll-call votes in the House of Representatives. The model explains only a fraction of the variation in presidential success rates, and only the constant is statistically significant. Nevertheless, this finding comports with the congressional decisionmaking literature, which demonstrates that representatives rely on many other cues before they respond to presidential signals (Kingdon 1981; Matthews and Stimson 1975).

Bureaucratic Outputs

I examine two types of cases litigated by the Civil Rights Division—criminal and civil—to assess the impact that presidential signals have on civil rights bureaucratic outputs. The CRD litigates criminal cases whenever the use or threat of force surrounds a civil rights violation. Juries hear criminal cases, the government has limited rights to appeal a criminal acquittal, and the remedy sought is usually a fine or imprisonment. Conversely, judges hear civil cases, and the government has a right to appeal them.

The amount of civil and criminal civil rights litigation is consistent with the history of federal civil rights policy. Table 4.6 shows that criminal cases were most numerous during the Johnson and Nixon adminis-

Table 4.5 Presidential Success on House Civil Rights Policy Roll-Call Votes

	Parameter Estimate	Standard Error	t-statistic
Signals	0.05	0.21	0.25
Veto threat	−18.48*	8.57	−2.15
Civil Rights Act 1964	−1.18	15.18	−0.08
Presidential party seats (%)	0.39	0.38	1.03
Past success	−0.30	0.29	−1.06
Media attention	0.06	0.06	0.94
Presidential approval	0.01	0.25	0.03
Constant	57.66*	18.16	3.17
R-square	.19		
F-statistic	1.94		
White's test	27.43		
N	67		

Notes: * $p < .05$.
Honeymoon dropped to account for heteroskedasticity in the full model.

Table 4.6 Yearly Average Number of Civil Rights Cases Litigated in
US District Court, 1958–2002

President	Criminal Cases	Civil Cases
Eisenhower (1958–1960)	1.0	16.3
Kennedy	26.7	38.7
Johnson	371.2	82.2
Nixon	139.3	203.8
Ford	74.0	407.5
Carter	78.0	297.3
Reagan	87.1	486.4
G. H. W. Bush	70.8	737.25
Clinton	73.6	645.25
G. W. Bush[a]	55.0	624.0

Source: Department of Justice, *Annual Report of the Director,* 1958–2000 (Washington, DC: US Government Printing Office).

Notes: Numbers are administration averages of the number of criminal and civil cases (where the government is the plaintiff) litigated in US district court.

a. Numbers for George W. Bush are for 2001 and 2002.

trations. Civil cases, in which the government is a plaintiff, trend upward over time. Since the Johnson administration, subsequent administrations have prosecuted more civil cases than previous administrations. The trend only begins to change with the Clinton administration.

Criminal cases. I model the number of criminal cases litigated yearly in US district courts against several independent variables. The dependent variable is logged (see Equation 4.1) in the supportive signals model because heteroskedasticity is a problem (see Appendix B). Criminal cases are a function of presidential signals and several other independent variables. Media attention to civil rights, congressional signals through hearings, Supreme Court signals, presidential approval ratings, and interest group activity may motivate bureaucrats to enforce criminal civil rights policy. Civil rights legislation sets legal parameters for CRD activity, so I model the Civil Rights Acts of 1964 and 1991. These statutes are step functions, coded "one" for each year it is the dominant civil rights statute on the books. I also model the Civil Rights Act of 1964 as a pulse function, given its immediate impact on criminal civil rights prosecution. Finally, budgets are relevant as more appropriations potentially increase CRD activity. This model is represented mathematically in Equation 4.1.

$$\ln (\text{Cases}) = B_0 + B_1 \text{Signals} + B_2 \text{CRA1964(step)} \qquad \textbf{4.1}$$
$$+ B_3 \text{CRA1964(pulse)} + B_4 \text{CRA1991} + B_5 \text{Court Cases} + B_6 \text{Approval}$$
$$+ B_7 \text{Media Attention} + B_8 \text{Congressional Hearings} + B_9 \text{Budget} +$$
$$B_{10} \text{Interest Group Membership} + \varepsilon$$

Supportive signals are an effective means of presidential influence over criminal civil rights cases filed in US district court. Table 4.7 shows that pro–civil rights signals increase the number of litigated criminal cases. A one-page discussion of civil rights by presidents leads to a 1 percent change in the number of criminal civil rights cases litigated in US district court. In a typical year, one page on civil rights policy leads to nearly one more criminal case filed by the CRD. From a different perspective, presidents deliver more than fifteen pages of supportive civil rights signals in a typical year. In an average year, therefore, presidential signals lead to a 15 percent increase in cases, or about seventeen criminal cases litigated in US district court. More attention to civil rights policy has an even larger impact by individual presidents.

What does this result mean? Simply, the president's statements signal to the Civil Rights Division that the president and his administration will support criminal civil rights litigation in federal court. The CRD, in turn, litigates more criminal cases, because positive and supportive statements on policy motivate bureaucrats to carry out their duties more vigorously. Simply put, signals persuade CRD lawyers to do more of what they would otherwise do: prosecute civil rights violations. These

Table 4.7   The Effect of Positive Signals on Criminal Cases, 1958–2002

	Parameter Estimate	Standard Error	t-statistic
Positive signals	0.01*	0.004	2.05
CRA 1964 (pulse)	3.31*	0.43	7.65
CRA 1964 (step)	1.75*	0.23	7.61
CRA 1991 (step)	−0.01	0.18	−0.03
Supreme Court cases (pro)	−0.02	0.01	−1.37
Presidential approval	0.01	0.01	1.41
Media attention	0.001	0.002	0.59
Congressional hearings	0.003	0.004	0.80
Budget Δ	0.01	0.02	0.61
Membership	0.000003*	0.000001	2.18
Constant	0.68	0.72	0.94
R-square	.89		
Adjusted R-square	.85		
F-statistic	23.34*		
Ljung-Box Q	12.52		
White's test	17.40		
Mean of criminal cases	111.84		
N	42		

Notes: * $p < 0.5$ (one-tailed).

The dependent variable is logged to account for heteroskedasticity. Although comparable criminal cases numbers are available through 2002 (see Appendix A), Supreme Court cases are not. This model, therefore, excludes Supreme Court cases in 2001 and 2002.

findings demonstrate support for two hypotheses: (1) more attention leads to greater influence, and (2) positive signals increase criminal cases litigated by the CRD in US district court.

Qualitative evidence also supports the inference that presidents who support an agency's policy area will increase its morale and also its output activity. Ramsey Clark noted in an oral history that Johnson's late 1963 address on civil rights had a motivational impact on the Justice Department and the Civil Rights Division:

> You see, in the late fall of 1963, [Johnson] made very clear by addresses to a joint session of Congress and otherwise his determination to continue to seek enactment of the civil rights act of '63, rather an extraordinary expression of determination and effort. "Did this have an effect on the morale in the Justice Department?" "Well, yes. I don't believe there was any doubt here. . . . I don't remember any doubt that there was full commitment from the President." (Ramsey Clark Oral History Interview I 1968: 10)

Johnson not only motivated bureaucrats through a particular address, he also made criminal prosecution of federal civil rights violations an administration priority (Graham 1990: 237). He emphasized this frequently in his signals and the civil rights legislation he signed. Concomitant with greater positive presidential attention to civil rights policy, the CRD dramatically shifted its focus and altered its priorities to litigate more criminal cases. Presidential leadership helped create an environment that moved division lawyers from their desks to vigorously litigate criminal violations of newly passed civil rights statutes.

One statute of extraordinary importance to federal litigation of civil rights crimes is the Civil Rights Act of 1964. The act's initial passage (pulse function) leads to an immediate increase of 331 percent in criminal cases litigated in 1964, and its extended influence (step function) over the entire series equals a permanent change, an increase in the number of cases litigated by about 175 percent. Based on the average yearly criminal cases, the pulse dummy causes an initial increase of 370 cases in the CRD's criminal litigation activity; the step function leads to an increase of about 196 criminal cases over the remaining years in the model.

The Civil Rights Act of 1964 expectedly had both initial and sustaining effects on CRD activity. The act expanded the division's authority immensely and gave the Civil Rights Division clear prosecutorial authority over a wider range of criminal civil rights violations. The significance of the CRA of 1964, however overwhelming, does not preclude presidential signaling influence over the CRD. The number of criminal cases had already begun to rise significantly in the early 1960s under the guidance of the pro–civil rights Kennedy administration. They also begin to fall with less presidential attention to civil rights (see Figure 4.1).

The overwhelming influence of the 1964 pulse function suggests, however, that the immense activity surrounding the fervor of a new administration and an expansion of power was fleeting. Neither the act nor Johnson's influence was continuous (see Figure 4.1). The number of criminal cases litigated fell throughout the Johnson administration along with Johnson's decline in political capital. After 1965, the president spoke less on civil rights as his credibility declined amid riots and the Moynihan Report on the degenerating black family (Graham 1990: 177). His words had less motivation over bureaucrats in an area growing in controversy. Furthermore, the CRD was not equipped to sustain its peak efforts during the mid-1960s. Small budgets, conflicting presidential responsibilities, and differing CRD priorities also contributed to an overall decline in criminal case activity. According to Graham (1990):

> The Civil Rights Division was one of seven major divisions in the department, and in 1967 it employed only 87 lawyers; the division's fiscal 1967 budget was only $2.5 million, which was less that 1 percent of the total budget for Justice. Yet the small division had to cover seven broadly defined and increasingly active areas of civil rights

Figure 4.1 Yearly Presidential Signals on Civil Rights Policy, 1948–2004

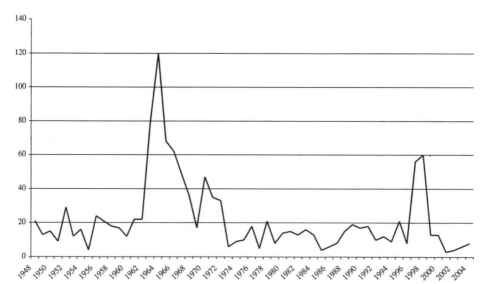

jurisdiction and litigation. Of these, the President had assigned top priority to voting rights, school desegregation, and criminal law enforcement cases involving violence, local defiance, and intimidation. These were hot areas of pressing public and political concern where blowups were frequent and dangerous and Congress was quick to blame the President. (236–237)

Notwithstanding a significant and positive impact of interest group membership, no other variable in the model has a statistically significant impact on criminal cases.

Another hypothesis explores negative civil rights policy signals. Presidents who oppose civil rights through signals should negatively influence the number of criminal cases. Because bureaucrats have discretion, however, they will be less likely to follow negative signals than positive signals. Negative signals contradict the basic mission of the Civil Rights Division to pursue and protect the civil rights of all Americans. Indeed, presidential opposition to civil rights through signals has a statistically insignificant, however negative, impact on the number of criminal cases filed in US district court (Table 4.8). This supports the proposition that presidents are much less effective threatening

Table 4.8   The Effect of Negative Signals on Criminal Cases, 1958–2002

	Parameter Estimate	Standard Error	t-statistic
Negative signals	−0.01	0.01	−1.11
CRA 1964 (pulse)	3.74*	0.44	8.48
CRA 1964 (step)	1.71*	0.25	6.80
CRA 1991 (step)	−0.06	0.20	−0.30
Supreme Court cases	0.004	0.01	0.47
Presidential approval	0.01	0.01	1.48
Media attention	0.003	0.001	1.82
Congressional hearings	0.01	0.005	1.23
Budget Δ	0.01	0.02	0.56
Membership	0.000002*	0.000001	2.02
Constant	0.54	0.73	0.74
R-square	.87		
Adjusted R-square	.82		
F-statistic	19.57*		
Ljung-Box Q	10.40		
White's test	14.66		
N	42		

Notes: * $p < .05$ (one-tailed).
    Although comparable criminal cases numbers are available through 2002 (see Appendix A), Supreme Court cases are not. This model, therefore, excludes Supreme Court cases in 2001 and 2002.

the bureaucracy than they could be motivating CRD lawyers to pursue civil rights policy vigorously. Even popular presidents have a difficult time decreasing CRD activity through negative signals.[17]

One reason why opposition signals may not have significantly affected CRD activity is that if presidents are to influence the bureaucracy through signals, they must signal frequently. The Nixon presidency is a particularly interesting case of presidential opposition to civil rights, but one without much of an impact on the CRD. Nixon opposed civil rights in an unfocused and inattentive manner. The CRD actually litigated a fairly high number of cases during the Nixon administration. Indeed, more litigation relative to fewer Nixon speeches coincides with the conclusion that "career lawyer-bureaucrats in the Civil Rights Division who were 'disgruntled' over the new Nixon-Mitchell policies were firming up the third anchor of an 'iron triangle'" (Graham 1990: 362). With all the domestic and foreign distractions to the Nixon administration, "it is small wonder that the Nixon administration found it so difficult to govern effectively or to forge a coherent legislative program. But much of the incoherence was internal to the Administration. It had no consistent history of civil rights, and especially during the crucial first year, no one seemed to be in charge" (Graham 1990: 364). The Nixon administration did not have a coherent and effective civil rights signaling strategy with which it could curtail CRD criminal litigation. Without presidential leadership to incite public criticism, CRD lawyers used their discretion to pursue criminal cases in spite of the Nixon administration's preferences.

Negative signals are unlikely to affect the implementation of public policy. All bureaucrats have discretion to ignore presidential directives when those orders conflict with the agency's core mission. Indeed, negative presidential signals have no demonstrable or statistically significant impact on criminal cases litigated in US district court, according to Table 4.8.

Nevertheless, the evidence does not preclude presidential signaling in opposition to civil rights. If presidents hope to dissuade the Civil Rights Division from litigating criminal cases, they might be able to do so through signals as long as they speak in opposition much more extensively than any president has since 1948. The negative, yet statistically insignificant, coefficient for signals that oppose civil rights suggests, on the one hand, that during the course of this study presidents were unable to use opposition signals effectively. On the other hand, they may be able to use negative signals to affect the implementation of civil rights policy in the bureaucracy if they exceed a minimum threshold of attention. Given the valence nature of civil rights policy, however, and the lack of an incentive, therefore, for presidents to speak out against civil rights, negative signaling will likely not be a successful strategy for this policy area.

Civil cases. Presidential signals might also have significant influence over civil cases filed in US district court. The dependent variable for this model is the number of civil cases commenced in US district court in which the government is the plaintiff.[18] I examine cases in which the Civil Rights Division actively brings suit in court, as opposed to cases in which the government is the defendant, because defendant cases are reactive and are theoretically unaffected by presidential signals intended to motivate lawyers to prosecute civil rights violations.

To account for the autocorrelation present in the civil cases series, I model a lagged dependent variable in Table 4.9. When variables display trends, as the civil cases series does, successive values tend to be related to each other or to display autoregressive tendencies. Modeling a lagged dependent variable mimics a stationary AR(1) process with a near unit root (Enders 1995: 213) and effectively controls for nonstationarity in the series that could contribute to spurious regression (Granger and Newbold 1974). The information in Table 4.9 shows that the lagged dependent variable is highly significant, and the trend is thus a product

Table 4.9 The Effect of Positive Signals on Civil Cases, 1958–2002

	Parameter Estimate	Standard Error	t-statistic
Civil cases, t-1	0.82*	0.11	7.33
Positive signals	−0.57	1.33	−0.42
CRA 1964 (pulse)	127.00	129.93	0.98
CRA 1964 (step)	149.89	81.22	1.85
CRA 1991 (step)	17.57	54.94	0.32
Supreme Court cases	−7.16*	3.44	−2.08
Presidential approval	2.12	1.73	1.23
Media attention	−0.13	0.43	−0.28
Congressional hearings	−0.54	1.14	−0.47
Budget Δ	−11.07	6.14	−1.80
Membership	−0.0001	0.0003	−0.19
Constant	−36.36	187.72	−0.19
R-square	.92		
Adjusted R-square	.90		
F-statistic	33.17*		
LM F-test (5 lags)	0.87		
White's test	23.40		
N	42		

Notes: * $p < .05$ (one-tailed).
Dependent variable is the number of civil cases filed by the government (as plaintiff). Although comparable criminal cases numbers are available through 2002 (see Appendix A), Supreme Court cases are not. This model, therefore, excludes Supreme Court cases in 2001 and 2002.

of short-term bureaucratic inertia.[19] Bureaucratic inertia explains much of the variation in the civil cases series, as a model with only a lagged dependent variable produces an R-square of 0.92. With this being the only significant variable, my hypotheses do not hold for civil cases tried in US district court. Presidents simply do not have direct influence over civil rights cases commenced in US district court.

Conclusion: Signaling Is Uncomplicated

This chapter shows substantial support for congressional and bureaucratic responsiveness to signals on a policy area that is salient, yet uncomplicated. In the Civil Rights Division, presidents have been able to increase the litigation of criminal cases in US district court through positive signals. Positive signals motivate CRD lawyers to litigate criminal cases more vigorously than they would without presidential leadership, yet presidents have little success coercing the Civil Rights Division into inaction through statements critical of the government's involvement in civil rights policy. Nevertheless, presidents have virtually no impact over the prosecution of civil suits related to civil rights violations.

Presidents have had mixed success affecting congressional civil rights activity. Primarily, signals influence the congressional civil rights policy agenda. Although this finding is consistent across both houses of Congress, the effectiveness with which signals increase the president's success rate vary substantially by house of Congress. Signals have virtually no impact on roll-call vote success rate in the House of Representatives, even though signals have a direct impact on Senate civil rights roll-call votes.

The case of civil rights policy demonstrates the potential that signals have as a source of presidential influence in Congress and the bureaucracy. Depending on whether one sees the glass as half empty or half full, one will see significant or only marginal signaling effects on civil rights policy. Simply put, presidential signals have an impact on congressional and bureaucratic outputs, even though this influence varies by institution. These findings provide support for the theory of presidential signaling as a generalizable alternative to the going-public argument. The next two chapters seek to illuminate the range of the president's power of public signaling, and whether it varies by other policy areas.

Notes

1. Executive Order 9981, July 26, 1948.
2. Media attention, according to the number of articles covering race list-

ed in the *Reader's Guide to Periodical Literature*, increased significantly in 1995. Public salience also increased slightly in 1997, according to Gallup's "Most Important Problem" series.

3. Shortly after Kennedy's assassination on November 22, 1963, Speaker Jesse Unrah urged immediate action on civil rights in a letter to President Johnson. He noted that civil rights must capitalize on the "sympathy factor" associated with the Kennedy assassination (this letter can be found in the LBJ Library as: Jesse Unrah to the president, November 26, 1963, Legislative Background Civil Rights Act of 1964 Box 1, Executive, LE/F211-4).

4. The preclearance provision requires states to submit any changes they make to voting laws to the federal government for approval before those changes may be enacted.

5. See *Missouri ex rel. Gaines v. Canada* (305 US 337 1938), *Sweat v. Painter* (339 US 629 1950), and *Brown v. Board of Education* (347 US 483 1954), among others.

6. Although President Clinton's "conversation" had little impact on legislation in Congress, it appears to have increased slightly the public importance of civil rights. Gallup's "Most Important Problem" series, for example, showed an increase in the percentage of the public who viewed race as the most important problem facing the United States over the course of 1997, the year in which President Clinton implored Americans to have a "conversation on race." The percentage rose from 2 in January, to 3 in August, and finally to 5 in December. The percentage declined back to 2 percent in April 1998.

7. Although the DOJ had authority to prosecute criminal violations of civil rights, this power was very limited prior to 1957 (Landsberg 1997: 174). Moreover, there is no record of criminal civil rights cases being filed in US district court prior to 1961.

8. Cohesion refers to bureau members' commitment to an organization and its goals (Meier 1993: 72).

9. Landsberg (1997: 79) observed that early court precedent in the prosecution of civil rights violations gave the Civil Rights Division and the executive branch considerable "judgement and discretion" in pursuing and filing civil rights cases.

10. Although Aberbach (1990) found that most congressional hearings are positive, research on civil rights oversight is limited. I therefore leave open the possibility of positive or negative oversight effects.

11. Two documents support staff emphasis on signals for civil rights legislation. The first is a memo from Lee White to Bill Moyers (December 30, 1964) concerning progress on what would be the 1965 Voting Rights Act. White suggested that the president "could in a speech or statement call attention to the importance of registration and indicate that 1965 was to be a year of test and if there were not any substantial improvements he would feel it desirable for the Congress to consider legislation along these lines in 1966" (this memo can be found in the LBJ Library as: Lee White to Bill Moyers, December 30, 1964, Voting Rights Act of 1965, Box 2). The second document is a memo concerning a January 1964 cabinet meeting that also emphasized the importance of public statements to the president's legislative and bureaucratic strategy: "It may be helpful to have a firm statement of presidential policy regarding strong efforts to employ and promote on the basis of ability and without regard to race, color, or creed" (this memo can be found in the LBJ Library as: Lee White to the president, memo, January 6, 1964, cabinet meetings). Although neither of these doc-

uments explicitly stated that presidential signals can affect legislation, their presence in White House operations suggests that White House staff at least thought that statements were important to the president's civil rights policy agenda and its success.

12. One executive order, No. 11478 (August 8, 1969), incorporated most of what Nixon called the Philadelphia Plan.

13. Whereas Nixon supported goals and timetables in 1969, he opposed "quotas" for hiring. In a Labor Day message on September 3, 1972, for example, Nixon said, "We believe that a person's ability and ambition should determine his income, and that his income should not be redistributed by Government or restricted by some quota system" (*Public Papers of the Presidents: Nixon, 1969–1974*). Edsall and Edsall (1992: 97) even claimed that Nixon turned against his Philadelphia Plan, although I cannot find an explicit statement by Nixon that actually renounces minority-hiring goals.

14. Presidents who spoke against civil rights policy did so on specific issues to which a majority of Americans were opposed. Presidents Nixon and Ford, who have the highest percentage of statements opposing civil rights, spoke out against a specific area of remedying segregation that was opposed by a high percentage of the public. Moreover, Presidents Reagan's and Bush's opposition to affirmative action was supported significantly by white Americans. Public opposition to particular aspects of civil rights policy for minorities gave certain presidents leeway to speak out against it. This also suggests that presidents may have responded to the measurable salience of civil rights policy and did not influence it (see Eshbaugh-Soha and Peake 2004).

15. Modeling the president's roll-call vote success as a dichotomous variable (1 if the president won the vote, 0 if he did not) produces a similar model. The probability of success increases as presidents signal more on civil rights policy.

16. Another explanation for this impact is multicollinearity. Correlation coefficients demonstrate that percentage of presidential seats, presidential approval ratings, and signals are all positively related. In bivariate regressions, seats have a positive impact on roll-call vote success. Yet, controlling for either presidential approval or signals flips the sign on the president's party seats in the Senate.

17. The same is correct for supportive signals. Interacting presidential approval with the number of signals—whether positive or negative—does not increase presidential influence over the Civil Rights Division. In other words, popular presidents are not more likely to decrease (increase) CRD activity if opposed to (supportive of) civil rights policy.

18. The number of "cases commenced" as opposed to "cases terminated" allows a more direct assessment of presidential influence. Terminated cases may hinge more on the skill of the prosecutor, the judge, and the quality of the case. I am not arguing that presidents influence the process of civil rights litigation but rather that presidents can set the table for more or less litigation. The difference is likely negligible in a quantitative model but theoretically important nonetheless.

19. Budgets could affect the number of civil cases litigated, and both series seem to trend together over time. Yet a Johansen Cointegration test fails to reject the null of no cointegration.

5

SALIENCE MATTERS

ON JUNE 13, 1989, PRESIDENT GEORGE H. W. BUSH USED THE MAJESTIC backdrop of the Teton Range to advertise new and extensive amendments to the Clean Air Act (CAA). He proclaimed that "nature needs our help . . . [and we need to] do our part to improve and preserve our natural heritage, the very air we breathe, from coast to coast, for another five generations and beyond" (*Public Papers of the Presidents, 1989–1993*). With this speech and many to follow, President Bush informed Congress and the Environmental Protection Agency that his clean air plan intended to reduce acid rain (by decreasing allowable sulfur dioxide and nitrogen oxide emissions), to reduce smog-producing emissions, and to promote alternative fuels. Bush eventually signed the amendments on November 15, 1990, leading to cleaner air and more enforcement activity in the EPA. The question that I am concerned with is: Do speeches like the one Bush gave in Wyoming have any impact on the clean air policy activities of legislators and bureaucrats?

Complexity Coupled with Salience

Clean air policy provides conflicting incentives for presidential leadership and policy responsiveness. On the one hand, clean air policy is salient. Air pollution is not only a health issue, whereby most prefer to breathe clean air, but also an environmental and economic one. For these reasons, clean air policy meets Gormley's definition of a salient policy, that it affects a "sizeable portion of the population" (1986: 598). On the other hand, the regulation of air pollution is a complex policy area. Being complex, clean air policy requires expertise and technical understanding. It is EPA bureaucrats, those monitors of industrial power plants, who are charged with the task of interpreting data. They must use their technical understanding of air pollution to ensure compliance with federal clean air statutes. Complex policies limit presidential leadership and influence and curtail the activities of legislators. Yet when a policy is also salient—as clean air is—presidents have an opportunity to signal their preferences and influence the adoption and implementation of clean air policy. Indeed, it is only when clean air policy has been periodically salient (covered by the news media, that is) that presidents have led and legislators have adopted additional clean air standards to be implemented by the Environmental Protection Agency.

Responsiveness to presidential signals appears most likely on policies that are not only salient but also uncomplicated. Even though legislators and bureaucrats have been responsive to presidents' signals on civil rights policy, it is unclear whether this influence will translate into a policy area that is also complex. Is presidential signaling an uncomplicated matter, as suggested by the findings in Chapter 4, or does salience play a vital role in this relationship? In other words, does salience matter to presidential leadership of Congress and the bureaucracy?

A History of Clean Air Policy

The twentieth century witnessed substantial variation in federal interest in clean air regulation. The federal government largely ignored clean air policy until the 1950s and did not establish enforceable federal air pollution standards until the Clean Air Act of 1970 (R. Cohen 1995; Bryner 1995; Davies and Davies 1975; Jones 1975; Landy, Roberts, and Thomas 1994; Lowry 1992; Kraft and Vig 1990; Ringquist 1993; Vogel 1986). Like most of the industrialized world, the United States had done little to combat air pollution prior to 1970. Most regulation on air pollution had occurred at the local level, in cities that had dirty air from industrial manufacturing. Substantive clean air legislation failed to pass Congress before the 1950s because environmental regulation was not perceived to be a federal problem.

The 1950s brought air pollution regulation to federal attention. Congressional initiative, along with some positive presidential leadership, led to the first major federal statute designed to address the air pollution problem. Although the Air Pollution Control Act of 1955 established an air pollution research program at the federal level, it did little to expand federal powers to combat air pollution (Davies and Davies 1975). A lack of leadership, whether from Congress or the presidency, meant that air pollution remained a local policy problem.

Federal regulation over air pollution grew in the 1960s when several key clean air bills became laws. In February 1963, President Kennedy called for Congress to expand the federal government's role in matters pertaining to air pollution. Led by Senator Edmund Muskie (D-Maine)—chair of the newly created Subcommittee on Air and Water Pollution—Congress passed the Clean Air Act of 1963, which legislated greater federal enforcement authority over air pollution. Although this act gave federal abatement authority when air pollution endangered "the heath or welfare of persons in a State other than that in which the discharge . . . originates" (quoted from Jones 1975: 75) and encouraged the automobile industry to develop cleaner exhaust systems, it failed to significantly expand the federal air pollution role in two ways. First, the 1963 act maintained state and local primacy over forms of air pollution. Second, no national air quality or emissions standards were set by the 1963 act (Jones 1975: 76). In addition, air pollution was a health, not an environmental concern, and was regulated by the Department of Health, Education, and Welfare.

The Air Quality Act of 1967 further expanded the role of the federal government in matters concerning air pollution. Championed again by Edmund Muskie, the act expanded federal grants to states so that they could better implement air quality standards and set compliance deadlines for state pollution control plans. It also gave the Health, Education, and Welfare secretary the authority to impose regional standards if the states failed to set their own. The act failed to mandate national emissions standards, however, through which the federal government could best control the enforcement of air pollution regulations. Indeed, it failed to break the incremental nature characteristic of federal clean air legislation for the previous twenty years.

Although Rachel Carson's *Silent Spring* is credited with first placing the environment on the national agenda in 1962 (see R. Cohen 1995: 13), it took the federal government until 1970 to pass substantive pollution control measures that mandated national air quality standards and emissions controls. Owing in part to potential Nixon-Muskie presidential campaign battles in 1972, the Clean Air Act Amendments of 1970 were an example of who could outdo whom. Nixon sought to trump Muskie's policy entrepreneurial advances by providing spoken leadership on clean air. Although Muskie had been an environmental advocate throughout the 1960s, Nixon prodded Congress to take much bolder environmental action in his 1970 State of the Union address to Congress. Nixon asked for a stronger federal role as Muskie continued to push his incremental approach to fighting air pollution (Landy, Roberts, and Thomas 1994: 29). Muskie would not be outdone, nonetheless, and his revised bill went beyond even Nixon's calls for stringent standards and federal enforcement procedures. Out of this competition came the Clean Air Act Amendments of 1970, which intended to "protect and enhance the quality of the Nation's air resources so as to promote the public health and welfare and the productive capacity of its population" (quoted in Bryner 1995: 100). It also established National Ambient Air Quality Standards (Portney 1990: 31) and emissions compliance guidelines.

Before President Nixon even signed the Clean Air Act Amendments into law, he created the EPA.[1] Through an executive reorganization, Nixon consolidated several environmental programs, including pesticide, waste management, and water management, under the EPA. In addition, the EPA would have enforcement authority over the subsequently passed Clean Air Act Amendments (Landy, Roberts, and Thomas 1994: chap. 2). The EPA is primarily responsible for setting and implementing standards and guidelines legislated by the Clean Air Act. However influential Nixon actually was in their enactment, the Clean Air Act Amendments of 1970 and the Environmental Protection Agency gave Nixon a solid environmental policy record on which he courted the environmental vote during his 1972 landslide reelection campaign.

Despite advancements in clean air policy during the early 1970s, clean air enforcement lost some of its bite over the next two decades. The Clean Air Act of 1970 attempted to reduce air pollution beyond the immediate capabilities of bureaucrats and technicians to do so (Jones 1975: chap. 8; Kraft and Vig 2000: 17). These impracticalities coupled with resistance from automobile manufacturers led Congress to extend emissions requirement deadlines in 1977.[2] Several Supreme Court decisions also limited EPA's ability to successfully enforce key provisions of the 1970 amendments (see *International Harvester v. Ruckelshaus* [1973], for example).

With the election of Ronald Reagan in 1980, efforts to further reduce air pollution came to a standstill. Reagan's appointments and budget cuts effectively limited the EPA's effectiveness in enforcing clean air law (see Kraft and Vig 1984; Wood 1988). EPA staff morale and credibility also suffered under Reagan's first EPA administrator, Anne Gorsuch. Potential clean air legislation stalemated over committee conflicts and the perception that Reagan would veto any clean air legislation (R. Cohen 1995: chap. 3). The only substantive air pollution legislation that Congress produced during the Reagan years was an extension of the deadlines provided for under the 1977 Clean Air Act Amendments (R. Cohen 1995: 38). This was clearly not a significant move to regulate clean air. Nevertheless, the public and a growing coalition in Congress pushed to fill the clean air void. With the election of George H. W. Bush in 1988 and his clean air proposals in 1989, Congress was well on its way to passing new clean air legislation. It did so and President Bush signed into law the Clean Air Act Amendments of 1990 on November 15, 1990.

Bush made a concerted effort as nominee and president to support efforts to update clean air regulations. At his opponent's polluted home harbor, Bush sent a signal to voters, legislators, and bureaucrats during the summer of 1988 that he would be nothing less than an "environmental president." Bush acted on his promise by sending a comprehensive clean air bill to Congress on June 12, 1989. Although Bush resisted many congressional initiatives and did not play an active role in its development (R. Cohen 1995), he signed the Clean Air Act Amendments of 1990, the widest expansion of air pollution regulation since 1970. Nevertheless, Bush's environmental presidency may best be characterized as mixed. Division within the Bush White House, including internal criticism by John Sununu and Richard Darman of EPA director William Reilly, may have limited Bush's ability to lead the initial implementation of the 1990 act. In addition, his campaign strategy to label Bill Clinton and Al Gore as environmental extremists undercut Bush's perception as a strong leader on clean air (see Sussman and Kelso 1999: 118; Switzer 1998: 55). Spurred by industry influence, Vice President Dan Quayle's Council on Environmental Quality also resisted many facets of the Clean Air Act's implementation (Switzer 1998: 178). Although criticized throughout the Reagan and Bush years, Bush made "environmentally" efficient, market-based air pollution regulation, including emissions trading credits, the regulatory model of subsequent administrations.

Unlike prior administrations, the Clinton presidency produced no major advances in clean air legislation. Clinton, whether because of a Republican-controlled Congress or the extensiveness of the 1990 amendments, neither offered a clean air legislative proposal nor supported one in Congress. The Clinton administration used an administrative and incremental strategy to advance its constituents' environmental and clean air concerns. It administered regulatory reforms in the EPA, making it more efficient and responsive to pollution needs (Rosenbaum 2002). Clinton also successfully countered Republican efforts to cut budgets of many environmental programs (Kraft and Vig 2000: 15).

President George W. Bush has had a similarly mixed record on clean air policy. George Bush's top environmental proposal, his "Clear Skies" initiative, would have furthered the use of emissions reductions credits and trading to combat air pollution. Specifically, the proposal would have "scrap[ped] several pollution control requirements for coal-fired power plants in favor of a cap-and-trade program for emissions of mercury, nitrogen oxides, and sulfur dioxide" (Kriz and Sangillo 2005). The Bush administration has opposed any clear air (or environmental) policies that it believes may place the United States at an economic disadvantage. This is one of the reasons cited for withdrawing from the Kyoto Protocol and for the apparent reneging on a 2000 campaign promise to regulate carbon dioxide emissions. A lack of consistent presidential leadership on carbon dioxide led to some confusion and perhaps to the resignation of George Bush's first EPA director, Christine Todd Whitman (Suskind 2004: 101). Indeed, it was the carbon dioxide issue that prevented the president's proposal from being voted out of committee.[3]

Since the 1960s, presidents have played an important, yet limited, role in the adoption and implementation of clean air legislation. Clearly, no major legislation has passed Congress without clear presidential support for clean air initiatives. Presidents have also had success advancing the implementation of clean air statutes, as when Nixon created the EPA, and limiting the EPA's enforcement of clean air regulations in the early 1980s (Wood 1988). This history shows, however, that Congress has played a particularly important role in clean air legislation and implementation. Despite the potential for presidential influence over clean air policy, competing congressional attention to clean air regulations may preclude presidential influence. Public opinion may also be a mitigating factor in the president's influence over clean air policy in Congress and the bureaucracy. Although presidents have been able to rally public support for environmental protection (Vig 2000: 99), they may not be able to do so on a consistent basis. Nevertheless, the salience of clean air legislation and enforcement varies episodically with presidential attention to air pollution regulation,[4] suggestive of the potential for presidential influence over the adoption and implementation of air pollution through signals.

Clean Air Policy in Congress

Congress initially adopted a piecemeal approach to combating air pollution. With passage of the 1955 act, the Clean Air Act of 1960, and the Air Quality Act of 1967, legislators began to recognize the potential health problems caused by dirty air. But in part owing to industry resistance (Jones 1975) and imprecise solutions for air pollution, Congress granted states primary authority to voluntarily submit plans for the regulation and limitation of air pollution.

Later clean air statutes allowed for more federal intervention. The Clean Air Act Amendments of 1970 established national ambient air quality standards and set compliance deadlines. Although President Nixon created the Environmental Protection Agency, Congress developed a cordial and helpful relationship with the EPA by granting significant discretion to the agency and favoring environmental regulation overall. The relationship continued even though Congress extended compliance deadlines and weakened some emissions standards in the 1977 amendments to the Clean Air Act. Several attempts to further weaken the Clean Air Act in the early 1980s were rebuffed in committee. In addition, Congress passed and President Bush signed the most comprehensive statute with which the EPA could limit air pollution. Two legislative entrepreneurs were particularly influential in congressional initiative on clean air policy. Senators Edmund Muskie and George Mitchell both made national clean air legislation their top priority and pushed for renewed and continued federal involvement.

Notwithstanding extensive congressional involvement over air pollution legislation, presidential signals may guide and influence congressional action on clean air policy. Because presidents are legitimate actors of the legislative process, Congress welcomes presidential priorities amid their own collective action problems (see Moe 1989). Presidential signals inform legislators whether presidents will support or oppose a bill. If presidents signal their support for a clean air bill, Congress can move confidently toward its passage. Each significant advance in clean air regulation is associated with presidential interest in it. Presidents Eisenhower, Kennedy, Johnson, and Nixon all voiced support for clean air legislation before Congress deliberated and debated the issue. George H. W. Bush made environmental protections a campaign issue and eventually signed the Clean Air Act Amendments of 1990. Pro-environmental legislators seized the opportunity for expanding federal air pollution regulations once President Bush had signaled his support for amendments to the Clean Air Act. With presidential support, legislators will act on their preferences, knowing that they have a good chance of achieving their own clean air policy goals.

When the president does not signal his support for a bill, legislators have to weigh the costs of pursuing legislation that might either stalemate without presidential leadership or might face a presidential veto. As witnessed during the 1980s, legislators who supported further clean air restrictions did not pursue them then because they knew that President Reagan was opposed to such legislation. Although several legislators thought strict air pollution regulations were needed, they were not optimistic about strengthening air pollution regulations with

Reagan in the White House (R. Cohen 1995). Henry Waxman, a strong supporter of air pollution regulations, did not propose significant overhauls to federal clean air laws, even though he preferred active federal involvement. Instead, he reacted to a president intent on cutting environmental spending by preventing further erosion in the federal government's air pollution regulatory authority (R. Cohen 1995). Potential clean air legislation hibernated in a Democratic-controlled Congress until a clean air–friendly George H. W. Bush was sworn in as president. In short, even if Congress has historically dominated the development of clean air policy, it has been unwilling to pursue major advances in air pollution regulation without explicit presidential leadership. Therefore, as presidents provide leadership over clean air policy through their public signals, they should affect their success over roll-call votes in Congress.[5]

The episodic dynamics of clean air policy aid presidential influence in Congress. Environmental and clean air policies follow cycles of public opinion, and they are only measurably salient periodically. When the public expresses concern for air pollution and the environment, Congress tends to enact favorable clean air legislation. Congress passed significant extensions to the Clean Air Act in 1970 and 1990 when public interest in the environment was quite high. Presidents have also tended to emphasize clean air when public opinion supported or media paid attention to clean air regulations. When salient to the public in the early 1970s and late 1980s, Richard Nixon bested Edmund Muskie's clean air proposal and George H. W. Bush proposed amendments to the Clean Air Act.[6] When public interest in environmental regulations was much lower in the late 1970s, conversely, President Carter quietly signed the 1977 amendments that extended emissions and pollution control deadlines at the behest of industry.

Presidential signals should have an impact on congressional clean air activities, all else being equal. Yet legislators have their own concerns that may conflict with the president's, rendering presidential signals inconsequential in their decisions. Legislators need constituency support to achieve their primary goal of reelection. Especially when presidential and congressional preferences for clean air policy conflict, legislators are likely to respond to their constituency's cues, not the president's signals, when an issue is salient (see Miller and Stokes 1963). Nevertheless, the historical evidence shows a clear pattern of presidential involvement over clean air policy: Congress has not pursued clean air legislation without presidential support (see R. Cohen 1995). Hence, presidential signals will likely have some impact on congressional roll-call votes.

Clean Air Policy in the Bureaucracy

To ensure that the air is clean, the federal government has sought to regulate pollution from industry and automobiles. Prior to the Nixon administration, federal responsibility to regulate air pollution resided in Health and Human Services or in the Department of Health, Education, and Welfare. During the Nixon administration, the Environmental Protection Agency assumed primary authority to regulate air pollution and to implement the Clean Air Act Amendments of 1970. With this act, the federal government assumed a primary role in the regulation of air pollution. Hence, this discussion of clean air policy in the bureaucracy focuses on the EPA and its responsibility for enforcing national ambient air quality standards.

The Environmental Protection Agency

Created through an executive reorganization during the Nixon administration, the EPA is responsible for implementing a range of environmental statutes dealing with air and water pollution, pesticides, and solid waste. The EPA's primary activity is enforcing pollution provisions of many environmental statutes. In coordination with state agencies, the EPA enforces federal air pollution standards set forth in the Clean Air Act.

Enforcement of clean air legislation can be an arduous and sometimes lengthy process. During the first few years of enforcing clean air regulation, the EPA had to compile a list of potential polluters, determine the minimum level of emissions allowed for that source, and acquire emissions reports from particular sources.[7] After determining that a violation had occurred at a specific source, the EPA had to issue a notice to that source and, at first pass, require the remedy within thirty days. If the offense was of sufficient gravity, an EPA administrator could issue an administrative order and demand compliance within a reasonable time frame. The EPA brings civil action if the source persists in its violation of clean air regulations (see Melnick 1983: 196–205).

The EPA serves both Congress and the presidency. Historically it has been responsive to congressional influence (Marcus 1980; Ringquist 1995; Ripley and Franklin 1991),[8] as key members of Congress created and drafted the legislation guiding EPA activity. In addition, Congress appropriates funds, amends governing statutes, and oversees EPA activities. The presidency also shapes the EPA. Richard Nixon created the EPA with an executive order and was instrumental in shaping the Clean Air Act of 1970. Despite more consistent congressional interest in clean air policy over time, several reasons, including presidential involvement in the creation of the Environmental Protection Agency, suggest some potential for signaling influence over the enforcement of air pollution regulation.[9]

Reasons for Presidential Influence Through Signals

Presidential signals should influence the EPA for the same reasons highlighted in Chapter 3. The EPA is amenable to political persuasion because it must respond to its external political environment. As chief executive, moreover, the president is the legitimate leader of the executive branch, and bureaucrats are bound to follow his directives. Although the president's formal tools of control—appointment, removal, and budget powers—may affect the implementation of clean air policy, they are not always sufficient for presidents to affect clean air regulations (Wood 1988; Wood and Waterman 1994). As a result, the president must lead and communicate preferences to ensure effective policy implementation (Edwards 1980, 2000). Presidents need their constitutional legitimacy *and* policy signals to inform and persuade policy actors and affect clean air outputs.

The EPA needs power to function effectively, and the presidency is relevant to an agency's implementation capabilities. As constitutional manager of clean air policy, the president is situated to either withhold or provide support for the agency's activities, thereby affecting its power to implement policy. Through positive signals, presidents inform EPA inspectors that they have presidential support of their mission. By providing consistent leadership and instilling a cohesive message among bureaucrats, presidents can motivate inspectors to enforce their mission vigorously, which will increase EPA enforcement activity. The opposite is unlikely to happen: owing to bureaucratic discretion, negative signals should not decrease the EPA's policy activity. Only significant hammers—such as massive budget cuts or unfavorable appointees (Wood 1988)—will have such an effect.

Positive signals are likely to be influential because they can help the EPA set priorities that are consistent with its mission. Presidents who set priorities may allow an agency to use its scarce time and resources more wisely. Like all federal agencies, the EPA has limited staff and resources. The EPA, in particular, has been significantly understaffed and funded since the 1980s (Kraft and Vig 2000: 19). A president who signals his preferences consistently and continuously to the EPA may be able to lead the agency to administer its regulatory responsibilities more efficiently. Signals can focus the EPA on the importance of clean air and increase its enforcement frequency. Presidential support can motivate the EPA to focus on clean air policy, knowing that if it follows the president's lead he will not cut its budget, appoint an incompetent director, or otherwise curtail its power. Signals may be particularly successful at focusing the EPA on clean air enforcement, given its responsibilities for water and noise pollution (see Rosenbaum [1991: 98–99] for a comprehensive list of EPA regulatory responsibilities). Signals advocating vigorous enforcement of clean air legislation help the EPA focus on the enforcement of air pollution laws amid its many other responsibilities.

The nature of clean air policy, that it is salient yet complex, provides conflicting incentives for bureaucratic responsiveness. On the one hand, salience requires bureaucrats to "look over their shoulder" and respond to presidential leadership. On the other hand, the technical complexity needed to understand how to regulate air pollution correctly encourages bureaucrats to ignore presidential preferences and to implement their policy mission without the guidance of the chief executive. To determine if one of these characteristics may drive bureaucratic behavior, it is worth discussing, then controlling for, the measurable salience of clean air policy.

Simply put, when environmental policy is measurably salient to the public, elected democratic officials have incentives to discuss, adopt, and encourage the implementation of clean air regulations. At these times, when clean air policies are clearly in the news and therefore on the minds of presidents and other politicians, politicians may endorse the adoption and implementation of clean air regulations and, at the same time, raise the awareness of bureaucrats responsible for regulating air pollution. Once the issue has been called to their attention, bureaucrats should respond by "looking over their shoulders" and listen for presidential signals. Moreover, because environmental policy follows only periodic attention cycles (see Downs 1972), public concern for clean air policy may temper both congressional and presidential control over the implementation of air pollution regulations, so that presidential signals may affect EPA activity primarily when clean air is salient.[10]

Despite incentives for both Congress and the presidency to oversee and direct clean air policy when its salient characteristics dominate the decisionmaking of bureaucrats, presidents are more likely to guide the implementation of clean air policy than are legislators. The literature suggests that an agency's creator has significant and sustained influence over that agency. President Nixon created the Environmental Protection Agency through an executive reorganization, so that the presidency, not Congress or the courts, laid the organizational foundation for the EPA's activity. Presidential influence over the EPA's creation "hardwired" it for presidential control over the long term. When a political principal hardwires, or creates an agency according to his or her own political and policy preferences, the principal creates within the agency a means of responsiveness (Macey 1992). As a result, an agency's internal structure and environment "mirror" the politics at enactment so that those instrumental in the agency's creation will be represented through its structure and process, protecting the creator's interests against "policy drift" (McCubbins, Noll, and Weingast 1989).[11] The presidency was vital to the creation of the EPA, so future presidential influence and involvement in its activity are probable. Notwithstanding presidential influence in the EPA, dual principals limit the potential for political control overall, especially if they have different ideological perspectives (Moe 1985; Krause 1996). Therefore, congressional hearings are still likely to affect EPA activity.

Limits to Presidential Signals

Other characteristics of clean air policy indicate that presidents might have some difficulty affecting EPA enforcements. For one thing, clean air policy is a complex regulatory policy. Presidents are unlikely to dedicate their limited time and resources to understanding the technical specifics of national ambient air quality standards and the level of automobile emissions allowed in different regions. Presidents must understand the importance of many policy areas, not specialize in the technical specifics of air pollution. Moreover, complexity encourages active industrial involvement that could limit presidential signals and their impact on enforcement activity (Gormley 1986). By definition, enforcement of clean air regulations by the EPA means that industry will be hindered, at least in the short term. Industry often has the resources to affect policy implementation (Meier 1985), however, and to influence EPA activity (see Rosenbaum 1989). Automobile manufacturers and other interested parties lobby legislators to oversee the EPA to limit regulation. They also engage in public relations campaigns to increase the public costs of burdensome air pollution restrictions. Given the direct losses industry could incur with strict enforcement of clean air laws, their influence, not the president's signals, could have a more direct bearing on the EPA's enforcement activity. The bottom line is that if industry does not wish to comply with federal regulation of air pollution, the EPA does not have enough money or manpower to ensure that it always complies.

Technological uncertainty and complexity also give the EPA much discretion to resist political and presidential control (see, among others,

Wood and Waterman 1994). The EPA works with national ambient air quality standards and has the technical understanding to apply these standards to different regions with distinct air pollution problems. Presidents simply do not have the time or resources (many do not have the interest) to understand the technical complexity of clean air policy. When it comes to implementation of clean air regulations, therefore, bureaucrats have an informational and expertise advantage to which elected officials, including presidents, may defer (Gormley 1986). It follows, therefore, that EPA bureaucrats might resist the president's leadership policy, given their discretion in the implementation of a complex policy area.

Finally, the fluctuating salience of clean air policy means that presidents will not consistently influence the EPA. Environmental policy is tied, like no other policy, to the cycles of issue evolution and public agendas (Downs 1972; Henry and Gordon 2001). Public interest in environmental politics has increased when the federal government has debated or proposed major environmental legislation. The early 1970s witnessed widespread public concern about many environmental issues, as did 1990, when the Clean Air Act was amended. Although the public consistently favors environmental protection, it is rarely intensely in favor of it. Termed "passive consensus," the public is concerned about the environment, but not immensely so, allowing politicians to ignore the environment when public salience is low and to focus on other issues (Dunlap 1989). When environmental policy is not salient to the public, politicians do not have as much incentive to pursue it, and industry may actually drive its adoption and implementation. Presidential signaling over clean air policy is likely an episodic, not a consistent, political event. Therefore, when the public is passive toward clean air policy, as it usually is, presidents are unlikely to affect the enforcement of clean air regulations through signals. Yet when clean air policy is salient, presidential signals should affect EPA outputs.

Congress and the Courts

Other principals besides the presidency may also influence air pollution regulation. Congress could affect clean air outputs through oversight hearings and key statutory interventions. Through their oversight authority, congressional committees can shape bureaucratic behavior and activity. Congressional oversight has been a particularly useful strategy since the 1970s (Aberbach 1990; Weingast and Moran 1983), as Congress has become more decentralized. Legislative entrepreneurs also prefer an active role in overseeing agencies because it gives them an opportunity to make a name for themselves by publicly supporting or opposing bureaucratic activity (Baumgartner and Jones 1993). When clean air policy is salient, when legislative entrepreneurs have a public opportunity to expand the scope of conflict, more hearings on air pollution regulations should shape EPA clean air enforcement activity.

Congress has influenced clean air regulations through legislation since the 1950s. Congress was instrumental in shaping the EPA's standards for regulation through the Clean Air Act Amendments of 1970 (see Macey 1992; McCubbins, Noll, and Weingast 1989) and its legislation of several "hammer" clauses that demand strict agency compliance to statutory deadlines and goals. Congress mandated that the EPA establish national ambient air quality standards within thirty days of passage of the 1970 amendments and develop technology standards for automobile emissions in five years. Only subsequent legislation (the 1977 amendments) or Supreme Court decisions (*International Harvester v. Ruckelshaus* [1973], for example) could change these and other statutorily defined compliance objectives. Congress is also free to change the procedures by which the EPA operates, further enhancing its control (see McCubbins, Noll, and Weingast 1989). In some instances, a few key legislators have been crucial to the adoption of the clean air acts that guide bureaucratic action. Policy entrepreneurs Muskie in 1970 and Mitchell in 1990 provided leadership to ensure passage of major clean air legislation. Other committee chairs and leaders have also altered the course of clean air policy outputs (Bryner 1995; R. Cohen 1995). Overall, legislative incentives to oversee the EPA and congressional prominence in crafting environmental legislation suggest that Congress can affect the enforcement of air pollution regulations just as presidents might.

The institutional makeup of Congress also *limits* the potential for congressional influence over clean air enforcement, however. Since passage of major environmental legislation in the 1960s and 1970s, Congress has become more decentralized. There is not one committee on the environment. Rather, several committees handle various aspects of different environmental regulations, including air pollution. An oversight hearing on the EPA and air pollution may be quieted by a different message from another, equally influential committee. The impact of external influences, including environmental and industrial lobbyists, may also dissuade Congress from taking an active role in environmental policy without persuasion from pressure groups (R. Cohen 1995). In addition, the technical nature of air pollution regulation means that individual legislators will take much less of an active role in crafting legislation and in understanding the nuances of regulatory enforcement (Ringquist 1995: 167).

Being a key institution in the interpretation of EPA rules, the courts have affected the regulation of air pollution. US district courts and, to a lesser extent, the US Supreme Court have set guidelines and limited EPA authority to enforce clean air statutes (see Melnick 1983). The discretion allotted to the EPA through environmental legislation contributes to the interpretation of administrative rules and procedures by the courts. Melnick (1983) concluded that the judicial branch has more often hindered than expanded the regulation of air control policy. It has also limited the discretion of administrators to bargain with industry by restricting such bargaining to the compliance deadlines legislated by Congress (see Wenner 1989: 251–255). Nevertheless, the complexity of clean air policy and judges' limited expertise in air pollution means that "judges usually uphold agency decisions" (Melnick 1983: 53).

Although the judicial branch is important to the EPA and clean air regulations, measuring difficulties limit its inclusion in this chapter's model of clean air enforcements. First, clean air cases at the Supreme Court level are rare. Segal and Spaeth, in their judicial database (Spaeth 1999), identified roughly eleven cases since 1957 that were related to environmental protection in their categories of environmental protection (category 933) and pollution (category 934) (see Appendix C).[12] Many significant clean air regulation cases also occur in US district court; these cases may or may not affect national clean air enforcement. Second, a limited number of important cases tend to drive the judicial impact on EPA decisionmaking and discretion (Melnick 1983: 54). These cases helped shape EPA enforcement criteria and may have influenced the level of its activity. Because many of these cases occurred prior to 1977, no measure of these cases will model EPA enforcements since 1977.

Findings

Clean air policy is an area that historically shows mixed presidential leadership. Although Eisenhower, Kennedy, Johnson, Nixon, and Bush all signed major clean air legislation, ambitious and conscientious members of Congress championed most of these proposals. Presidents may have, nevertheless, facilitated legislators' efforts. Presidents may have used their signaling powers to affect clean air policy in both Congress and the bureaucracy. I first present descriptive evidence of presidential signaling on clean air policy and then examine several quantitative models of signals and clean air policy.

Descriptive Evidence

Presidents speak periodically about clean air policy, an area to which presidents do not pay regular attention. Table 5.1 shows that two presidents who were particularly influential in the passage of major clean air legislation—Nixon and George H. W. Bush—delivered more positive clear air policy signals than any other president. Johnson spoke about clean air to a small but noticeable extent as he lent public support to the Air Quality Act of 1967. Presidents Ford and Carter sent a fair number of clean air signals as well. Ford urged Congress to pass an amendment to the 1970 version of the Clean Air Act in light of energy shortages and price spikes. Unlike most presidents in this study, however, Gerald Ford sought to limit the reach of clean air regulations, rather than extend them. Carter also spoke about clean air in relation to his energy program. Aside from several "Energy Emergency" statements that allowed state governors to suspend clean air standards for thirty days amid rising

Table 5.1 Yearly Average Signals on Clean Air Policy by Presidential Administration

President	Total Average	Support	Neutral	Oppose
Eisenhower	0.9	0.9 (100 %)[a]	0 (0.0 %)	0.0 (0.0 %)
Kennedy	2.0	2.0 (100.0)	0 (0.0)	0.0 (0.0)
Johnson	7.6	6.0 (78.9)	1.4 (18.4)	0.0 (0.0)
Nixon	13.3	10.5 (75.3)	2.5 (18.8)	0.3 (2.2)
Ford	8.0	0 (0.0)	1.7 (21.3)	7.7 (96.3)
Carter[b]	13.8	8.5 (61.8)	1.3 (9.4)	4.0 (29.0)
Reagan	6.1	2.5 (40.8)	2.5 (40.8)	1.1 (18.0)
G. H. W. Bush	29.8	25.0 (83.9)	4.3 (14.4)	0.5 (1.7)
Clinton	8.5	7.7 (90.6)	0.8 (9.4)	0.1 (1.2)
G. W. Bush[c]	8.25	6.0 (72.7)	0.5 (6.1)	2.0 (24.2)

Notes: Numbers are administration averages of the number of pages in the *Public Papers of the Presidents* on which presidents mention clean air policy.

a. Numbers in parentheses are the average percentage of all positive, neutral, or negative clean air policy signals.

b. Carter has a high number of opposition signals because of his "Energy Emergency" statements that gave the governors of several "mideastern" states the discretion to suspend clean air regulations for thirty days.

c. Numbers for George W. Bush are through 2004.

energy prices, Carter was in favor of regulating air pollution. He advocated an energy plan to use available resources, including alternative fuels, in accordance with reasonable clean air standards mandated by the 1970 amendments to the Clean Air Act.

Presidents Reagan, Clinton, and George W. Bush offered similar clean air strategies, despite their different perspectives. On the one hand, President Reagan opposed clean air regulations even though he did not actively signal this preference. Clean air policy is a valence issue because, on the surface, everyone values and supports clean air. Hence, presidents who oppose clean air regulation are unlikely to use a public strategy to realize their policy goals. When President Reagan spoke about clean air, for example, he did so symbolically, without substantive rhetoric and promise for action (Eshbaugh-Soha 2001). Clinton, on the other hand, signaled at a moderate frequency in favor of clean air regulations. Nevertheless, Clinton did not propose any further clean air regulations in the legislative arena. Burdened by a Republican-controlled Congress, he sent several signals a year opposing potential cuts in the EPA's budget and supported EPA director Carol Browner and her promise of efficient, yet effective, regulation of air pollution. Finally, although George W. Bush proposed his own revision to the Clean Air Act, his "Clear Skies" initiative, he has not discussed clean air policy frequently. Indeed, George W. Bush's devotion to clean air signals is average when compared with all presidents, but well below the yearly signals devoted by presidents who supported revisions to the Clean Air Act.

Two presidents who clearly used signals to affect clean air policy were George H. W. Bush and Nixon. Both presidents supported clean air legislation publicly and signaled their support for clean air legislation frequently. Although legislators played key roles in the development and adoption of clean air legislation, these presidents did more than just signal their preferences as Congress deliberated the issue. President Nixon, for example, used the State of the Union address and other speeches that pushed Senator Muskie to advocate even stricter air pollution legislation (R. Cohen 1995). Moreover, George H. W. Bush made clean air policy a campaign issue before legislation was even submitted in Congress. Scholars also point out that one reason why clean air was on the legislative agenda was that Bush was not Reagan. A moderate President Bush signaled through his public statements his desire for comprehensive clean air legislation and, in turn, encouraged legislators to prioritize amendments to the Clean Air Act. Bush and Nixon also supported the implementation of air pollution regulations. Nixon, in particular, used the bully pulpit to inform members of Congress of his intentions to reorganize the federal environmental bureaucracy and to create the Environmental Protection Agency.

Legislative Activity

Legislative attention to clean air policy has fluctuated over the course of this study. Initially, Congress passed incremental federal regulatory laws to combat air pollution. Following the Clean Air Act Amendments of 1970, Congress resumed this strategy by maintaining existing policies and renewing them in the short term (Kraft 1990). Significant clean air legislation follows episodic cycles of public opinion, so we might expect presidents to increase their roll-call vote success when they signal their preferences on clean air policy. But have presidential signals influenced clean air roll calls? To answer this question, I model presidential signals separately by house of Congress because the percentage of presidential party seats in Congress is the strongest determinant of presidential success on roll-call votes.

Aside from different percentages of party seats, the models for the House and Senate are similar. The dependent variable is the percentage of legislators who voted in favor of the president's position, and the unit of analysis is the vote. Presidential signals are the number of statements presidents make on clean air policy during the eight months prior to each vote.[13] I also model presidential approval, measured as the percentage indicated on the date prior to each vote, and media attention. I interact signals with media attention to produce a salience measure. Ordinary Least Squares (OLS) regression estimates the impact of presidential signals and other independent variables on the president's roll-call success over clean air policy (see Appendix B).[14] Equation 5.1 shows the basic model.

$$\text{Vote Success} = B_0 + B_1\text{Signals} + B_2\%\text{Seats} + B_3\text{Success}_{t-1} + \\ B_4\text{Media Attention} + B_5\text{Approval} + B_6\text{Veto Threat} + B_7\text{Honeymoon} + \varepsilon \qquad \textbf{5.1}$$

The Senate.   The Senate has played a central role in the development and enactment of clean air policy. Senators Muskie and Mitchell, for example, were crucial to the success of two major clean air bills. Senator Muskie had significant influence over clean air legislation in the 1960s and in crafting the Clean Air Act Amendments of 1970. Although George H. W. Bush clearly signaled his support of clean air legislation early in his tenure, George Mitchell pushed amendments to the Clean Air Act through the Senate (R. Cohen 1995). Nevertheless,

Presidents Bush and Nixon spoke frequently about clean air regulations (see Table 5.1) and supported their passage. Given the potential for affecting success in the Senate through clean air signals, what do the numbers say?

I first examine the relationship between signals and several control variables and the president's success on clean air roll calls. First, signals have no apparent impact on the president's success on clean air roll calls (Table 5.2, Model A). They do relate positively to success but not significantly so. The same is true for the president's Senate party coalition, which is related positively, but not significantly, to success. Second, I model the president's success as a function of salience (Table 5.2, Model B). Signals, after all, might only be influential over clean air policy when it is salient; signals might only influence the president's success when interacted with media attention. The salience interaction positively affects success, even though it is not quite statistically significant for a one-tailed test. Moreover, it adds nothing to either the R-square or F-test, indicating that this measure does not add explanatory power to the president's success on clean air roll-call votes in the Senate. In addition, both models have relatively high R-squares without having many significant variables. Multicollinearity is therefore a likely problem in the Senate roll-call models. Besides the constant, only presidential approval ratings significantly affect the president's success rate on individual roll-call votes in both models, but the coefficient is negative and, thus, in the unexpected direction.

Table 5.2 Presidential Success on Senate Clean Air Policy Roll Calls

	Model A	Model B
Signals	0.15 (0.47)	
Presidential party seats (%)	0.69 (1.21)	0.66 (1.20)
Past success	−0.28 (−1.06)	−0.24 (−1.05)
Media attention	−0.02 (0.43)	
Presidential approval	−1.35 (−1.97)*	−1.19 (−2.36)*
Signals * media attention		0.001 (0.62)
Constant	130.69 (1.82)*	124.60 (1.87)*
R-square	.50	.50
F-statistic	3.63*	4.75*
White's test	3.26	2.83
N	24	24

Notes: * $p < .05$ (one-tailed).

t-scores in parentheses. Senate clean air roll-call votes occurred in 1966 (one vote), 1967 (one vote), 1974 (one vote), 1980 (one vote), 1988 (one vote), 1990 (sixteen votes), and 2003 (three votes). Veto, honeymoon, and Clean Air Act 1990 dummies are not applicable to sample of votes.

The House. Unlike the Senate, in which key members have played central, nationally prominent roles over the adoption of clean air legislation (R. Cohen 1995), the House of Representatives has played a more modest role. Because of this, presidents may be more likely to influence clean air policy in the House of Representatives than in the Senate. Cue theory suggests, after all, that legislators are more likely to use presidential cues absent cues from their own colleagues. Nevertheless, key committee members, such as Henry Waxman and John Dingel, have influenced developing clean air policy consistent with their different constituencies, whether stricter standards in southern California or automobile manufacturing interests in Michigan. Congressional makeup also shapes the likelihood that presidents will be successful over clean air roll-call votes, so long as they support clean air legislation. Usually, air pollution regulation or environmental policy is an area that Democrats support (Kraft and Vig 2000). Because the Democratic Party controlled the House of Representatives in all years in which major clean air legislation came to the floors of Congress, presidents who propose clean air legislation should receive favorable support from the House of Representatives.

I present two analyses of presidential influence over individual clean air roll-call votes in the House of Representatives. The first model relates signals and several control variables to the president's clean air success in the House (Table 5.3, Model A). Consistent with my expectations, signals relate positively and significantly to the president's success on individual clean air roll-call votes. One additional signal on clean air policy leads to an increase of nearly 3 percent in the president's success on clean air roll-call votes. This finding is confirmed when signals are interacted with media attention (Table 5.3, Model B). As the media cover more stories on clean air policy in combination with more presidential signals, the president's success increases on clean air roll-call votes in the House. Moreover, the salience interaction brings the percentage of House seats held by the president's party to a statistically significant level. When presidents signal their clean air preferences when the policy is measurably salient, the congressional makeup matters more to the president's success. Controlling for "salience," every additional percentage of House seats held by the president' party leads to a nearly 2 percent increase in the president's success.

Like the Senate model, nevertheless, these findings should be interpreted with caution. This sample of roll-call votes is very small. With an N of only 14, the impact of signals and the interaction of signals and

Table 5.3   Presidential Success on House Clean Air Policy Roll Calls

	Model A	Model B
Signals	2.97 (3.01)*	
Presidential party seats (%)	1.01 (1.22)	1.59 (2.07)*
Past success	0.24 (0.27)	–0.62 (–0.85)
Media attention	0.32 (0.50)	
Presidential approval	–2.36 (–1.01)	–4.01 (–2.13)*
Honeymoon	38.98 (0.75)	62.72 (1.51)
CAA 1990	–55.39 (–1.93)*	–62.47 (–2.47)*
Signals * media attention		0.05 (3.41)*
Constant	66.96 (0.63)	194.02 (2.20)*
R-square	.82	.80
F-statistic	3.89	4.74*
White's test	13.31	10.13
N	14	14

Notes: * p < .05 (one-tailed).

t-scores in parentheses. House clean air roll-call votes occurred in 1965 (two votes), 1967 (one vote), 1969 (one vote), 1970 (two votes), 1976 (three votes), 1977 (two votes), 1990 (one vote), and 1995 (two votes). Veto threat dropped from model.

media attention cannot be included in the same model. Because of these data limitations, it is impossible to model all theoretical expectations about signals, salience, and the president's success on roll-call votes. The interaction flips the direction of some variables, further complicating interpretation of this small N model. I present an alternative solution to this problem in Chapter 7.

Congress. To lessen the multicollinearity problem in the Senate models and to limit the impact of a small N present in the House of Representatives models, I pool all data points in Table 5.4.[15] In both models, signals and the president's party coalition in Congress positively and significantly affect his success on clean air roll-call votes. In Model A, an additional signal on clean air policy increases the president's success on individual roll-call votes by nearly 2 percent. Moreover, 1 additional percent of presidential party seats leads to an additional 2 percent increase in the president's success. Model B demonstrates that these effects also hold when signals are interacted with media attention. These findings do not comport exactly with my expectations, as I hypothesized that signals should only have an impact on the president's success in Congress when the news media pay substantial attention to clean air policy. Signals, nevertheless, have an independent and direct impact on the president's clean air success in Congress.

Table 5.4   Presidential Success on Congressional Clean Air Policy Roll Calls

	Model A	Model B
Signals	1.45 (2.15)*	
Congressional party seats (%)	1.84 (4.16) *	1.84 (4.47) *
Honeymoon	−14.86 (−1.01)	−13.63 (−1.13)
Veto threat	−15.70 (−1.07)	−13.07 (−1.02)
CAA 1990	−64.03 (−2.73) *	−72.70 (−3.21) *
Presidential approval	−0.71 (−1.47)	−0.77 (−1.72)
Media attention	0.23 (0.76)	
Past success	−0.74 (−1.75)	−0.75 (−1.95)
Signals * media attention		0.02 (3.48) *
Constant	48.48 (1.47)	66.41 (2.12) *
R-square	.60	.61
F-statistic	5.44*	5.96*
White's test	9.89	9.40
N	38	38

Note: * $p < .05$ (two-tailed).
t-scores in parentheses.

Bureaucratic Outputs

The number of EPA enforcement outputs over time helps assess presidential signaling influence over clean air bureaucratic outputs. This primary dependent variable, supplied by Wood (1988), is the number of monitoring activities undertaken by the EPA from 1977 to 1989 (Figure 5.1). "Monitoring activities are enforcement actions taken to assure that air pollution sources remain in compliance with the law . . . [they] consist of the sum of all EPA inspections, compliance monitor reports, compliance tests, and routine surveillance actions" (Wood 1988: 220; see Wood and Waterman 1994). The second dataset involves similar data supplied directly to me by the EPA: compliance and violation enforcement data recorded from 1989 to 1998 (see Figure 5.2 later in chapter). I analyze these data separately because the EPA has altered its enforcement data collection, making these series incompatible.

Of the independent variables, signals are the primary variable in the clean air enforcement models. Presidential signals are the total pages—whether positive, negative, or neutral—that presidents devote to clean air policy in their public papers. Like all other continuous variables in the models, signals are quarterly; they are also lagged one time-point to meet the time-order rule of causality.

Signals are not the only means of presidential control in the Environmental Protection Agency. The president's appointment and budgetary powers provide presidents with less-public sources of influence and control over the EPA. Presidential appointees help presidents

Figure 5.1 Quarterly Clean Air EPA Monitoring Reports, 1977–1989

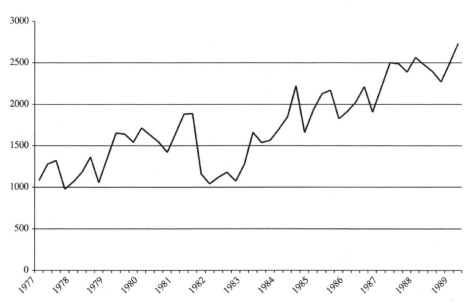

influence the bureaucracy, without presidents needing to make a significant personal effort at control. A political appointee may influence EPA activity in line with the president's policy preferences. Although Reagan's first EPA director, Anne Burford, did not significantly influence clean air enforcements, his second director, William Ruckelshaus, did (Wood 1988). The appointment measures are step function dummy variables coded one when a director actively heads the EPA.

Budgets are also important to agency outputs. An increase allows agencies to do more of what they do; budget cuts prevent bureaucrats from doing their jobs effectively. Indeed, Reagan's 1982 EPA budget cuts limited the EPA's ability to effectively monitor and enforce air pollution regulations (Wood 1988). I include a budget step function for the quarters when Reagan's 1982 fiscal year budget adversely affected EPA enforcement activity (see Wood 1988).

The remaining variables are also important controls of presidential signaling influence. As detailed in Chapter 3, presidential popularity as well as congressional, media, and interest group involvement may all affect EPA activity. Media attention is particularly important because policy salience, according to my theory, is crucial to the potential for political influence over EPA activity. This model is expressed mathematically as the transfer function shown in Equation 5.2.

$$Y_t = B_0 + (1-\omega_{01}B)X_{1-k} + (1-\omega_{02}B)X_{2-k} + (1-\omega_{03})X_{3-k} + (1-\omega_{04})X_{4-k} + \quad \textbf{5.2}$$
$$(1-\omega_{05})X_{5-k} + (1-\omega_{06})X_{6-k} + (\omega_{07}/1-\delta_{17}B)X_{7-k} + \varepsilon_t$$

where Y_t = quarterly EPA monitoring counts
  X_1 = supportive signals
  X_2 = congressional hearings
  X_3 = media attention
  X_4 = presidential approval ratings
  X_5 = Real gross domestic product (GDP)
  X_6 = step function interventions: 1982 budget; Burford and
    Ruckelshaus
  X_7 = signals, media attention interaction ("salience")
  k = number of lags

Some presidential influence: 1977–1989. Bureaucratic inertia and memory explain much EPA enforcement activity. Both the first-order autoregressive and fourth-lag moving average parameters are positive and significant and explain a good deal of the variance in EPA monitoring.[16] Thus, despite factually correct claims, such as Bush's own inference that his policies increased EPA enforcement activity over one year, from 1989 to 1990 (Switzer 1998: 56), presidents might have only a small impact on enforcement activity, whether through signals, appointments, or budgets. Indeed, Reagan's use of budget cuts and ideological appointments to exert influence over the EPA's clean air enforcement activity may be more an aberration than a consistent expectation of control. This comports with other research, including Wood's (1988) finding of some, however fleeting, presidential influence over the EPA. It also compares with EPA staff survey responses; EPA staffers rank presidents in the middle tier as to which principals they listen and respond to frequently (Waterman 1999).

Table 5.5 presents a preliminary model of clean air policy enforcements. Several variables are statistically significant. In particular, the Ruckelshaus appointment had an enormous positive impact on EPA morale, leading to increased enforcement of air pollution regulations. Two variables that have been significant in other research (Wood 1988), but are not in this model, are the step functions for Anne Burford and the fiscal 1982 budgets. The lack of significance is likely a function of less-refined time points used here than in previous analyses (Wood 1988).[17] Although the signals coefficient (Table 5.5) does not reach conventional levels of statistical significance, it is positive. This suggests the statistical potential for presidential signaling influence, influence that may be dependent on clean air's measurable salience (as my theory predicts).

Table 5.5   The Effect of Positive Signals on EPA Clean Air Monitoring Activity,
1977–1989 (Model 1)

	Parameter Estimate	Standard Error	t-statistic
Positive signals $_{t-1}$	26.60	20.89	1.27
Burford (step)	213.50	246.27	0.87
Budget (step)	−166.26	174.35	−0.95
Ruckelshaus (step)	733.22*	309.48	2.36
Presidential approval	1.24	7.13	0.17
Media attention	2.36	5.17	0.47
Congressional hearings $_{t-1}$	4.69	5.31	0.88
Membership Δ	−0.001	0.001	−0.71
Real GDP % Δ	−0.98	7.66	−0.13
Constant	1298.56*	377.79	3.43
AR1	0.71*	0.13	5.27
MA|4|	0.33*	0.17	1.95
R-square	.85		
Adjusted R-square	.80		
Mean of dependent	1761.42		
Standard error of estimate	215.71		
Box-Ljung Q	15.62		
White's test	17.82		
N	50		

Note: * p < .05.

Table 5.6 tests this condition by including an interaction term between supportive signals and media attention. Including an interactive effect between signals and salience produces a model in which supportive signals do have a positive and significant impact on EPA's monitoring activity over time. Every page that presidents devote to support of clean air policy in the *Public Papers of the Presidents* during the prior quarter leads to an increase of over fifty-one monitoring reports, or about a 3 percent increase on average. This coefficient means that from 1977 to 1989, the presidency was effective in motivating EPA bureaucrats to monitor air pollution violations more vigorously, typically in concert with significant media attention to clean air policy. Supportive signals sent are more likely to affect EPA activity significantly when controlling for the interactive effects of media attention and signals. But because this impact is modeled as a zero-order transfer function, these effects are of a short duration. In other words, signals motivate EPA bureaucrats to enforce clean air policy vigorously, but bureaucrats realize that presidential attention may be fleeting and therefore only react to signals in the short term.[18]

Theoretically speaking, when presidents signal their support for clean air policy as media discuss it, the motivational effects of signals

Table 5.6   The Effect of Positive Signals on EPA Clean Air Monitoring Activity, 1977–1989 (Model 2)

	Parameter Estimate	Standard Error	t-statistic
Positive signals $_{t-1}$	51.27*	21.24	2.41
Signals * media (salience) ω_0	0.69*	0.33	2.08
Signals * media (salience) δ_0	–0.92*	0.05	–17.10
Burford (step)	142.03	242.57	0.59
Budget (step)	–104.05	166.46	–0.62
Ruckelshaus (step)	665.69*	301.29	2.21
Presidential approval	0.31	6.62	0.05
Media attention	1.52	4.86	0.31
Congressional hearings $_{t-1}$	2.52	4.95	0.51
Membership Δ	–0.001	0.001	–1.27
Real GDP % Δ	–3.16	7.20	–0.44
Constant	1347.82*	353.17	3.82
AR1	0.75*	0.13	5.97
MA|4|	0.25	0.17	1.44
R-square	.88		
Adjusted R-square	.83		
Mean of dependent	1761.42		
Standard error of estimate	199.68		
Box-Ljung Q	8.72		
N	50		

Note: * p < .05 (two-tailed).

are compounded, furthering the positive impact that presidents have on EPA activity. Indeed, supportive signals seem most likely to penetrate multiple layers of a federal bureaucracy when they are associated with media attention. So even though signals have only a fleeting impact, the importance of salience to the EPA is more important. In sum, positive signals are influential but mainly when signals are delivered when clean air policy is also salient.[19]

What about the hypothetical relationship between negative signals and bureaucratic activity, that there should not be a relationship? Table 5.7 supports this hypothesis, that negative signals do not coerce the EPA and encourage it to enforce clean air legislation less. This is owing, in part, to the fact that the president's ability to coerce the EPA through public criticism is rarely effective and may be risky and costly. As a valence issue, clean air is not something that can be actively and publicly opposed.[20] Even popular presidents who oppose clean air enforcements have no impact on EPA activity through signals. More important, bureaucrats have discretion to resist presidential overtures when such overtures conflict with their policy mission. Only with significant use of other tools at their disposal, such as budget cuts, will presidents likely curtail an agency's activity with which they disagree. This is consistent with what we saw with the Civil Rights Division in Chapter 4.

Table 5.7   The Effect of Negative Signals on EPA Clean Air Monitoring Activity, 1977–1989

	Parameter Estimate	Standard Error	t-statistic
Negative signals $_{t-1}$	52.04	47.33	1.10
Burford (step)	355.63	259.48	1.37
Budget (step)	−213.01	179.74	−1.19
Ruckelshaus (step)	786.22*	318.76	2.47
Presidential approval	−2.29	7.34	−0.31
Media attention	−0.01	5.32	−0.001
Congressional hearings $_{t-1}$	5.95	5.18	1.15
Membership Δ	−0.001	0.001	−0.51
Real GDP % Δ	0.92	7.71	0.12
Constant	1506.85*	403.16	3.74
AR1	0.76*	0.13	5.71
MA|4|	0.32	0.18	1.79
R-square	0.85		
Adjusted R-square	0.80		
Mean of dependent	1761.42		
Standard error of estimate	217.02		
Box-Ljung Q	13.48		
LM test (5 lags)	3.27		
White's test	12.81		
N	50		

Note: * p < .05 (two-tailed).

Limited presidential influence: 1989–1998.   Although presidents used their positive signals to influence clean air enforcements during the late 1970s and 1980s, the future picture for presidential signaling influence over the EPA's handling of clean air may not be so rosy. Figure 5.1 showed EPA air pollution monitoring levels from 1977 to 1989. Significant and irregular variance in the graph implies the potential for presidential influence, as Table 5.6 demonstrated. Figure 5.2 shows EPA compliance and enforcement data from 1989 to 1998. These data are more seasonal and predictable. Indeed, the noise model for the latter series accounts for nearly 97 percent of the variance (Table 5.8).[21]

What do these seasonal enforcement patterns mean? One possible hypothesis concerns the age of the EPA. Bernstein (1955) argued that regulatory bureaucracies develop according to a life cycle, in which they enter into and pass through four stages: youth, gestation, maturity, and old age. The EPA may have passed through its youthful and gestation stages into maturity. At this third stage, an agency "relies more and more on settled procedures and adapts itself to the need to fight its own political battles unassisted by informed public opinion and effective national leadership" (Bernstein 1955: 87). As implied by the content of Figure 5.2 and Table 5.8, the EPA may well have entered a mature stage of development. In its air pollution regulatory activity, the EPA has become

Table 5.8   A Model of EPA Clean Air Enforcements, 1989–1998

	Parameter Estimate	Standard Error	t-statistic
Constant	3480.86*	1377.43	2.53
AR1	0.36*	0.18	2.05
SAR4	1.14*	0.03	33.49
SMA|4|	–0.43*	0.20	–2.13
R-square	.96		
Adjusted R-square	.96		
Mean of dependent	9680.57		
Standard error of estimate	541.89		
Box-Ljung Q	6.82		
N	88		

Note: * p < .05 (two-tailed).

so accustomed to implementing the Clean Air Act that its enforcement follows seasonal patterns of air pollution and enforcement. The EPA may be less amenable to presidential, congressional, and public influence because it has settled into a routine of enforcement. It has learned and effectively mastered the art of air pollution regulation so that this inertia as well as seasonal patterns of hot weather and more pollution— not external influences—drives EPA behavior. This does not mean that

Figure 5.2 Quarterly EPA Enforcement Activity, 1989–1998

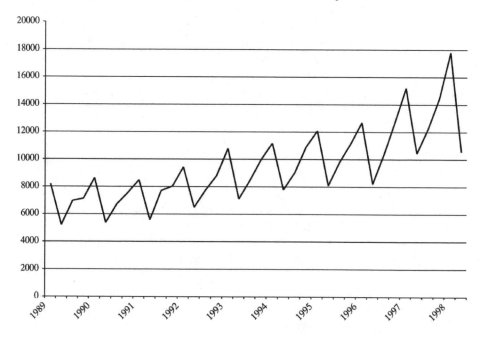

political actors cannot control the EPA. Only a significant hammer, such as severe resource cuts, may be shock enough to sway the EPA from its present course of clean air enforcement activity. Absent a drastic means of influence, politicians may be unable to influence the apparently impervious clean air activity of the Environmental Protection Agency.

Conclusion: Salience Trumps Complexity

As expected, presidents have significant, yet mixed, influence over clean air policy outputs. In Congress, the president's signals increase his success on clean air roll-call votes in the House but not in the Senate. This finding holds once the president's success is modeled against the impact of the president's signals on roll-call votes in both houses of Congress, combined. As in the House of Representatives, signals also increased the president's success on all clean air roll-call votes in this additive model. These positive effects of signals on the president's success persist whether or not clean air is measurably salient at the time of floor votes.

In the bureaucracy, presidents have been successful in motivating EPA agents to enforce clean air regulations more vigorously. The relationship is related to news coverage of clean air, whereby the episodic nature of clean air policy increases the impact of the president's signaling effectiveness. As expected, a newsworthy issue encourages bureaucrats to "look over their shoulders" and respond to presidential leadership. When clean air is not of national concern, bureaucrats rely more on their discretion and expertise than on presidential leadership to implement the complexity of air pollution regulations. As the two different clean air series show, however, future presidents may be unable to affect clean air enforcements through signals. The EPA seems entrenched significantly enough in its quarterly enforcement activity that only severe constraints on the EPA's ability to carry out these consistent activities will alter the future course of the series.

My findings also enlighten Wood's (1988) and Wood and Waterman's (1994) claims about the impact of Reagan's inauguration on EPA activity. "If the EPA bureaucracy was an agent responding passively to initiatives promulgated singularly by an executive principal, then enforcement activity should have dropped following the Reagan inauguration" (Wood and Waterman 1994: 119). Furthermore, "on the increase in EPA enforcements following the Reagan inauguration, it is clear that early executive leadership was ineffective" (Wood and Waterman 1994: 123). Signals, a clear indication of a president's public leadership on an issue, were not part of Reagan's strategy on clean air. He signaled his preferences only ten times in 1981, and only four of those discouraged air pollution regulation. We did not see a drop in enforcement activity upon Reagan's inauguration because Reagan did not provide the leader- ship necessary to induce such change. Although Reagan's inauguration could be seen as a negative signal, as Wood and Waterman did, I have hypothesized and confirmed support for the argument that negative sig- nals will not dissuade bureaucrats from implementing their mission. Especially when bureaucrats disagree, presidential intentions are not sufficient to alter the behavior of bureaucrats. What is needed is active use of presidential powers, such as the budget (Wood 2000b; Wood and Waterman 1994), when goals conflict or motivational leadership through signals when policy preferences converge. In other words, the EPA was able to ignore Reagan's and Burford's attempts to undercut agency activity until the 1982 fiscal year budget, which severely constrained the EPA's ability to implement clean air regulations effectively.

Overall, presidential signals provide presidents with a source of influence over policies that are salient, yet complex. Because salience matters, this impact is tied to the policy's measurable salience, particu- larly in the bureaucracy. The inevitable periodicity of clean air policy salience means that presidents have been less willing to use their public signals to affect clean air as they had used them on civil rights policy. Infrequent attention to clean air policy may be a function of the com- plexity of clean air policy, which tempers the president's interest in air pollution controls. Yet presidential leadership makes the reality of clean air legislation and EPA enforcements more or less plausible depending on how often the president signals his support.

Notes

1. President Nixon signed the Clean Air Act Amendments of 1970 into law on December 31, 1970. The EPA was created when Reorganization Plan 3 became effective on December 2, 1970.

2. Congress gave in to industry pressure in the 1977 amendments by extending compliance deadlines and relaxing some emissions standards. Nevertheless, Congress also strengthened the EPA's hand by adding civil penal- ties and construction ban sanctions to the agency's enforcement arsenal.

3. The proposal died in the Senate Environment and Public Works Committee in March 2005.

4. Gallup's "Most Important Problem" series shows peaks of public con- cern for clean air policy during the late 1960s and early 1970s as well as during 1989 when Bush proposed his clean air legislation.

5. Recent clean air legislation—George W. Bush's "Clear Skies" initia- tive—had to wait for a similar congruence before his initiative was even debat-

ed in committee. After Republicans took back control of the Senate during the 2002 congressional elections, Senator James Inhofe replaced the more liberal Senator Jim Jeffords as chair of the Environment and Public Works Committee, producing a committee vote, albeit a defeat, in March 2005. The theory of presidential signaling predicts this lack of success in part because Bush did not use his signals to lead his clean air policy priority through the Senate.

6. I do not assess the causality of salience. In other words, I do not know if presidential attention caused clean air to be salient or if clean air salience caused presidential attention. I simply note that presidential attention to clean air policy coincides with the public's concern (but see Eshbaugh-Soha and Peake [2004] for evidence that both congressional and presidential attention to clean air increased media attention to it).

7. The initial "set-up" cost is one reason why there are no reliable and consistent enforcement data prior to 1977.

8. This may be more a function of each branch's ideology over time than of something inherent in either branch's organizational or institutional makeup. A regulatory agency should respond more to an institution dominated by Democrats and liberals who favor environmental restrictions (Congress) than an institution occupied predominately by deregulators and free marketers (presidency).

9. Congressional support of the EPA may be a function of Democratic control of Congress rather than something inherent in clean air policy that favors legislative influence.

10. I am not arguing that presidents can increase the salience of clean air policy—a necessary assumption of the going-public model. Rather, presidents take advantage of the dynamics of clean air policy and focus their energy on its adoption and implementation when the public supports it.

11. McCubbins, Noll, and Weingast (1989) attributed these factors to congressional influence. There is no logical reason why they cannot be applied to presidential influence, especially considering President Nixon's role in the creation of the Environmental Protection Agency. The "hardwiring" argument made by Macey (1992) applies to interest group involvement. Once again, there is no reason why presidents cannot be similarly advantaged (see Moe 1989).

12. The Segal and Spaeth dataset was available online at http://polisci.msu.edu/~pljp/sctdata1.html. As of September 2005, this link no longer appears to be active. I had previously downloaded and saved the Supreme Court database through 2000 and am happy to provide these data.

13. Lacking a clear theory, modeling the influence of signals eight months prior to a roll-call vote is reasonable. Presidents often propose a policy toward the beginning of each year, whether in a State of the Union address or a Special Message to Congress. Congress, if it acts at all, will rarely act immediately. Proposals that linger across congressional sessions, moreover, are unlikely to receive the sustained interest of legislators. It follows that signals within about one year should have the most impact on the president's success on clean air roll-call votes. To test this inference, I ran separate models with signals of four-, six-, or ten-month lags. Compared with these models, the eight-month lag provides the best statistical explanation of signals and their impact on clean air success in Congress. Besides, an eight-month lag also captures Bush's entire signaling effort over the 1990 Clean Air Act.

14. Logit is not appropriate because the president is successful on all but three Senate clean air roll calls.

15. After all, one of the best cures for multicollinearity is more data points.

16. The autoregressive-moving average (ARMA) terms alone explain over 79 percent of the variance.

17. Using quarterly data was necessitated by the infrequency with which presidents have signaled their clean air policy preferences.

18. A delta coefficient in a transfer-function model (see Equation 5.2) measures the dynamic impact of an independent variable on a dependent variable. A delta ranges in value from −1 to 1, with a negative value indicative of oscillation in the variable's influence until it reaches a new equilibrium. Typically, deltas measure decay or duration of an intervention in an impact assessment model (see McCleary and Hay 1980). Although unconventional, the delta seems to stabilize the model. Several renditions of this model are highly autocorrelated. An alternate model produces significant positive and negative signals coefficients, both positive and at time t. Lagging both variables, as expected theoretically, induces autocorrelation. Finally, the interactive impact is the result of $\frac{\omega}{1-\delta}$, which equals $\frac{.69}{1+.92} = 0.36$.

19. The positive signals coefficient must be confusing to some considering that the Reagan administration comprises a large portion of the time series. Reagan should have had a negative impact on EPA monitoring activity through his signals. This is the case. A Reagan interaction with positive signals on clean air policy produces a negative, albeit insignificant, coefficient. Clearly, Presidents Carter and George H. W. Bush, who were mostly positive on clean air, drive the findings in Tables 5.5 and 5.6.

20. The Reagan interaction raises another point: bureaucrats who know the president's preferences through other means (for example, budgets, appointments, or reorganizations) will not be motivated by signals.

21. Figure 5.2 and Table 5.8 present only one picture of EPA enforcements since 1989. Counts of selected enforcement orders (generally administrative orders, indicated by EPA action codes 7B, 8A, or 8B) reveal seasonal regularities but also more variation in enforcements than the counts revealed in Table 5.8. A regression on these counts produces some influence of positive signals but only in the current, not the previous, quarter.

6

THE LIMITS OF SIGNALS

DURING THE SUMMER OF 2005, FARMERS THROUGHOUT THE MIDWEST and much of the southwest endured hot temperatures and well below average rainfall. For much of the summer, the drought conditions as reported by the National Oceanic and Atmospheric Administration for many of these farmers were extreme or severe, and the drought was expected to be ongoing through October 2005.[1] Most Americans sympathize with the plight of the family farmer and support government payments to farmers when faced with hardship.[2] Yet despite the opportunity that drought conditions provided for at least symbolic presidential leadership, President George W. Bush did not issue a single public statement on domestic farm policy, price supports to farmers, or the plight of drought-stricken farmers in the hottest months of 2005.

Naturally, for signaling to be an effective source of power of public policy, presidents must dedicate enough of their public speeches to that policy area. If presidents are inattentive to a policy area, legislators and bureaucrats will be unlikely to look for presidential leadership on that issue. For much of the past twenty-five years, presidents have not attended frequently to domestic farm policy. This suggests that presidential signals may have little impact on the domestic farm policy process, whether in Congress or the US Department of Agriculture (USDA). The fact that domestic farm policy is not a type of policy that conditions the propensity for presidential influence further undermines its likelihood.

A History of the US Farm Program

Modern farm policy began during the 1930s when severely depressed farm prices prompted strong federal action. Responding to the crisis, the

73rd Congress passed and President Franklin Roosevelt signed the Agricultural Adjustment Act (AAA) in May 1933. The AAA was intended to stabilize farm prices through federal regulation of the farm commodities market. The act encouraged farmers to agree about prices and marketing strategies. Farmers were also paid if they voluntarily reduced their production acreage. Both strategies increased prices out of the agriculture market crash of the early 1930s.

Because the Supreme Court declared parts of the original agriculture statute unconstitutional,[3] Roosevelt signed the Agricultural Adjustment Act in 1938, as Truman did in 1949, with an emphasis on price supports. The 1938 act created price supports to increase farm income at 52 to 75 percent of parity, or the level of farm income between 1910 and 1914 (Moyer and Josling 1990: 106). Price supports were enforced by the Agricultural Adjustment Administration in accordance with voluntary agreements by farmers to reduce acreage of crops and "to store crops on the farm with advance payments to producers for the crop" (Tweeten 1979: 458). Farmers received price supports so long as they abided by planting restrictions set by the secretary of agriculture in accordance with federal law. The 1938 act established the basic price and production control system under statute for the next fifty years (*Congressional Quarterly Almanac* 1996: 3-15).

Agricultural price supports changed during World War II, as the government offered assistance at about 90 percent of parity. The 1949 Agricultural Act reverted to prewar levels of 52 to 75 percent of parity. The 1949 act also gave the secretary of agriculture greater flexibility in setting support payment levels and required Congress to update farm legislation every five years. Otherwise, farm law would revert to the "permanent" provisions of the 1949 act (*Congressional Quarterly Almanac* 1996: 3-17). Subsequent agriculture acts passed in 1954 and 1958 also continued to support prices on grain and other commodities.

Price supports have led to mixed success for the US farmer. They worked well for farmers and the federal government through the 1940s, as world food stocks were low and markets tight. Farmers made a solid living, and the federal government ensured adequate food supplies for the US consumer. Price supports began to be ineffective as the world market changed, however. Farmers produced enormous surpluses throughout the 1950s (Moyer and Josling 1990), and the federal government had no policy to distribute the surpluses. In addition, the federal government could not cease supporting farmers because, at least in the short term, the US farmer could have been hurt enormously.

Tweeten (1979: 465) argued that two approaches to farm policy are plausible, neither of which US farm policy follows. One requires controlled production along with price supports. The other leaves production and prices to market forces; more product leads to lower prices that discourage future planting. "A Democratic Congress and Republican Secretary of Agriculture Benson concocted an unworkable combination: price supports with ineffective controls at an inopportune time when the technological revolution had struck agriculture full force," however. In other words, price supports encouraged farm production in a market economy not fully engaged in the international trade of agriculture, which resulted in government expenditures to store surplus crops (Destler 1980: 28) and support farm income. Price supports that inflated grain commodities much higher than market prices also discouraged US farmers from seeking legitimate export opportunities.

The next wave of agriculture policy distributed commodity surpluses created by past policies. The Kennedy administration began food distribution programs such as food stamps, school lunches, and Food for Peace. Farm policy of the 1960s also encouraged farmers to export farm commodities and alleviate surplus burdens on federal expenditures. The federal government also gave farmers incentives to produce nonsurplus crops through the Emergency Feed Grain Act of 1961. In 1963, the USDA set price supports at much lower levels and began supporting farmer income through direct payments (Moyer and Josling 1990: 107).

The 1965 Agriculture Act also shifted the federal government role over agriculture policy, yet maintained commodity supports as a central component to US farm policy. A key component of these reforms was to reduce federal expenditures on farm policy, provide incentives for farmers to produce less in order to be competitive on the world market, and encourage commodity exports. The act also introduced deficiency payments to farm policy. Deficiency payments consider the market price for a commodity. If farmers sell at a market price less than a USDA-determined target price, the government pays farmers the difference.

This shift in farm policy, from payments based on parity to deficiency payments and other near-market solutions, is usually explained as a product of declining rural influence over Congress and the federal agriculture bureaucracy. A decline in the US farm population (Ulrich 1989) and the subsequent decrease in rural representation relieved Congress of some of its farm-constituency representation and allowed for these reforms in the implementation of agriculture policy. Fewer farmers also meant less "pressure group" influence over the secretary of agriculture and his price support payment discretion. Nevertheless, commodity supports remained intact, in part owing to the relative strength of agriculture interests and the entrenched subgovernment nature of the policy (Browne 1988; Lowi 1979: 72–75; Ripley and Franklin 1991: 85).

Price supports remained central to US agriculture policy throughout the 1970s. Several pieces of legislation further reduced farmer reliance on federal price supports. The 1970 act, for example, added a "set-aside" program to price supports. Farmers could receive compensation for taking a portion of their land out of production, raise whatever they wanted, and receive a market price for their crops. The Agriculture and Consumer Protection Act of 1973 replaced old supports for major commodities—wheat, corn, and so on—with "target prices." The bill encouraged farmers to play the market but provided a safety net when market prices plummeted.

Other aspects of these and other bills encouraged exports. Exports simultaneously freed the government from having to purchase surplus products and allowed farmers to be more market oriented in their sales. Given world famine and international need for US crops, the deficiency payment system was a boon to the US farmer; US agriculture had many markets to exploit. As Third World food production increased and markets were limited by US foreign policy decisions (such as the Soviet grain embargo), however, US commodity exports fell in the 1980s (Moyer and Josling 1990: 111), leading to yet another crisis in US agriculture.

The 1985 farm bill sought to remedy the continuing plight of US farmers. Escalating international competition, overproduction and surpluses, farm debt, and massive federal expenditures on farm subsidies curtailed by rising budget deficits (Ripley and Franklin 1991: 94; see Browne 1988: 217–220) all contributed to attempted change in the direction of agriculture policy. The five-year, 1985 farm bill maintained a 10 percent decline in price support loans, increased agricultural export activity, and reduced corn and wheat acreage to reduce these commodity surpluses (Ripley and Franklin 1991: 96). The commodity program altered farm policy only superficially, as existing price supports and income payments to farmers were preserved. The bill succeeded in rescuing the US farmer from depression but at a substantial cost of $88.6 billion over five years. Once again, the changing agriculture policy environment was not sufficient to derail agriculture interests entrenched in a strong subgovernment comprising agriculture interest groups, the USDA, and key congressional subcommittees.

With farm legislation due for renewal during a Republican-controlled Congress, the 1995 farm bill debates were poised to produce pure market-based agriculture reforms. Indeed, the 1996 farm bill is the most recent effort by Congress to wean farmers off of federal support payments and encourage market-based agriculture. Republican legislators sought to reform and limit federal farm payments. In the so-called

Freedom to Farm Act, Congress replaced traditional price and control legislation with a system of fixed, declining payments to farmers over seven years. Democrats vowed to repeal the 1996 legislation if reelected to a majority in Congress; President Clinton even made future "farmer safety net" legislation a condition of signing the bill. The 107th Congress effectively overturned the 1996 act and reinstated price supports for most commodities (Meier 1995). The president signed this bill, which provided in six years a total of $46 billion for commodity price supports. Nevertheless, the 1996 reforms were a worthwhile experiment in light of the consensus among scholars (and among key Republican members of Congress) that the US farm program, despite its successes, is generally a failed policy. It remains to be seen, furthermore, what impact the 2002 farm bill (signed as the Farm Security and Rural Investment Act on May 20, 2002) has had on either extending or curtailing the intentions of the "Freedom to Farm Act."[4]

Ripley and Franklin (1991) summarized succinctly the failure of US farm policy:

> U.S. agricultural policy for the preceding fifty years had not produced clear or prioritized goals. As a result, farmers received a variety of federal payments to produce surplus crops that lowered market prices and tended to push farm income down. That downward pressure was in turn dealt with by increasing the amount and range of payments. A seemingly endless cycle of feckless but costly programs ensued. (95)

Most other research concurs that US agriculture has not been consistently helpful to the US farmer (Browne 1988; Moyer and Josling 1990; Tweeten 1979; Ulrich 1989). Although price supports tend to boost farm income in the short term, political and fiscal constraints limit their consistent success. At times, US agriculture has been held hostage to an international agriculture economy that dictates much lower market prices than what price supports can offer. A complicated policy that regularly contributes to economic difficulty is politically risky and does not encourage presidential interest or influence. The subgovernment nature of US farm policy further suggests that presidents have not been influential over the history of commodities programs.

Farm Policy in Congress

Congress has traditionally played a prominent role in agriculture policy. During the 1930s, many legislators' electoral fortunes hinged on the prosperity of the US farmer. Many congressional districts were rural, and a prosperous farm economy was good insurance for legislative reelection. The farm lobby also played a key role in the development of the farm program. The farm lobby advised congressional committees on appropriate directions in farm policy. Indeed, novel ideas, such as price support, government payments, and commodity controls, grew out of this relationship.

Another by-product of early farm policies is a lack of presidential influence. Although Roosevelt and Truman made farmers an important constituency and their preferences a top policy priority, legislators crafted and debated legislation shaped by the advice of farmers and members of the farm bureaucracy. Without an initial foothold in its development, and lacking a reason to throw their hats into the ring, presidents have left farm policy to the three actors in the agriculture policy triangle: legislators, bureaucrats, and lobbyists. Nevertheless, a few important factors related to the decline of congressional interest in farm policy lead to the potential, however limited, for presidents to affect farm policy legislation through their signals.

Although most agriculture policy is hammered out in subcommittee in consultation with the preferences of the farm lobby and the USDA, the presidency has some potential to influence farm legislation. Jones (1961) noted that members of the House Agriculture Committee follow several "cues" when they vote on agriculture policy. First, legislators consider constituent interests. When committee members have a clear cue from their constituencies to support or oppose agriculture legislation, they will rely primarily on those cues. Second, when the measure has little direct impact on constituency interests, or the member does not recognize the bill's relationship to his or her constituency, party becomes the primary decision cue. This analysis is consistent with other studies on cues and congressional decisionmaking (Kingdon 1981; Matthews and Stimson 1975).

The potential for presidential influence lies in the second means of legislators' decisions. Since farm population and the number of farms have declined, fewer legislators represent primarily agricultural districts. Legislators will follow other cues, such as party, to vote on farm policy. Presidents act as party leaders in government, and theoretically this stature gives reason why presidents' agriculture signals could be effective in Congress. If legislators look for party cues to vote on farm policy, presidents may fulfill legislators' rational need for information and direction. If presidents are to influence farm policy in Congress, therefore, they need party to circumvent traditional constituency cues on the farm program. As party leader, presidents may therefore provide cues to same-party legislators as to how to vote. Nonetheless, attempts to drive farm policy by partisan politics have also failed (Hansen 1991: 163), and legislators and presidents who do not directly represent a farm constituency have little or no incentive to tackle the complex, difficult, and unrewarding area of farm payments and price supports.

Farm Policy in the Bureaucracy

The federal bureaucracy responsible for agriculture policy is the large and very diverse US Department of Agriculture. The secretary of agriculture, political head of the USDA, leads the development of agriculture policy (Moyer and Josling 1990: 127). The USDA houses several agencies, bureaus, and corporations responsible for the implementation of US agriculture policy. The Farm Service Agency (FSA) is the primary implementer of price support programs.

Created in 1994 with the Department of Agriculture's Reorganization Act of that year, the FSA is responsible for providing a "safety net" to US farmers in lieu of recent changes to the farm bill. In part its mission, as described on the USDA Web site at http://www.fsa.usda.gov/pas/about_fsa/mission.htm, is to:

> ensure the well-being of American agriculture, the environment and the American public through efficient and equitable administration of farm commodity programs; farm ownership, operating and emergency loans; conservation and environmental programs; emergency and disaster assistance; domestic and international food assistance and international export credit programs . . . [and] provide a safety net to help farmers produce an adequate food supply, maintain viable operations, compete for export sales of commodities in the world marketplace, and contribute to the year-round availability of a variety of low-cost, safe, and nutritious foods.

The FSA's mission will change as political support for the farm bill declines in Congress. Providing a "safety net" for US farmers is clearly language adopted by President Clinton in his response to the "Freedom to Farm" Act of 1996 and seems to be the motivation for changes in the 2002 farm bill. Simply, as rural population declines and support in Congress for the farm bill wanes, the FSA will invariably provide less support to the farmers who may need it.[5]

The Farm Program

To determine the effects of presidential signals on agriculture policy, I will focus on the farm program revised in 1938 under the Agricultural

Adjustment Act. A prominent component of this act and its extensions and revisions allocates federal funds to augment farm incomes. Government payments to farmers act primarily as an income stabilization mechanism. The federal government also uses this money for disaster relief programs or to aid farmers who experience short-term crop difficulties.[6] Although the specifics of price supports (such as payments at what percent of parity, target prices, set-asides, or fixed payments) have changed over time, the basic process of government payments to farmers has remained the same.

Until the 1990s, the federal government used some form of price support to increase farm income when commodity prices were low. Initially, the USDA calculated price supports according to a percentage of parity set by Congress. Volatility in market prices required a knowledgeable and informed individual to set price supports for each commodity. Congress considered this need in the Agriculture Adjustment Act of 1949, which placed the responsibility for determining and distributing price support payments with the secretary of agriculture.

Despite discretion and authority over the implementation of farm policy programs, the secretary is not in a position to dictate all components of the farm program. For instance, the secretary sets payment levels and production controls, but they must be consistent with federal agriculture law.[7] Furthermore, he or she cannot force compliance unless farmers approve mandatory participation rules through referenda.[8] Instead, the USDA abides by the 1938 Agricultural Adjustment Act that stipulated voluntary compliance with farm subsidy and price support programs. None of the production controls are mandatory; farmers can opt out of federal farm subsidy programs, but, of course, those who do so forgo any payment income. Farmers must abide by certain legislated rules and requirements to receive payments.

The secretary of agriculture's discretion over government payments to farmers has varied with each new piece of farm legislation.[9] In the 1970s, for example, Congress granted itself more control over farm payments by establishing fixed "target prices" for each commodity. Target prices were based on the national average cost for producing each commodity (*Congressional Quarterly Almanac* 1981: 537). If the market failed to meet the target price, farmers could collect deficiency payments (the difference between market and target prices). In other words, government reduced support payments to farmers when commodity prices were high or when farmers earned a reasonable income without government help (Meier, Wrinkle, and Polinard 1995: 438). This basic formula held until 1996. In 1983, Reagan's farm program used commodities, not cash, to supplement farmer income. Payment in Kind

(PIK), as it was called, allowed the secretary of agriculture to pay farmers in surplus commodities that farmers then would sell at market price. The 1990s witnessed erosion of the secretary's discretion over basic commodity price supports. Congress set fixed payments to farmers in the 1996 farm bill, payments that were to be set by Congress yet again in early 2002 (Davis 2001).

Although Congress has gradually wrested control of the income support component of the farm program from the bureaucracy,[10] several components of the federal program of payments to farmers still allow for some discretion by the secretary of agriculture and farm policy bureaucrats. Congress enacts several minor components (loan deficiency payments, water programs, support if crops are afflicted with particular diseases) in every farm bill from which farmers can benefit if only they know that they qualify.[11] It is the job of some USDA bureaucrats to "get the word out," to inform farmers and various farm groups that these changes have been made and that farmers A and B qualify if they only fill out the appropriate applications and paper work. These programs require outreach on the part of street-level bureaucrats in the USDA.[12]

In addition, the farm program allows bureaucratic discretion over a portion of these payments. Several farm-related situations arise every year that require immediate action on the part of farm policy bureaucrats. For example, Congress appropriated no money in 1996 for farmers whose wheat was afflicted by karnal bunt fungus and who had to have their farms quarantined. The USDA, bureaucrats in the Farm Service Agency in particular, made a rule to compensate farmers. Secretary of Agriculture Daniel Glickman also signed a "declaration of emergency" that authorized the transfer of funds—from within the USDA—to use in the fight against karnal bunt fungus. In situations like this,[13] the secretary either transfers funds (as above) or the Commodity Credit Corporation (CCC) borrows money from the Treasury and then is reimbursed by Congress through appropriations. Although Congress has influence in these relief-type scenarios, the USDA actually spends money first under its own discretion. Besides, Congress is intentionally vague in many areas. When they do appropriate money for non–fixed payment expenditures, they do so by acre. Congress certainly does not know the acreage, so they appropriate an estimated amount of money. The USDA then either uses its discretion to restrict the availability (if appropriations are not sufficient) or pays out and transfers or borrows money to cover the costs. When there is excess, either in terms of surplus commodities or appropriations, the USDA can also transfer funds to other programs such as food stamps.

Again, bureaucrats have some discretion over government payments to farmers. They can make rules to pay for immediate or pending problems, they can increase or decrease the incentives to participate in various programs, or they can borrow money to pay for projects that they deem reasonable. Farm policy bureaucrats do not have a large amount of discretion of payments to farmers, but they have enough to at least allow for the possibility of signaling influence. Like civil rights policy, presidential leadership (signals) could motivate these farm policy bureaucrats to independently fix short-term agriculture problems, without recourse to congressional appropriations and leadership.

Presidential Influence

Applied to the US Department of Agriculture, the theory of presidential signaling in the bureaucracy holds that presidents should have influence over farm policy outputs for several reasons. First, the USDA is not impervious to political influence. It, like all other agencies, needs political support and cooperation to implement its mission effectively. The USDA cannot ignore either Congress or the president, given their separate powers to reward or punish. Congress, of course, passes budgets and approves appointments. Presidents propose budgets and appoint leaders to positions in the department. Because the agriculture bureaucracy is susceptible to political influence, presidents have the potential to influence the implementation of agriculture policy through their signals.

Second, the president's constitutional legitimacy over the USDA means that USDA bureaucrats might respond to his signals. The president is chief executive of the bureaucracy, and the USDA is subordinate to the presidency. Coupled with the assertion that presidential legitimacy gives the bureaucrats a reason to respond to cues (see Matthews and Stimson 1975), presidential signals might affect farm policy outputs. Indeed, with more attention given to farm policy preferences through signals, presidents can lead the agriculture bureaucracy through signals. The president's authority over the bureaucracy is a fundamental means by which presidents can be sure that bureaucrats consider their policy wishes.

Third, the USDA needs power to function effectively. Bureaucratic power is a necessary component for the effective implementation of policy. Presidents may be able to use their signals to encourage bureaucrats to respond to their farm policy preferences precisely because presidents are important to the distribution of bureaucratic power (Meier 1993; Rourke 1969). Bureaucrats desire resources and autonomy to implement their policy missions. Through signals, presidents may increase agency morale or cohesion and motivate bureaucrats to distribute more payments to farmers in need. If presidents oppose the farm program through statements critical of farm payments and price supports, they are unlikely to discourage farm policy bureaucrats from spending scarce federal dollars on welfare for farmers by threatening a substantial decline in their budget or other sources of bureaucratic power if they do not. Consistent with other policy areas, only positive, motivational signals should have an impact on the implementation of the farm program; negative signals should not be influential. Moreover, much research shows limited evidence that the president is an important actor in the development of agriculture policy, one to whom bureaucrats look for support and guidance (Schlozman and Tierney 1986: 272).

Other Influential Institutions and Events

Most scholars concur that Congress is the dominant institution affecting the adoption and implementation of agriculture policy (Meier 1995; Ripley and Franklin 1991). Congress has devoted much attention to farm legislation in part because it must renew it at least every five years. In addition, legislators from rural districts and states have had personal and electoral incentives to satisfy their farming constituencies. The number of rural representatives has clearly declined over time, but enough legislators have agricultural interests in their districts to consider farming interests when the farm bill is up for renewal or when the farming community is in need. Because the secretary of agriculture has had discretion in distributing payments to farmers since 1949, legislators need to oversee USDA activity to influence the distribution of government payments to farmers.[14] Congressional attention to farm policy through committee hearings should have some impact over the level of government payments to farmers.

Several key statutes and policy innovations are also important to farm policy and the level of government payments to farmers since 1950. All extensions and alterations of the Agricultural Act should be important to government payments. I model dummy variables for statutes in 1985, 1990, and 1996 (see Meier, Wrinkle, and Polinard 1995: 441). All legislation dummy variables are step function variables for the years in which they were active extensions of farm policy, usually about five years. I also model a pulse function dummy for 1983. President Reagan offered the PIK program as an alternative to direct payments to farmers. PIK paid farmers in surplus commodities to avoid further increases in budget deficits and reduce massive crop stockpiles. Nearly 80 percent of farmers participated, and in 1983, 73 percent of net farm income came from government payments (Meier, Wrinkle, and Polinard 1995: 432). Clearly, Reagan's PIK program should lead to an increase in government payments to farmers.

Other external factors could also affect agriculture policy outputs. In particular, the state of the economy and the number of farms could affect presidential signaling influence. First, if the economy is in decline, presidents may shy away from discussing farm policy, just as presidents avoid appearing in public when the economy sours (Hager and Sullivan 1994). If farmers are poorer financially owing to a sagging economy, and presidents speak less when economic indicators are not favorable, presidents might avoid signaling their preferences on farm policy, negating any potential impact on legislation. Second, the number of farms has been in decline at least since the early part of the twentieth century (Ulrich 1989) and could be a mitigating factor in the adoption and implementation of farm policy. A declining number of farms and a smaller rural population mean that legislators and presidents have fewer farmers to represent. With fewer farmers to represent, legislators or presidents will likely focus their legislative or leadership efforts on other policies that can secure more votes from their constituencies. If presidents have little to gain from discussing farm policy because there are fewer rural constituents, signals cannot have an impact on Congress or the bureaucracy. Absent presidential attention and leadership, signaling cannot be a successful strategy.

Limits to Presidential Influence over Farm Policy

Unlike the other two policy areas in this study, the nature of agriculture policy strongly precludes presidential influence through signals or other means. First, the farm program is not salient to the public. According to Gallup's "Most Important Problem" series, for example, farm policy had been important to more than 4 percent of the US public only once since 1956. Farm policy is not usually salient because changes in government payments to farmers rarely affect consumer prices substantially. Presidents are unlikely to dedicate their limited time and resources to farm policy, absent a public incentive to advocate and pursue changes in the farm program. Because the farm program, including government payment levels and target price information, is not important to the general public, presidents have little incentive to talk about and therefore influence it.

Second, farm policy is a technically complex policy area (Meier 1995: 134). Agriculture is a complex industry, in which farmers have to make decisions not only about fertilizers and crop production but also about whether to accept payment from the government for their commodities and, if so, how much. Farm policy requires experts to set the level of government payments, calculate future target prices, and assess the policy's potential impact on the economy. Indeed, the complexity of farm policy may be a significant reason why it has failed to benefit farmers consistently over time (see, among others, Meier 1985). It is unlikely that most presidents have the time or the incentive to learn about the technical aspects of the farm program and communicate exactly why government payments should increase or decrease according to world commodity markets.

Agriculture policy also operates in a subgovernment.[15] This means that congressional committee members adopt policy in conjunction with agriculture agencies and the farm lobby. Subgovernments, by definition, exclude extensive presidential influence. Instead, members of congressional committees and subcommittees, outside interest groups, and the agency itself dominate the adoption and implementation of farm policy (Ripley and Franklin 1991). The agriculture subgovernment was most cohesive during the 1930s and 1940s when the foundations of US farm policy developed. Through the 1960s, the farm lobby maintained a monopoly on policies that affected farmers (Hansen 1991: 187–189). As rural representation declined, however, and the farm lobby became less useful to legislators' farm policy decisions, the agriculture subgovernment weakened, and the congressional requirement to renew farm legislation became the reason to entertain farm interests (Hardin 1978). This does not mean that presidential involvement has filled the declining influence of Congress. Rather, the importance of agriculture to the federal government has declined overall, just as congressional representation of farming communities, the size of the rural population, and the importance of agriculture to the US economy have declined. Multiple subgovernments further compound this problem (Meier 1985: chap. 5). Presidents might be effective infiltrating one tight network of policy interests, but to influence multiple groups who also affect each other's decisions is unlikely.

Past research confirms an absence of presidential influence over the farm program. Meier, Polinard, and Wrinkle (1999) dismissed presidential influence in their discussion of federal farm credit policy. Instead, they argued, congressional involvement and bureaucratic discretion are the political factors that drive agricultural debt. Studies that find influence determine that the president's impact is rare: Reagan's Payment in Kind program and the president's party affect payments and loans to US farmers (Meier, Wrinkle, and Polinard 1995: 441).

Anecdotal evidence shows that presidential involvement and influence over farm policy are not significant. Presidents do not devote much of their limited time and resources to the adoption or implementation of the farm program. Ripley and Franklin (1991: 94) noted that the Reagan administration's proposed changes to agriculture policy during the 1985 farm bill debate were dead on arrival in Congress owing to a lack of personal presidential involvement in the plan. Reagan did not even mention the bill in his 1985 State of the Union address (*Public Papers of the Presidents: Reagan* 1985), a clear indication that farm policy was not on Reagan's policy agenda (see Light 1999).

Signaling theory maintains that for signals to be effective, for legislators to look for and use them when adopting farm policy, presidents must provide public leadership. Without adequate attention to farm policy, presidents are unlikely to provide a definitive cue to legislators who may be looking for leadership on farm policy. Simply put, "wise politicians choose their arenas carefully." When it comes to farm policy, "more often, [politicians] have bigger games to play" (Hansen 1991: 163). Presidents should have little or no signaling influence over farm policy outputs in Congress mainly because they have no incentive to wage the battle and because the risk for failure—and to the president's credibility—is high (Meier, Wrinkle, and Polinard 1995: 431–432). The descriptive evidence in the next section confirms a lack of presidential influence by demonstrating an absence of presidential attention to farm policy since the Johnson administration.

Findings

The history of agriculture policy, the dominance of congressional interests, and the policy's complexity yet lack of salience suggest that presidential farm policy signals will have little influence in both Congress and the bureaucracy. To test if this is accurate, I first present descriptive evidence of the president's signaling activity since 1950. I also quantitatively analyze the effects signals have had on the level of government price support payments to farmers and their impact on agriculture rollcall votes in Congress.

Descriptive Evidence

Table 6.1 shows the yearly averages of the number of pages that presidents devote to the farm program.[16] Eisenhower averaged the most statements on agriculture with over twenty-one pages per year. The

Table 6.1   Yearly Average Signals on Farm Policy by Presidential Administration

President	Total Average	Positive	Neutral	Negative
Eisenhower	21.5	18.4	3.0	0.1
		(85.5 %)[a]	(14.0 %)	(0.5 %)
Kennedy	20.0	16.7	3.0	0.3
		(83.5)	(15.0)	(1.5)
Johnson	13.6	9.6	3.8	0.2
		(70.6)	(27.9)	(1.5)
Nixon	6.7	3.7	2.8	0.2
		(55.2)	(41.8)	(3.0)
Ford	5.5	1.0	1.5	3.0
		(18.2)	(27.3)	(54.5)
Carter	10.8	7.8	2.5	0.5
		(72.1)	(23.1)	(4.6)
Reagan	8.4	1.8	3.4	3.3
		(20.9)	(40.3)	(38.8)
G. H. W. Bush	7.5	3.5	3.8	0.3
		(46.7)	(50.0)	(3.3)
Clinton	6.1	4.9	1.1	0.1
		(80.3)	(18.0)	(1.6)
G. W. Bush[b]	9.5	7.5	1.75	0.25
		(78.9)	(18.4)	(2.7)

Notes: Numbers are administration averages of the number of pages in the *Public Papers of the Presidents* on which presidents mention farm policy.

a. Numbers in parentheses are the average percentage of all positive, negative, or neutral farm policy signals.

b. Numbers for G. W. Bush are through 2004.

number would be much higher if years in which farm legislation was not before Congress were excluded from the average. Eisenhower devoted over forty pages to agriculture policy during 1954 and 1956, years in which Congress considered farm legislation (Figure 6.1). He usually supported traditional price supports and subsidies even though he often argued for a lower parity percentage than farmers might have preferred. He also supported early market reforms in the form of flexible supports that fluctuated with market supply and demand.

Kennedy and Johnson also had reasonably high levels of interest in agriculture policy. They supported traditional price supports and pursued solutions to growing farm commodity surpluses. Both presidents agreed to open more markets through Food for Peace programs and to expand food stamp distribution and school lunch programs. Indeed, these presidents spent a considerable amount of time devising ways to use commodity surpluses created by past policies that encouraged a large amount of planting and harvesting.

Presidential interest in farm policy waned considerably beginning with the Nixon administration. Nixon was the first president in this study

Figure 6.1 Yearly Presidential Signals on Farm Policy, 1950–2004

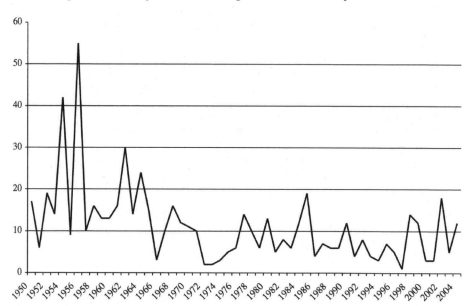

not to give a special message to Congress on agriculture. Since the 1970s, only President Carter has given considerable support to agriculture policy, part of this owing to his own personal interest in the area. Other presidents talked about agriculture but were mostly symbolic and neutral in their comments. Both Presidents Reagan and George H. W. Bush enjoyed lending support to an audience of farmers. Jokes about thirty-eight inches of rain in one night and "that 'ol tractor" received a round of laughter, even though neither regularly expressed focused policy leadership. President Clinton rarely discussed farm policy until the late 1990s, when he assured farmers that they would not be left without a safety net after dramatic changes in farm policy. Finally, President George W. Bush urged Congress to pass (in early 2002) and claimed credit for (in late 2002) the required renewal of the Agricultural Adjustment Act, the 2002 Farm Security and Rural Investment Act. (This accounts for the slight increase in average statements on agriculture on Table 6.1.) These statements were usually quite brief (about a page or less) and general, although very positive.[17] Other than touting this bill again during his reelection campaign in 2004,[18] George W. Bush has hardly made domestic agriculture policy a priority, despite his public claims to the contrary.

There is a clear trend downward over time in presidential public statements on farm policy (Table 6.1 and Figure 6.1). This is not surprising given the decline in rural population and the number of farms, as well as overall congressional dominance of agriculture policy (see Porter 1978). With less of the nation residing in rural areas, presidents simply have a smaller farm constituency to represent. With fewer voters who understand farm policy and vote for or against a president based on his plan for farmers, presidents have little reason to speak about price support and commodity subsidies. A strong regional aspect to domestic farm policy (cotton in the south, corn in the midwest, or wheat in the plains) also limits the incentive for presidents, who are national leaders, to adopt farm policy as a priority (Member of Congress [Texas] interview 2005). Moreover, the decline in agriculture-related employment has shifted what power remains over agriculture policy to those few agriculture committee members who have an electoral interest in cultivating the support of farmers.

The comparative dearth of recent interest in agriculture among most legislators means that presidents could seize a signaling opportunity, if only they showed interest in agriculture policy. The descriptive evidence suggests, however, that presidents do not devote much of their public discussions to farm policy (Table 6.1). Indeed, presidents have rarely made farm policy an agenda priority since the 1950s. Several pieces of major agriculture legislation were infrequently mentioned by presidents and not pursued vigorously in public.[19] President Johnson delivered the last special message to Congress on agriculture in 1968.

Again, a declining farm population, a lack of public salience (or concern for prices or supply, which are low and abundant), policy complexity, and political risk (without potential payoff) are all plausible explanations for the declining trend in presidential interest in agriculture policy. The lack of consistent attention to farm policy over time (Figure 6.1) implies that presidents should not have much influence over agriculture policy. After all, the key to presidential signaling influence is attention and leadership.

Legislative Activity

Congress has shown constant interest and control over agriculture policy. In part to avoid reverting to the permanent statute on farm policy, the Agricultural Act of 1949 (*Congressional Quarterly Almanac* 1996: 3-17), legislators have renewed and revised agriculture laws about every five years. Presidents have also chimed in, on occasion, but there have been several years in which major agriculture legislation passed Congress without a whimper of interest from the White House. Because presidents have generally been inattentive to agriculture policy, it is unlikely that they have had much influence over its success in Congress.

As with any policy, and agriculture policy in particular, signals should have different effects in the two houses of Congress. After all, party is the driving mechanism behind presidential-congressional relations, and the percentage of seats held by the president's party has varied by house over the past fifty years. I therefore analyze presidential signaling effects separately in the Senate and House of Representatives. As with civil rights policy, I examine the president's success rate and his agenda-setting impact on farm policy roll-call votes. The Heckman selection equation is detailed in Appendix B.

The Senate. The Senate has maintained influence over agriculture policy. With a declining rural population, however, many senators have fewer electoral and policy incentives to follow the complexities of farm policy on a regular basis. Despite the decline in US agriculture over time, however, the Senate still has powerful members from farm states who could shut the president out of farm policy debates. Both Tom Harkin of Iowa and Saxby Chambliss from Georgia, for example, often play prominent roles in farm policy (Davis 2001: 1630). Their leadership might preclude the influence of presidential signals in the Senate. The five-year farm bill renewal cycles might also preclude presidential influence. Nevertheless, just as members of Congress have ignored clean air legislation without expressed presidential support (see Chapter 4), these key senators may be reluctant to bring farm bills to a vote if they do not have presidential support. As such, if presidents provide sufficient leadership on agriculture policy, senators might listen to signals.

Table 6.2 shows results from two equations: the determinants of the president's average success rate on agriculture roll-call votes in the Senate and a Heckman selection model that estimates those variables that are purported to influence whether or not farm policy comes to a vote in the Senate. The president clearly has difficulty increasing his success on farm policy roll-call votes with signals. Signals are insignificant, even though they are in the expected direction. The only variable that has even a marginal impact on the president's roll-call success in the Senate is the state of the economy. When the economy improves from one year to the next, presidents have greater flexibility to oppose or support payments to farmers. Finally, veto threats are significant and in the negative direction. According to Table 6.2, a veto threat in a given year actually leads to an average success rate of about 25 percent less than in years in which presidents do not threaten to veto farm legislation. Presidents have less success in years when they threaten vetoes

Table 6.2   Presidential Success on Senate Farm Policy Roll Calls, 1950–2004

	Parameter Estimate	Standard Error	t-statistic
Total signals	0.07	0.50	0.15
Past success	−0.68*	0.31	−2.23
Presidential approval	−1.36*	0.64	−2.13
Media attention	0.39	0.24	1.67
Presidential party seats (%)	0.27	0.36	0.76
Honeymoon	7.86	5.81	1.35
Veto threat	−24.68*	13.29	−1.86
Real GDP % Δ	2.62*	1.00	2.63
Number of farms	0.004	0.01	0.65
Constant	150.81*	64.31	2.35
Heckman Selection Model			
Total signals	0.05	0.04	1.33
Presidential approval	0.03	0.02	1.55
Presidential party seats (%)	−0.02	0.03	−0.79
Past success	0.004	0.01	0.26
Constant	−1.27	1.48	−0.86
N (censored N)	54 (28)		
Wald χ^2 (9)	19.71*		
σ (sigma)	15.85*		
Log likelihood	−135.02		

Note: * p < .05 (one-tailed test).

because they usually threaten to veto legislation when their preferences conflict with those of the Senate. Hence, the president's average roll-call success rate is likely to be much lower in conflictual years, when presidents threaten to veto legislation, than in years when the Senate and president agree on farm policy.[20]

Although also in the expected direction, presidential statements also fall short in affecting the Senate's yearly farm policy agenda. In most respects, a lack of agenda-setting influence by the president is consistent with the required renewal of the Agricultural Adjustment Act. The AAA is slated to expire (and be renewed) approximately every six years. A deterministic timetable such as this precludes presidential leadership of farm policy in most instances. Only when an agricultural disaster requires immediate government action might presidents set the congressional farm policy agenda. In recent years, the Reagan administration's Payment-In-Kind program, but no other presidential proposal, has had the potential to impact the congressional farm policy agenda.

That signals come close to influencing the Senate's farm policy agenda leaves open the possibility that presidential signals could also affect presidential success on individual farm policy roll-call votes, however unlikely. Table 6.3 confirms that presidential signals have no

Table 6.3   Presidential Success on Senate Farm Policy Roll-Call Votes

	Parameter Estimate	Standard Error	t-statistic
Signals	−0.58	0.46	−1.27
Veto threat	−13.50*	7.20	−1.89
Honeymoon	−7.76	6.05	−1.28
Presidential party seats (%)	0.07	0.22	0.30
Past success	0.16	0.19	0.85
Media attention	0.10	0.18	0.53
Presidential approval	−0.09	0.17	−0.50
Number of farms	0.002	0.004	0.58
Real GDP %	0.26	0.74	0.35
Constant	46.68*	22.77	2.05
R-square	.17		
F-statistic	2.51*		
N	96		

Notes: * p < .05 (one-tailed).
Robust Standard Errors account for heteroskadasticity.

demonstrable impact on the president's success rate in the Senate. The signals coefficient, indeed, is in the unexpected, negative direction and does not approach conventional levels of statistical significance, even for a one-tailed test. Clearly, the Senate does not respond to cues from the president regarding his position on domestic farm policies.

The House. Political science research does not differentiate the degree to which the Senate and House of Representatives differ on their farm policy leadership. Just as Congress is an important component of the agriculture subgovernment, and the Senate is unlikely to respond to presidential signals, it is also probable that presidential signals will not be influential in the House. The decline of both rural population and the relative importance of agriculture to the US economy, however, means that fewer representatives will have a direct electoral incentive to champion farm policy. The House may therefore find it necessary to listen to presidential signals, as fewer members have cues from their constituencies to listen and respond to.[21]

The data show that the House of Representatives pays little attention to presidential signals on farm policy (Table 6.4). Although positive, signals have no significant bearing on the average yearly success presidents have on agriculture roll-call votes. This may be a function of declining farm interests in the House, whereby the majority of representatives look to expert members of agriculture committees to inform their votes on farm policy. Because presidents are generally disinterested in farm policy (see Table 6.1), representatives have little incentive to

Table 6.4   Presidential Success on House Farm Policy Roll-Call Votes

	Parameter Estimate	Standard Error	t-statistic
Signals	−0.004	0.46	−0.01
Veto threat	−4.59	7.67	−0.60
Honeymoon	1.42	5.76	0.25
Presidential party seats (%)	0.60	0.35	1.69
Past success	−0.44	0.28	−1.56
Media attention	0.37	0.24	1.57
Presidential approval	−0.26	0.28	−0.92
Number of farms	−0.01	0.01	−1.34
Real GDP %	2.39*	1.17	2.03
Constant	68.08*	29.86	2.28
R-square	.14		
F-statistic	1.16		
White's test	41.62		
N	76		

Note: * $p < .05$ (one-tailed).

search for presidential leadership when better cues are available from their colleagues.

Of importance, however, is the effect of the economy on farm policy. The yearly change in gross domestic product (real GDP) has a positive and significant impact on presidential success. Clearly, a strong economy benefits presidents in relation to their success on farm policy in the House of Representatives. When the economy is doing well, presidents are better situated politically to support or oppose farm policy. They have fewer political risks in a strong economy. When the economy is weak, however, presidents have less political capital to persuade members of the House that they should support the president's position. They might also run the risk of angering and alienating a diminished yet still powerful interest group in the US farm lobby.

Much like presidential influence in the Senate, presidential signals have no impact on the House's domestic farm policy agenda, either. The Heckman selection model, in Table 6.5, shows that presidential signals do not increase the likelihood that the House will vote on domestic farm policy in a given year. All in all, presidents avoid domestic farm policy and legislators are unresponsive to the president given farm policy's complex and unsalient nature.[22]

Bureaucratic Outputs

To assess presidential signaling over farm policy, I examine yearly government payments to farmers. Government payments to farmers have

Table 6.5   Presidential Success on House Farm Policy Roll Calls, 1950–2004

	Parameter Estimate	Standard Error	t-statistic
Total signals	1.01	0.63	1.59
Past success	−0.42	0.36	−1.17
Presidential approval	−0.16	0.46	−0.36
Media attention	−0.14	0.28	−0.49
Presidential party seats (%)	0.13	0.56	0.23
Honeymoon	2.89	8.49	0.34
Veto threat	7.32	10.78	0.68
Real GDP % Δ	2.52*	1.09	2.31
Number of farms	0.01	0.01	1.02
Constant	52.71	45.92	1.15
Heckman Selection Model			
Total signals	0.02	0.03	0.52
Presidential approval	−0.02	0.02	−0.94
Presidential party seats (%)	−0.02	0.02	−0.85
Past success	−0.002	0.01	−0.15
Constant	1.18	1.48	0.80
N (censored N)	54 (26)		
Wald χ^2 (9)	9.42		
σ (sigma)	18.00*		
Log likelihood	−153.09		

Note: * $p < .05$ (one-tailed).

been a mainstay of the agriculture program, even though the substance of the payments has changed. Since 1996, for example, most government payments to farmers have been fixed payments set by Congress. These payments were designed to subsidize the farmer, not the crop production typical of previous price supports, as he or she transitions to a free market. Direct payments increased after 1996 as the transition to a free market proved more difficult than legislators imagined. The transition halted in 2002 as Congress reinstated some traditional crop subsidies.

Total payments include other payments, such as disaster assistance payments and aid to farmers who experienced karnal bunt fungus, a disease that afflicts wheat. In years prior to 1996, payments comprised deficiency payments from the target price program, commodity surplus payments to farmers (under Reagan's 1983 Payment in Kind program), and aid to farmers who stored surplus commodities. As the information in Figure 6.2 shows, government payments to farmers increased substantially during the farm recession of the mid-1980s. Farmers were less dependent on federal support in the 1950s and 1960s when agriculture comprised a larger percentage of the US economy. The independent

**Figure 6.2 Yearly Government Payments to Farmers,
1950–2004 (1990 constant dollars)**

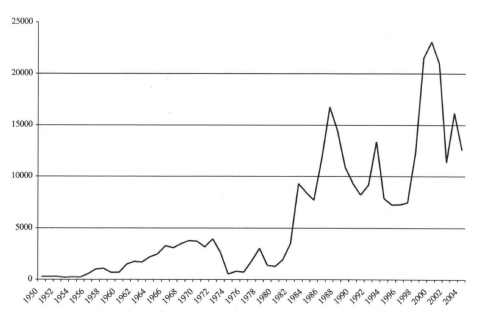

variables include congressional, presidential, media, economic, and
interest group influences, as expressed in Appendix A.

Two components comprise congressional influence. The first component is the number of congressional hearings on farm policy. The
more hearings Congress has about farm policy and government payments, the more likely those hearings are to affect the secretary of agriculture's decision about whether to increase or decrease payments to
farmers. The second component is the fact that Congress regularly
updates and revises the Agriculture Act that allocates and guides government payments to farmers. Four such acts, in 1985, 1990, 1996, and
2002, are modeled as step function dummies for years in which they are
statutory precedent. The year 1983 is also important, given Reagan's
Payment in Kind program (see Meier, Wrinkle, and Polinard 1995). I
also model another variable, the USDA's annual budget appropriated for
income support. Although Congress appropriates budgetary dollars,
budgets are also an indication of indirect presidential influence because
presidents propose yearly agency budgets.

A final component is the importance of farmer influence. A good
measure of agriculture interest group influence is the number of farms
per year. The number of farms has declined over time, consistent with

farmers' declining representation in Congress and their influence over legislation (Porter 1978). Fewer farms mean fewer farmers who join and fund interest group organizations. Less influence means lower price support levels. The economy is also important. Economic downturns during the early 1970s and 1980s caused Congress and the president to reconsider the type and size of government payments to farmers. Nevertheless, when the economy is in recession, legislators who support farmers probably push for more payments to offset their struggles. The discretion of the secretary of agriculture, usually a farmer himself or herself, surely leads to more assistance in times of economic difficulties. These variables are displayed mathematically in Equation 6.1.

$$\text{Payments} = B_0 + B_1\text{Signals} + B_2\text{AAA2002} + B_3\text{AAA1996} + \quad \textbf{6.1}$$
$$B_4\text{AAA1990} + B_5\text{AAA1985} + B_6\text{PIK1983} + B_7\text{Approval} +$$
$$B_8\text{Media Attention} + B_9\text{Congressional Hearings} + B_{10}\text{Budget}\Delta +$$
$$B_{11}\text{GDPD} + B_{12}\text{Farms} + \varepsilon$$

I model the relationship among the several independent variables—along with positive or negative signals—and government payments to farmers (in constant dollars) in Tables 6.6 and 6.7. These tables show that presidents have virtually no signaling influence over the US Department of Agriculture and its distribution of commodity payments to farmers. Presidential signals, regardless of direction, do not have a statistically significant impact on government payments to farmers. Even though negative signals correlate negatively with government payments (Table 6.7), positive signals are also related negatively to government payments (Table 6.6). Both coefficients are statistically insignificant, which underscores the limited influence of a president's signals on farm policy over the distribution of government payments to farmers.[23]

Congress is particularly important to farm payments over time, however, especially in terms of the guidance it provides the farm program through amendments and extensions to the Agriculture Adjustment Act. For all three models, key statutes are quite influential. Of these pieces of legislation, the 1985 farm bill (but not Reagan's Payment in Kind program) dramatically increased payments to farmers. Surprisingly, the 1990 and 1996 farm bills led to much higher payments as well. The 1996 farm bill was supposed to encourage farmers to engage in "free market" agriculture by weaning them off of crop subsidy payments. But a series of decreases in commodity prices led to a series of federal bailouts that actually increased the level of government payments to farmer (see Figure 6.1) in spite of the market-oriented intentions of the 1996 bill. As expected, the 2002 bill also increased pay-

Table 6.6   The Effect of Positive Signals on Government Commodity Payments,
1950–2004

	Parameter Estimate	Standard Error	t-statistic
Positive signals	–40.82	43.99	–0.92
2002 (step)	8301.90*	2488.73	3.34
1996 (step)	10670.43*	1693.76	6.30
1990 (step)	4532.72*	1743.38	2.60
1985 (step)	6689.29*	1908.52	3.50
1983 (pulse)	3761.00	2501.34	1.50
Presidential approval	98.94*	41.70	2.37
Media attention	–3.53	27.83	–0.13
Congressional hearings	8.03	31.84	0.25
Budget Δ	–0.11	0.07	–1.50
Real GDP % Δ	–96.73	90.21	–1.07
Number of farms	–2.20*	1.11	–1.99
Constant	3894.34	3379.05	1.15
AR1	0.75*	0.14	5.37
AR2	–0.55*	0.15	–3.63
R-square	.87		
Adjusted R-square	.82		
Mean of dependent	6225.15		
Standard error of estimate	2582.96		
Box-Ljung Q	7.25		
White's test	13.24		
N	54		

Notes: * $p < .05$.
The dependent variable is direct government payments to farmers. It is the total yearly dollar amount (in constant dollars) paid to farmers by the Farm Service Agency.

ments to farmers, as it reconciled the failure of the "Freedom to Farm" Act, which incorrectly concluded that most farmers could compete on the open market without government assistance. Although not statistically significant, congressional hearings are in the expected direction in all three models: more attention by Congress may lead to an increased desire to please its rural constituents by increasing payments to farmers.

One last variable is influential. Farm groups have always played an important role in the distribution of government payments to farmers. An increase in the number of farms leads to a decline in government payments. This is initially counterintuitive, as one would expect more payments when more farms are in operation. Nevertheless, it does make sense: when there were more farms, the US economy was more agrarian, farmers were better off financially, and they were less dependent on government support. When US farmers encountered bankruptcy and massive crop failure during the 1980s, they needed and the government provided more monetary relief. Hence, as farms have declined, payments have increased.

Table 6.7   The Effect of Negative Signals on Government Commodity Payments,
1950–2004

	Parameter Estimate	Standard Error	t-statistic
Negative signals	−188.52	209.10	−0.90
2002 (step)	7353.85*	2506.24	2.93
1996 (step)	10745.52*	1790.10	6.00
1990 (step)	4710.14*	1829.72	2.57
1985 (step)	7231.58*	2067.55	3.49
1983 (pulse)	4417.44	2555.22	1.73
Presidential approval	96.61*	42.58	2.27
Media attention	−14.07	23.98	−0.59
Congressional hearings	18.59	33.07	0.56
Budget Δ	−0.07	0.08	−0.85
Real GDP % Δ	−43.03	74.11	−0.58
Number of farms	−2.36*	1.17	−2.02
Constant	4386.32	3613.93	1.21
AR1	0.78*	0.14	5.45
AR2	−0.53*	0.16	−3.36
R-square	.87		
Adjusted R-square	.82		
Mean of dependent	6225.15		
Standard error of estimate	6067.66		
Ljung-Box Q	10.47		
White's test	22.76		
N	54		

Notes: * p < .05.
The dependent variable is direct government payments to farmers. It is the total yearly dollar amount (in constant dollars) paid to farmers by the Farm Service Agency.

Conclusion: A Lack of Influence

Signals are not a reliable tool for presidential influence over agriculture policy. In part because presidents have little incentive to signal their preferences on farm policy, signals are unlikely to, and in fact do not, influence the policy activities of either Congress or the bureaucracy. The answer to the question of whether presidential signals matter to policies that are not salient yet complex is a resounding no. Presidential signals do not increase the president's success on roll-call votes, his yearly success rate, or the domestic farm policy agenda of either house of Congress. Signals do little to increase the president's influence over the implementation of price support programs either.

Presidents have limited time and resources and will choose to lead on public policies that are likely to welcome presidential leadership. In part because agriculture is a complex policy issue that is not salient, presidents avoid the topic of farm policy when speaking from behind the presidential podium. Whereas former presidents frequently prioritized price supports for farm commodities, recent presidents have found little time to discuss the farm bill, save during election years when they appeal generally for the support of a diminished farm constituency. Subgovernments have long dominated the adoption and implementation of farm legislation, so a lack of influence is not particularly surprising. Moreover, the required renewal of the Agricultural Adjustment Act further complicates the president's incentive to sacrifice his prestige and reputation through public discussion of domestic farm policy and its impact on the US farmer.

Notes

1. The US Drought Monitor is available at http://www.drought. unl.edu/dm/monitor.html. These observations are taken from the August 2, 2005, report.

2. Eighty-eight percent of respondents answered "approve" to the following question: "When drought or floods damage farmers' crops, how do you feel about federal payments to help them stay in business? Do you approve, disapprove, or neutral?" The Tarrance Group conducted the "Farm Survey" between June 2 and June 21, 2001.

3. *United States v. Butler* (291 US 1 1936).

4. It is worth noting that when George W. Bush mentioned specifics of this legislation, he did not emphasize its $90 billion price-support allotment but rather its free trade and new-market exports aspects.

5. An example of declining farm representation in Congress occurred in the 2004 congressional elections. Texas's redistricting efforts pitted two pro-agriculture incumbents against each other in Texas's District 17 race. Charlie Stenholm, ranking member of the House Agriculture Committee, lost to Randy Neugebauer, a junior Republican member of that committee. Whereas West Texas farmers had two pro-agriculture representatives prior to the 109th Congress, afterwards they had only one. This trend is likely to continue as Congress looks for programs to cut amid growing federal budget deficits.

6. For example, a portion of government payments (1996–1998) assisted farmers whose wheat was afflicted with karnal bunt fungus.

7. Much of the secretary's discretion has diminished since the 1996 farm bill. Over the majority of my time series, 1950–1998, the secretary had much more discretion.

8. The farm lobby, the American Farm Bureau Federation in particular, actually used its referenda authority to reject a provision of the 1964 wheat program and defeat a major portion of the Kennedy administration's farm program (Hansen 1991: 151).

9. With that said, any time Congress fails to authorize new farm legislation every five years, federal farm policy will revert to the permanent provisions of the 1938 and 1949 Agricultural Adjustment Acts, which gave the secretary discretion to set commodity price supports at pre–World War II levels.

10. The location of the farm program in the USDA has changed over time.

A 1994 bill created the Farm Service Agency—formerly the Commodity Stabilization Service and then the Agricultural Stabilization and Conservation Service—that now administers government payments to farmers.

11. As an example, disaster assistance programs in livestock have actually increased since 1996.

12. With the advent of the Internet, outreach may consist largely of information posted at USDA.gov. Nevertheless, a bureaucrat is responsible for posting information and application instructions.

13. These situations happen quite frequently. Congress does not appropriate funds, yet the FSA makes payments to farmers based on needed changes in agriculture.

14. Government payments to farmers have been a mainstay of the agriculture program, even though the substance of the payments has changed. Since 1996, for example, most government payments to farmers have been fixed payments set by Congress. These payments total $5.6 billion in 1996, $5.4 billion in 1997, and $5.8 billion in 1998. Total payments include other payments, such as disaster assistance payments and aid to farmers whose wheat crop experienced karnal bunt fungus. In years prior to 1996, payments comprised deficiency payments from the target price program, commodity surplus payments to farmers (under Reagan's 1983 Payment in Kind program), and aid to farmers who stored surplus commodities.

15. Subgovernments are often confused with the "iron triangles" of some policy areas. Farm policy no longer fits this strict categorization of subgovernment politics. Hansen (1991) noted that the farm lobby had the most influence over farm policy during the 1930s and 1940s. Since the 1950s, the farm lobby has had to compete with other influential actors or institutions. As farm policy changed and as the farm lobby lost some influence, so did the subgovernment nature of agriculture policy.

16. I do not analyze exports, grain embargoes, and other agriculture-related policies. I only examine signals that mention the domestic price support component of farm policy. One may suspect that presidents pay significant attention to the foreign policy aspects of agriculture policy.

17. In December 2001, the Bush administration stated that it "opposed" both houses' versions of what would become the 2002 farm bill, even though the president was overwhelmingly positive, however general, in his support for the bill in early 2002.

18. Naturally, Bush delivered these speeches in core "red" states and battleground states such as Iowa.

19. For this inference, I compared Mayhew's (1991) list of important legislation with my own data on presidential policies (Eshbaugh-Soha 2005). One could also look at presidential box scores to notice a lack of presidential emphasis on agriculture.

20. The data might also explain the coefficient's direction. Since the dependent variable is a yearly average measure, many votes—including those that do not support the president's position—may occur prior to the veto threat. Even though the postveto threat votes may bring presidents greater support, the yearly average masks this potential finding.

21. The House of Representatives still maintains a strong cohort of legislators who are responsive to farm interest group and constituency concerns. Indeed, the House appeared to be moving more quickly than the Senate in renewing farm legislation prior to the 2002 fiscal year (Davis 2001: 1630).

22. It is worth noting that time series from 1950 to 2000 show a modest signaling impact over both the House and Senate's yearly farm policy agendas. Those results, having been examined now through 2004, were clearly time bound. This implies that President Bush has continued a trend of decreasing presidential influence over and interest in domestic farm policy since the late 1960s.

23. Some have suggested that all three directional signals should be included in one model. Doing so does not alter the substantive results of any of the coefficients as reported in separate tables. Presenting three tables instead of one should be easier for the reader to follow.

7

PRESIDENTIAL SIGNALING
AND PUBLIC POLICY

THIS BOOK HAS DEVELOPED AND TESTED A THEORY OF PRESIDENTIAL signaling in Congress and the bureaucracy. Simply put, legislators and bureaucrats should respond to presidential signals because they have a need for cognitive efficiency, and the president's role in the policy process gives them reason to respond to his signals. This theory has been subjected to quantitative tests and supported with qualitative evidence. The empirical chapters provide evidence that presidents can and do influence the adoption and implementation of policy through direct signaling even though this source of influence varies by policy area and across institutions. With that, signaling is a mixed source of power for modern presidents because signals are not always effective, nor do they guarantee presidential influence.

Just as this work disputes the conventional wisdom about how presidents use their speeches to govern, signaling theory does not eliminate the feasibility of going public as a viable strategy for modern presidents to successfully influence the policy process. Like most theories of presidential politics, alternative explanations are likely to inform and expand upon our current understanding of presidential speeches and policy; exceptions are also likely. This concluding chapter addresses the implications of and limitations to the theory of presidential signaling. At the same time, this book provides an answer to a conundrum of research on the public presidency. Because presidents cannot typically move public opinion with their speeches, presidents speak to inform legislators and bureaucrats of their policy priorities and affect the adoption and implementation of those policies. Public policy type is a primary determinant of this conclusion.

Policy Signals and Presidential Power

Presidential signals are a source of power, but signals clearly differ in their effectiveness by policy area, as predicted by the theory of presidential signaling. Signaling also varies by institution, as members of Congress and the bureaucracy have different incentives to respond to presidential leadership through signals. Table 7.1 summarizes and rankorders each policy area and institution according to its capacity for presidential influence: civil rights policy signals have the most influence over both Congress and the bureaucracy, signals are modestly effective over clean air policy in Congress and the bureaucracy, and farm policy signals have no impact on either institution. In recapping these findings, it is important to summarize the incentive of each institution—the presidency, Congress, and the bureaucracy—to engage each policy area.

Presidency

For presidential signals to affect a policy area, the president must first devote a sufficient amount of attention to it. We have seen, indeed, that presidential attention to a policy area is related to the president's propensity to influence the adoption or implementation of policy through signals. We have also seen that this varies significantly by policy area. Of the three policy areas, presidents have the most incentive to be attentive to civil rights policy. Civil rights policy is unique in that it presents two policy dimensions favorable for presidential influence through signals. First, a policy that has salient characteristics, such as civil rights, encourages presidential attention. Second, civil rights policy

Table 7.1   **Responsiveness to Presidential Signals by Policy and Institution**

	Civil Rights	Clean Air	Farm Policy
Congress			
House	Agenda only, not success	Increase in success	No impact
Senate	Agenda and increase in success	No impact	Marginal agenda only, not success
Bureaucracy	Positive signals increase criminal cases	Positive signals increase EPA enforcements when clean air is salient	No impact

Note: Signals also increase the president's success on clean air roll-call votes for the entire Congress.

is not complex. Presidents are generalists whose powers are more influential over issues that elicit an emotional response, rather than issues that require expertise to understand (see Corrigan 2000). Being uncomplicated, civil rights policy is an area that contributes to effective presidential signaling.

Given that civil rights policy has both characteristics that encourage presidential leadership, it is not surprising that presidents frequently signal their preferences on it, whether in support of or opposition to specific areas of civil rights. Even when legislation is not pending in Congress, presidents have spoken out against or in favor of desegregation, busing, and affirmative action. All presidents in this study have made at least symbolic reference to supporting equal opportunity for all Americans. As Chapter 4 argues, civil rights policy can be a valence issue. Even when a president may oppose the adoption or implementation of civil rights laws, he may not want to publicize these controversial views; this situation affects his propensity for influence through signals.

The fact that presidents have had slightly different reasons to signal their preferences on clean air policy affects their overall attention levels. Those dimensions likely to encourage presidential leadership do not always characterize clean air policy. Air pollution regulations are fairly complicated, meaning that presidents have less incentive to speak about them in public than they might about civil rights policy. Because of this, individual legislators and expert bureaucrats are likely to handle clean air policy anyway. However, clean air policy is generally salient, providing some opportunity for leadership. These conflicting incentives for presidential leadership make clean air policy a truly mixed area for presidential influence, a policy area that conditions substantial variation in presidential attention.

Because the salience of clean air policy varies over time according to the episodic nature of environmental policy, presidential attention and influence have also varied by clean air's measurable salience. Presidents adopted a clean air policy agenda when the environment was highly salient to the public or when congressional circumstances encouraged presidential leadership of the issue. At times they have been able to lead on this issue (Eshbaugh-Soha and Peake 2004). Presidents Nixon and George H. W. Bush both took advantage of cycles of environmental policy, signaled their preferences to Congress and the bureaucracy, and helped drive my conclusion that presidents have had some signaling impacts in both institutions. When clean air policy was not on the public or congressional agendas, presidents such as Johnson and Clinton rarely made public statements in favor of or against the regulation of air pollution. Just as clean air policy follows episodic cycles of public opinion, so do presidents adhere to issue attention cycles and discuss clean air episodically.

Of the three policy areas, agriculture policy is least likely to encourage presidential attention. Farm policy is not high in policy salience. Except in rare instances, such as during increased public awareness of farm debt in the mid-1980s, farm policy typically does not capture the nation's attention; it is seldom important to the media or public. Agriculture is also fairly complicated. The risks to presidential involvement in farm policy are far greater than the potential benefits presidents may receive from showing public leadership on income support payments to farmers. Presidents have been fairly consistent in their lack of concern about agriculture. Since the Eisenhower administration, presidents have had increasingly fewer reasons to discuss farm policy, given its dominance by the agriculture subgovernment. When presidents do discuss farm policy publicly, they have only limited influence over the congressional agenda (Eshbaugh-Soha and Peake 2004). This, more than any other reason, limits the potential for presidential influence over agriculture policy.

Because policy type and the larger contextual environment tend to condition the president's incentives to signal his policy preferences, presidential signaling is likely not a function of either presidential personality or style, per se, even though the characteristics of the individual president clearly influence whether he will or will not signal on a policy area. Undoubtedly, individual presidents matter because each differs in how he delivers a signal and how much he does so. Whereas President Reagan delivered fewer speeches in exchange for emphasizing a handful of issues through national addresses, President Clinton delivered countless speeches on a range of policies that were not necessarily core priorities. But just as the propensity of presidents to speak about an issue results from the president's own policy priorities and interests, the larger political and contextual environment also forces, or at least encourages, presidential leadership of specific policies. Presidents Nixon and George H. W. Bush prioritized clean air policy not because they had similar speaking styles or personal reasons for supporting environmental legislation but because context presented an opportunity for presidential leadership. At the very least, the topic of presidential style and its impact on the public presidency is worthy of further inquiry.

In addition, whereas the going-public model posits presidential power through speeches to be a fairly recent phenomenon, presidential signaling has beyond question been a source of influence for all modern presidents. We see this whether in terms of the lack of leadership provided by Eisenhower on civil rights and clean air policy (that public leadership perhaps could have paved a different path toward federal involvement in either area) or leadership provided by Kennedy and Johnson on civil rights or by President Nixon on clean air policy. Each of these instances of presidential signaling and influence occurred prior to the perception that going public was a result of the decentralization of Congress that occurred in the early 1970s (Kernell 1997; but see Powell 1999). Kennedy and Johnson both used their public speeches to set the civil rights agenda and eventually to urge Congress to support comprehensive civil rights reforms. They did so even during an era of a more centralized Congress, of institutionalized pluralism, that purportedly did not encourage presidents to make speeches for the purpose of influencing either the adoption or implementation of public policy.

Congress

Congress has its own incentives to be involved with a policy and respond to presidential leadership, each of which is conditioned, in part, by policy area. On the one hand, Congress should be responsive to presidential leadership on policies that are salient, yet not complex. Presidents are most likely to be attentive to these types of policies, making the impact of presidential signaling probable. On the other hand, legislators have strong electoral incentive to ignore the president on salient and uncomplicated policies. A primary concern of a member of Congress is his or her constituents, regardless of presidential prerogative.

Congressional responsiveness to a salient and uncomplicated policy, such as civil rights policy, is mixed. To be sure, presidential signals have a strong agenda-setting effect on civil rights policy in both houses of Congress. Yet signals have not increased the president's success rate on individual roll-call votes in both houses of Congress. Signals directly increase the president's success in the Senate, but not in the House of Representatives. These results suggest the opportunity for, but do not guarantee, congressional responsiveness to presidential signals on civil rights policy. Conflicting incentives to follow the president's lead ensure these results.

The complexity of clean air policy further compounds congressional responsiveness to presidential signals, despite its salience. Presidential influence over clean air roll-call votes in Congress is at once present, but limited. Clean air policy signals have a direct impact on the president's success on individual roll-call votes in the House of Representatives and in Congress as a whole, but not in the Senate. These findings are again suggestive; only more data points can confirm the president's signaling effectiveness over clean air policy and whether this influence does indeed vary by the issue's measurable salience as it does in the bureaucracy.

The weight of the evidence shows that, since 1950, legislators have been unresponsive to the president's farm policy signals. Simply, Congress dominates the adoption of farm policy absent presidential leadership on domestic farm policy issues. It does not expect presidential leadership, and thus we see no presidential influence over the agriculture legislative agendas of either the House or Senate. Without affecting when Congress thinks about domestic farm policy, it is also not surprising that signals have no impact on roll-call votes. This is consistent with past findings that show limited presidential influence—and congressional dominance—over farm policy issues. It is also consistent with a lack of presidential attention to domestic farm policy over time.

Beyond policy, partisanship conditions the relationship between presidential signals and Congress. When presidents disagree with Congress's policy leanings, they tend to engage in other, nonsignaling means to affect those policies, if they do so at all. Recall that Ronald Reagan opposed the renewal of the Voting Rights Act in the early 1980s (at least Congress's version of the renewal) and refrained from pursuing limits on clean air regulations through legislation. In both instances, Reagan faced a House of Representatives that would not overtly support either position of the Reagan administration. Congress, with roughly the same makeup, received George H. W. Bush's signals on clean air policy more favorably. Just as this book holds that policy matters to this relationship, so too does the relative partisanship between the president's signals and their receptivity in the legislative arena.

The recent increase in partisanship in Congress (see, among others, Bond and Fleisher 2000) seems to present conflicting opportunities for presidential leadership. On the one hand, conditions of unified government increase the chances that legislators will hear the president's signals. More ears that are receptive to the president's signals should contribute to more opportunities for presidents to affect policy through signals. On the other hand, higher levels of partisanship have decreased the possibility for bipartisanship and compromise. Signals from a Republican president seemed much less likely in 2004 to influence a Democratic member of Congress than signals used by a Republican to sway a Democratic legislator twenty years earlier. A member of Congress may simply be less likely to listen to a president who did not reach out to his side of the aisle, just as the tendency for presidents to reach over the aisle for votes seems less likely than during previous presidential administrations (Member of Congress [Texas] interview 2005).

Bureaucrats

Bureaucrats are most likely to follow presidential leadership on policies that have primarily salient characteristics. Indeed, as Chapter 4 demonstrates, bureaucrats are mostly responsive to presidential signals on civil rights policy, as positive presidential signals motivate Civil Rights Division lawyers to litigate criminal cases more vigorously than they would absent presidential leadership. Nevertheless, bureaucrats do not always respond to presidential signals, even on civil rights policy. In the Civil Rights Division, presidents are unable to sway the litigation of *civil* cases. Bureaucratic inertia and lawyers' propensity to prosecute more cases over time best explain the number of yearly civil cases filed in US district court. Presidents also have difficulty using signals to oppose the CRD and limit its prosecution of criminal cases. Negative signals are not influential and do not cause a statistically significant decline in criminal cases filed in US district court. When presidential and bureaucratic goals conflict, bureaucrats have substantial discretion to discount presidential preferences absent catastrophic budget cuts or reorganizations.

The importance of salience to clean air policy processes is especially relevant to bureaucratic responsiveness to presidential signals. EPA bureaucrats are most likely to increase their enforcement activity in response to the president's positive and motivational signals when clean air policy is also in the news. From 1977 to 1989, presidential signals in support of clean air encouraged the EPA to enforce clean air statutes more vigorously when those signals were interacted with media attention to clean air. Presidential influence over the EPA is only suggestive when clean air policy is not "measurably salient." Moreover, since the early 1990s, the EPA appears to have grown accustomed to its own enforcement activity, limiting the power of the presidency to affect its activities through public signals. Once again, the president's use of signals in the EPA is not guaranteed, but it has been a source of presidential influence, nonetheless.

An agency responsible for implementing a complex policy beyond the public's gaze is unlikely to respond to presidential leadership. Just as it is unlikely for presidents to speak about domestic farm policy in the first place, it is quite likely for bureaucrats to rely on their expertise to implement policy related to farm price supports. In short, presidential signals have not significantly affected the level of government payments to farmers over time. Instead, congressional leadership through legislative statutes explains most of the variance in payments to farmers.

Just as policy conditions the signaling relationship, partisanship also shapes the effectiveness of presidential signaling in the bureaucracy. Although more subtle than the influence of partisanship in Congress, partisanship at once limits and provides presidents with opportunities to affect the bureaucracy. Presidents are most likely to influence the bureaucracy through signals when they agree with the agency's mission. In other words, presidents who share the same ideology as an agency are more likely to agree with it and, therefore, to increase its policy activity than a president who disagrees ideologically with an agency's mission. Johnson influenced the Civil Rights Division with his positive signals, after all, whereas Reagan could not use coercive signals to undermine the EPA's mission to enforce the Clean Air Act. We should witness this across other policy areas, as well, subject to the limitations expressed in Chapter 5.

Limitations and Implications

This book underscores several contributions to the fields of US politics, the presidency, and public policy. First, presidential signaling is more than a theory of presidential influence in Congress. Whereas past research limited its scope to the impact of speeches on the president's success in Congress, this research also explores the relationship between signals and the implementation of public policy in the bureaucracy. The president's policy signals have an impact in both Congress and the bureaucracy.

Second, the theory of presidential signaling revises the role that the US public plays in the linkage between presidential speeches and their impact on public policy. The signaling effects presented in this volume are direct and do not require public involvement. This is a central contribution. Although past research required presidential speeches to be filtered through a public, often disinterested and uninformed about presidential politics and public policy, the argument presented here allows for presidential influence regardless of the public's involvement. Presidential signaling focuses on elite interactions, the relevance of public interest notwithstanding.

Third and quite important, the president's influence through signaling varies by policy area. The impact of signals is neither uniform nor consistent across civil rights, clean air, and farm policy. The adage that policy affects politics is very relevant to the president's public attempts to influence public policy. The broad framework that I have used to select three specific policy areas also means that my findings should be generalizable to other policy areas with similar characteristics. It also raises the possibility that public interest, even if not active, may be subsumed within the salience dimension of public policy.

Nevertheless, this book is not the final say on presidential policy signaling in Congress and the bureaucracy. The policy types themselves—salience and complexity—require further elaboration and understanding. Additional policies must be explored to ensure that the findings presented here are representative of the policy types, not the specific policy areas. The parsimonious nature of my models may present some problems of causality and inference. It ignores legislative liaison, an important, yet underexplored, aspect of presidential-congressional relations. Beyond modeling interventions, it does not consider the role that departmental secretaries or agency heads may play in the president's attempts to lead through signals. My findings also raise questions about democratic leadership and responsiveness surrounding the president's use of public speeches to affect policy. If presidents are typically concerned with elite responsiveness without regard for public support or opposition, then the theory of presidential signaling may be problematical for democratic theory.

Salience vs. Complexity

Salience and complexity dimensions of public policy not only help explain the effectiveness of presidential signals in the policy process but also refine our understanding of presidential-congressional relations. First, presidential approval ratings have distinct impacts when examined by policy areas. This is consistent with recent research (Canes-Wrone and de Marchi 2002). The findings for civil rights policy, for example, actually extend their findings. Even beyond Canes-Wrone and de Marchi's (2002) time frame, presidential approval has different impacts by policy area. This seems to confirm most research that insists that approval ratings matter (Edwards 1989) and to counter major findings that claim the president's public standing has little relevance—absent political party—to his success in Congress (Bond and Fleisher 1990).

Second, and most interesting, the importance of the president's party coalition in Congress to his legislative success seems to waver by policy area. Party makeup was most influential over clean air policy, moderately influential over civil rights policy, yet not relevant in the president's farm policy success. These findings suggest that policies with salient—but not complex—characteristics condition the relevance of the president's party coalition to his success in Congress. If this holds up over more rigorous and comprehensive examination, then no conclusions about the president's relationship with Congress should be accepted unless the conditioning effects of public policy are considered. Modeling key variations by public policy clearly refines our understanding of presidential-congressional relations.

The salience component to public policy remains an intriguing path for future study. Of all the explanations for why presidents have signaling influence over policy, salience tends to be the most consistent. Simply put, when an issue is salient, presidents tend to be more attentive to it, dedicate more resources to influence its adoption or implementation, and actively use their speeches to affect those policy outputs. The importance of salience to presidential influence over clear air policy confirms that salience is the dominant policy characteristic in the signaling relationship and that salience is the driving, conditioning characteristic behind presidential influence through signals.

Finally, this application of a salience-complexity policy typology builds upon Gormley's (1986) basic insight that political processes differ by a policy area's complexity and salience. Just as signaling varies by these policy characteristics, so it appears that the president's legislative success, the relevance of the president's job approval to his relationship with Congress, and the implementation of public policy do also. To be sure, Gormley (1986) has unearthed an important generalization about public policy, one that extends beyond the confines of regulatory policy alone.

Despite the promise of this book's findings, it remains to be seen whether my findings are specific to civil rights, clean air, and domestic farm policies or whether my findings are generalizable to most policy areas that exhibit similar salience and complexity properties. A future research project must examine a larger sample of congressional roll-call votes. This sample will not be constrained by specific policy areas but will include all roll-call votes along salience and complexity dimensions. Coding all roll-call votes according to their salience and complexity increases the yearly N on roll-call votes and allows a researcher to use more reliable methods unavailable for my specific policy area approach. A larger sample of roll-call votes will help determine if these findings are generalizable across salience-complexity policy dimensions or if the conclusions reflect the impact of signals on these specific policy areas. This research speaks to whether or not salience and complexity dimensions truly provide a broad framework for institutional analyses by policy area. Variation on these dimensions has suggested that the levels of impact for presidential signals differ by specific policy area and that presidents should have the most influence on votes where the policy is low in complexity and high in salience.

Legislative Liaison

This study, much like many other examinations of presidential-congressional relations, ignores the organizational side of presidential influence. Important organizational and less public factors may also influence the president's success in Congress, particularly the success of his public signals. Indeed, a member of Congress noted that his propensity to listen to and respond to the president's signals was a function, in part, of the outreach conducted by the president and his legislative liaison staff (Member of Congress [Texas] interview 2005). He was more likely to listen to President Reagan's than President George W. Bush's signals, in part, because Reagan encouraged compromise, whereas Bush did not. Private communications among the president, legislative liaison, and members of Congress help open up the possibility for receiving and responding to signals.

The president's legislative liaison works tirelessly behind the scenes to inform and persuade legislators of the president's policy preferences and top policy goals. The theory of presidential signaling maintains that a legislative liaison is one among many tools of presidential influence in Congress, so that a legislative liaison strategy complements presidential signals. Efforts by the White House to reach out to members of Congress through the Office of Legislative Liaison may themselves be useful signals to legislators.[1] Yet given the efficiency with which legislators hope to make decisions, according to signaling theory, legislators are just as rational and efficient to rely on the president's public statements, clear indicators of the president's commitment, concern, and leadership. Legislative liaison is also a comprehensive strategy that is most successful at the end of a congressional session (Light 1999), when both presidents and legislators try to complete previously unfinished business. Since I have selected policies based on their salience and complexity characteristics—not their level of priority for a president—it is difficult for my current model to incorporate a measure of legislative liaison, however important it may be to the president's success. Of course, not incorporating the organizational dynamics of presidential influence in Congress plagues nearly all large studies of the president's legislative success (see Bond and Fleisher 1990).[2]

The Impact of Political Appointees

Aside from the quantitative research that shows blunt, directional effects of presidential appointments on the bureaucratic policy activities (Wood and Waterman 1994), scholarship has not delved into the ways in which a department secretary's public statements may affect the policy activities of their bureaus and agencies. A secretary's public statements could act in one of two ways. First, they could elaborate upon and provide more specific direction and support for the bureaucracy after the president outlines a broad course of action. Second, they could be used in conjunction with presidential leadership, reinforcing the president's statements as he makes them. In either case, a department secretary's public statements could accentuate the president's leadership and further extend presidential influence over the bureaucracy. The idea behind signals' being effective, after all, is that if there are more of them, each individual bureaucrat is more likely to hear, understand, and respond to the president's preferences. If the department secretary employs a similar tool to communicate with street-level bureaucrats, then this should extend and amplify the president's influence over the agency. Although I suggest this only as a possibility, future research must explore the interactive relationship between a president's and department secretary's public signals on policy and how this may or may not increase presidential control of the bureaucracy.

Negative Signals

I have argued and provided evidence throughout this volume that negative presidential signals should not dissuade bureaucrats from implementing their missions and should, therefore, have no impact on bureaucratic activity. Yet, the same psychological forces that encourage bureaucrats to do more of what they already do after being urged by positive presidential signals to do so may also encourage bureaucrats to do less. Surely, repeated efforts on the part of presidents to criticize the federal bureaucracy in general as being wasteful and ineffective, a problem to reduce and do away with, and to criticize specific agencies in particular must have some impact on bureaucratic behavior. Perhaps there are conditions under which negative signals could be an effective tool for presidents to alter and change the direction of policy implementation in the bureaucracy.

Numerous explanations suggest why bureaucrats will resist presidential overtures that conflict with their core mission. First, bureaucrats have discretion to ignore presidential directives that conflict with their own policy goals. Bureaucrats simply do not need to follow—nor will they, according to Simon (1957) and other "bottom-up" organization theories (see Kaufman 1960)—presidential directives that do not significantly undermine the objective resources bureaucrats need to implement their policy mission. Second, the bureaucracy is inertial. It is much more difficult to alter standard operating procedures—the ways by which bureaucrats act and operate—than it is to encourage or facilitate those same procedures through positive rhetoric. Again, only when presidents employ a significant negative "hammer," such as drastic budget cuts, can presidents expect to break this inertia and undermine the bureaucrats' abilities to act. Third, the policy areas in this study are typically "valence" issues that discourage presidents from speaking out too often against them. It is politically difficult for presidents to proclaim their dislike for the implementation of broad ideals, such as equal opportunity for all and clean air to breathe.

Although compelling, these reasons do not eliminate the possibility of negative signals affecting policy implementation in the bureaucracy. Perhaps presidents can repeatedly bombard an agency with negative signals so that its bureaucrats will become so disenchanted, so unwilling to act on their mission that the president will have a negative impact on that agency's activities. The psychological effects that positive signals have, motivating bureaucrats to do more, should be reversed with negative signals, so long as presidents use them at a significant level or threshold. Keep in mind that the signaling relationship depends upon the signal user. Bureaucrats want to use positive signals from the president. Although they may not want to respond to negative signals, a sufficient number of such signals may require them to do so, as their morale and motivation to resist presidential coercion decrease. It is unclear to me what this policy area may be, but if the president has a public incentive to criticize the bureaucracy, then he may wish to dedicate enough signals to decry and ultimately dissuade bureaucrats from doing what they otherwise would do without presidential opposition through signals. I leave this research question for a future study.

The Pitfalls of Parsimony

Is signaling really unidirectional as I present it? Do presidents simply talk about policy and influence it? Is it not just as likely that presidents respond to policy environments in Congress and the bureaucracy and then signal to influence the direction of policy in those institutions? The policy process is an ongoing, cyclical, and dynamic process (Anderson 2000). Like the relationship between Congress and the public over the women's rights movement (see Costain and Majstorovic 1994), signaling may be a reciprocal or multicausal process, one that is more complicated than what I have modeled and tested in this book. Congress can affect the president, the media can affect Congress, and the president can affect the bureaucracy.

A president may survey the congressional environment and upon finding that Congress supports a policy area, he may advocate that policy. If a president knows that congressional support for a policy is likely, he is rational to speak about that policy because being successful on that policy is also likely. Surely President Nixon's clean air proposals were a response in part to congressional support for clean air legislation and Edmund Muskie's specific clean air act proposals. At times, their relationship was very competitive, with one trying to be more environmental than the other (R. Cohen 1995). Evidence indicates, however, that congressional attention does not affect presidential attention to civil rights, clean air, or domestic farm policy (Eshbaugh-Soha and Peake 2004).

Presidents may also respond to bureaucratic implementation. Sometimes the implementation of public policy may reveal problems with the original policy solution; these problems may require presidential attention. Limitations of previous clean air acts contributed to amendments in 1970, 1977, and 1990. The implementation of public policy may also inform presidents of bureaucratic intent and policy direction, with which presidents may disagree. Reagan after all, cut the EPA's budget and appointed an unfavorable director in response to its clean air enforcement activities of the 1970s. Unfortunately, there exists no reliable measure of bureaucratic attention to issues and, as some argue, bureaucrats implement first, then comment about their actions publicly (West 1995).

Given the importance of salience to the signaling process, media attention is also relevant to presidential signals. Chapter 4 reveals that Presidents Kennedy and Johnson signaled most frequently their civil rights policy preferences. Throughout the 1960s, the civil rights of African Americans were quite salient to the public. Major civil rights events, such as sit-ins, marches, and Supreme Court decisions, also shaped public attention. It is quite plausible that presidents may have responded to media attention. If so, then the media, not the president, ultimately drive signaling impacts in Congress or the bureaucracy. Being able to trace out the direct linkages among media attention, presidential signals, and their influence in Congress and the bureaucracy is clearly not possible with my parsimonious signaling model. Nevertheless, media attention had limited impacts in all three empirical chapters, and research shows that media attention does not alone drive presidential attention to these policy areas, including civil rights (Eshbaugh-Soha and Peake 2004).

Despite these possibilities of reciprocal or multicausal impacts, I have taken some steps to alleviate the difficulties present in my unidirectional signaling model. Basic time-order controls ensure that presidential signals have an intended impact. The time dimension to my quantitative models allows me to lag presidential signals and at least satisfy the time-order criterion for causality. Even though presidents may signal in response to the political environments in Congress and the bureaucracy, the time-order qualification is a simple and parsimonious way to test the relationship that I have hypothesized exists: presidents affect congressional voting and bureaucratic implementation with several tools, including their signals. Moreover, even if presidents respond to the congressional and bureaucratic environments, this does not preclude presidential signaling effects. The president may have responded to Congress, the bureaucracy, or the news media at one point; legislators and bureaucrats may still respond to presidential signals later in the policy process. When the signaling train began, presidents may have been responding to a political and policy environment in the Congress, bureaucracy, or news media. But without addressing the origins of a policy—without answering this chicken and egg question—I have made strides to simplify yet represent accurately the relationship between presidential signals and their influence over policy in Congress and the bureaucracy.

Other research is beginning to trace out the multidirectional relationships among presidential speeches, media attention, and congressional hearings (Eshbaugh-Soha and Peake 2004). Although presidents do affect media and congressional attention to policies with primarily salient characteristics, media attention also affects presidential attention to policies that are also uncomplicated. This research suggests that we are safe in arguing that presidential leadership is the driving force behind the signaling relationship, but the only way that we may be able to sort out the complexity of the signaling relationship may be through a formal model of presidential signaling. This is yet another avenue for future research.

Presidential Signals and Democratic Governance

The logic behind presidential signaling and the policy process purposefully excludes the public as *the* reason why legislators and bureaucrats will respond to presidential speeches. Presidents are not rational to rely on public support when the public is typically disinterested in politics, rarely watches presidential addresses, or is typically unaware of how the adoption or implementation of policies affects society. The public may listen to the president on occasion, but infrequent public attention cannot explain why presidents speak daily about their policy priorities. Presidents speak to inform political elites, those responsible for adopting or implementing the president's policy programs. Yet presidents must also speak to meet public expectations, and they are more likely to influence Congress or the bureaucracy on salient issues. If the public is going to respond to the president at all, it most likely will be on those issues to which the public may react strongly and hold the president accountable. Some believe that for the president to maintain public support, support he needs to be considered relevant to Washington politics, the president will speak publicly. But if the public is not the president's primary concern when he discusses policy in his public statements, what does this say about US democracy?

Initially, one may be concerned that signaling, therefore, is undemocratic. Signaling is based on the idea that public support is not a necessary condition for presidential speeches to affect public policy. Presidents attempt to move legislators and bureaucrats to support their policies, irrespective of public sentiment. If signaling does not require public support, as Kernell (1997) and others claim is required of going public, then is it an undemocratic source of presidential power?

The power of presidential signaling may still be considered a democratic power in part because the public always has the potential to influence politics. *If* the public cares to respond to presidents, as it did to Reagan's national addresses on tax cuts in 1981, then legislators are even more likely to listen to presidential speeches. The people may magnify presidential statements (Member of Congress [Texas] interview 2005), even though democratic governance—and the signaling relationship—cannot hinge solely on a disinterested public.

This study also accounts for the potential that the public may have on a policy—absent consistent and reliable public opinion data—through the policy itself, which shapes incentives for political action. Recall the importance of salience to the signaling relationship: Presidents are most likely to use their signals effectively on issues that are characteristically salient. Presidents are therefore concerned with public opinion, in the sense that they are most likely to speak about and influence the policy directions of those policies that fit into Gormley's (1986) salient category. Presidents have an incentive to speak about salient policies because the public also has an incentive (and may be most likely, at least potentially) to be involved in these policies. Presidents will engage these policies more than others because there exists a greater payoff—in terms of meeting public expectations, garnering public support, and winning reelection. But this does not mean that presidents can necessarily (or have to) move public opinion or otherwise affect news coverage of an issue to use their signals to influence policy on salient issues.

Moreover, presidents must be cognizant of the potential that public action has in a democracy. Inattentive publics (see Arnold 1990) wait in the shadows of political discontent, regardless of presidential prerogative. As Ronald Reagan claimed on April 28, 1981 (quoting President Theodore Roosevelt), "the American people are slow to wrath, but when their wrath is once kindled, it burns like a consuming flame." This is a threat, however inconsequential most of the time, of which politicians are very much aware. This threat exists, moreover, whether presidents themselves are responsible for kindling the flame. For all intents and purposes, the public acts independently of presidential attention, instead responding to desires inherent in the collective US experience. Nevertheless, salient policy types demand presidential, congressional, and bureaucratic attention precisely because federal officials could be held accountable to public demands (Gormley 1986). The public has influence over public policy, however infrequent (Brady 1988); representatives know this, and so they rely on broad indicators of when the public is most likely to react, revolt, or otherwise criticize policy decisions.

In short, the theory of presidential signaling posits a model of elite relationships, whereby presidents influence the policy decisions of legislators and bureaucrats through public speeches. Presidential signaling is not without a public dimension, nevertheless. The public shapes the incentives for politicians to act through public policies. Even though the president may be unable to move public opinion, salient policies provide incentives for presidents, legislators, and bureaucrats to respond to public preferences. In other words, the nature of the policy area—the reason why public policy is so vital to explaining institutional processes—shapes the behavior of political actors. We may not see political actors reacting to public opinion as they lead, vote, or implement, but the policy area provides different incentives to be responsive, just in case the "wrath" of the US people is indeed kindled near Election Day. The public still plays an active role in the actions of elected officials. Whether presidents may be able to manipulate public opinion and use it actively to increase their policy success is irrelevant to presidential signaling.

Referring once again to the question of democracy, of course a democracy calls upon its people to act democratically. If citizens do not live up to their democratic responsibilities, if they do not show interest in public policy, nor pay attention to presidential leadership, then it is only rational for a president to act as a trustee in representing public preferences. Yes, the public will potentially be the trigger in a politician's demise. But if the president's signaling strategy is undemocratic, then it is up to citizens in a democracy to change their behavior—doing so will clearly change the dynamics of presidential signaling and the causal linkage between presidential speeches and their impact over public policy.

Beyond Going Public

For decades now, presidency scholars have been intrigued by the president's use of public statements in his daily governing activities. Scholars have theorized why presidents give public speeches and how they might affect legislation. Research has also explored empirically the president's public statements and their relationship to the president's success in Congress. The literature is clear: presidential public statements are an important component to the president's governing strategy.

The literature has been unclear as to how presidential statements affect the president's influence over public policy. The dominant model—going public—theorizes an indirect link among the president's speeches, public opinion, and his success in Congress. Yet much research demonstrates that presidents cannot typically move public opinion and that the public, therefore, is inconsequential to the demonstrated link between presidential speeches and legislative success. Indeed, scholars who show a link between presidential speeches and success only assume that an indirect linkage model is appropriate, without testing the existence of such a link. An indirect linkage model such as these scholars posit is furthermore limited because it cannot account for the president's speeches and their impact on the bureaucracy.

Simply, if the president cannot move public opinion (Edwards 2003) or influence the news media on a consistent basis (Edwards and Wood 1999; Eshbaugh-Soha and Peake 2005), thereby expanding the scope of conflict and encouraging public involvement in the legislative process, then how can we conclude that the public plays a vital role in the president's quest for legislative success through public speeches?

This book adds a significant wrinkle to our understanding of the president's public speeches and their impact over the policy processes of the federal government. I have put forth a direct linkage model between presidential signals and the president's success in Congress. The president's public speeches are signals that reflect his policy preferences and concern for various policy areas. Because of their need for cognitive efficiency, legislators use presidential signals in their policy decisions. Moreover, presidents hope to influence a policy's implementation just as they hope to affect its adoption. The logic of presidential signaling, therefore, also applies to the bureaucracy. The impact of signals over bureaucratic and congressional policy outputs varies by policy area because different policies elicit different institutional and political responses. Even though signals are a mixed source of power in that they do not affect all policy areas and institutions equally, they have been directly influential over the adoption and implementation of public policy.

This book provides substantial evidence that presidential signals directly affect policy in Congress and the bureaucracy and that signaling theory is an alternative to the going-public model. Yet the results presented here do not eliminate the feasibility of a going-public strategy for presidents. We must explicitly test the going-public model to determine if and when presidents may be able to move public opinion and use public support as a means to coerce legislators into supporting their positions. Although this book provides support for an alternative model to going public, it remains to be seen if other presidents besides Ronald Reagan in 1981 have had success influencing public opinion according to a going-public strategy.

This project is, nevertheless, an improvement over past research because it builds a model and then tests that model. It is possible that evidence will support an indirect linkage among presidential statements, public opinion, and the president's success in Congress, however unlikely this may be (Eshbaugh-Soha and Peake 2004). Only when scholars test the going-public model properly will we be sure if indeed going public is a viable strategy that presidents may employ when they use their speeches to affect public policy.

Given significant public disinterest in politics and public policy, nonetheless, presidents are wise to use their speeches to inform the decisions of legislators and bureaucrats. Doing so may directly affect the adoption and implementation of public policy, depending on the nature of each policy area. Indeed, the threat of public concern—of public salience—for a policy issue is a catalyst for presidential signaling effectiveness. Even so, signals cannot be considered effective outside of the context of the political environment, as they are clearly not the president's only source of influence. Being mixed in their effectiveness, sending signals to policy elites is one among many strategies available to presidents as they strive to navigate successfully the difficulties of presidential leadership in the modern era.

Notes

1. The same argument could be made for another organizational component of the White House: the speechmaking and communications organizations. The Office of Communications and the White House Press Office have

undoubtedly shaped the president's ability to deliver speeches and to do so effectively. Arguably, the White House speech organization is one of the missing explanations for why presidents have been able to deliver more speeches but also perhaps why they have not been as influential as one might expect (Eshbaugh-Soha 2001).

2. This is not to say that these studies cannot account for legislative liaison and its potential impact on Congress. Bond and Fleisher (1990) could argue, for example, that legislative liaisons filter through party and committee leaders, thereby having a minimal impact on rank-and-file legislators.

Appendix A

Data Sources and Coding Decisions

Independent Variables

Presidential Signals

I measure presidential signals as the number of pages devoted per unit of time (year, quarter, and so on) to civil rights, clean air, or agriculture policy. I code signals from successive issues of the *Public Papers of the Presidents*. Each volume of the *Public Papers* has a subject index from which I compiled a list of key words related to each policy area. The key words for each policy area are listed in Appendix C. I then scanned each entry to ensure that the statement related to either civil rights, clean air, or agriculture policy. I also determined whether the statement was in support of government action, neutral to government action, or against it. These positions tend to follow standard liberal or conservative categories. Although the number of speeches or remarks is only marginally different from the number of pages devoted to a subject, which are barely different from the number of paragraphs (Barrett 2000), counting pages allows differentiation between a brief mention of a policy and a concerted effort by presidents to make a policy point. Coding pages, therefore, is appropriate given the importance my argument places on presidential attention to specific policies.

My coding scheme is different from that of many past studies that have utilized the *Public Papers of the Presidents*. Some scholars use only State of the Union addresses because they are nationally televised and most likely to be heard by the public (Cohen 1997). Yet presidents can project their preferences to Congress and the bureaucracy from a variety of public forums beyond the State of the Union address, including national addresses and ceremonial bill signings (Grossman and Kumar 1981: 238–240). Even though question-and-answer sessions have been excluded in some scholars' analyses of presidential statements (Barrett 2000; Fett 1994), press conferences are also a useful forum from which presidents may signal their preferences. Indeed, presidents have much control over their press conferences (Eshbaugh-Soha 2003). They can plant questions to make statements on agenda policy, decide which reporters to recognize, and decide when to notify the press of the conference's location and time (Grossman and Kumar 1981: 248). Moreover, presidents may be asked specific questions that can illuminate the president's policy preferences beyond the pre-rehearsed, sometimes symbolic comments made in prepared statements. Presidents are strategic actors and may find advantages in having reporters ask questions instead of relying solely on their own prepared statements to support or oppose a policy.

Again, I code any statement in which the president shows interest in a policy area. Recall that presidential signaling is a source of power for presidents, a resource they may use to influence simultaneously the adoption and implementation stages of public policy. Signals may be both broad and specific, directed toward Congress or the bureaucracy, because any mention of a policy area may be interpreted as a signal for action and because presidents only mention a policy area if they have a preference for that policy. Moreover, this inclusive approach to coding ensures that I am measuring what I theorize affects policy in Congress and the bureaucracy. I code not only spoken words but also written documents, which are both public statements.

Whereas bureaucratic models assess directional signals and their impact on outputs, congressional models assess total number of signals irrespective of direction. A president is successful on a roll-call vote if his position wins. A negative signal tells Congress to oppose a vote, a positive signal tells Congress to support a vote, and total signals tell Congress to support the president's position, whether it is positive or negative.

A comparison between Presidents Bush's and Johnson's different strategies of civil rights success provides support for using total signals. George H. W. Bush repeatedly criticized Congress for pushing a "quota bill" during debates on the Civil Rights Act of 1991; he chose a negative strategy. Nevertheless, Bush still wanted a civil rights bill and eventually won 67 percent of his civil rights votes in 1991. If a president speaks in favor of a bill, he too can be successful. Johnson won more than 95 percent of his 1964 civil rights votes using overwhelmingly positive signals. Whichever strategy presidents choose, the direction of their signals is not relevant to determining success because total signals tell Congress to support the president's position. Hence, the total number of signals devoted to policy, whether positive or negative, is the key independent variable in the congressional analyses.

All presidential signals have been taken from hardcover volumes of the *Public Papers of the Presidents* save 2002, 2003, and 2004. At this writing, the Public Papers are only available electronically in weekly form for these years at http://www.gpoaccess.gov/wcomp/index.html. Although the electronic versions of the *Weekly Compilation of Presidential Documents* mirror the hardcover volumes in font and format, so that page counts from this source would be equivalent to a page count taken from a hardcover volume, the weekly documents do not contain an index like that of the hardcover volume. To be able to update this study beyond 2001, therefore, I relied on key word searches to assess President George W. Bush's attention to civil rights, clean air, and domestic farm policies between 2002 and 2004. Care was taken to ensure comparability, even though the additional three years produced no demonstrable differences in the results. Civil rights policy signals were provided in part by Bohte (1997).

Veto Threats

Veto threats are a specific signal that presidents may send to Congress. Presidents occasionally threaten to veto legislation to try to persuade members of Congress to adopt a bill more consistent with the president's preferences. Indeed, this threat, not broad and informative signals, may increase the president's success on roll-call votes. When they threaten a veto, presidents are making legislators decide if they have enough votes to override the president's veto. Otherwise, legislators may be wise to consider the president's policy preferences to ensure that a compromise bill is signed.

To assess the impact that veto threats have on presidential success in Congress, I surveyed the *Public Papers of the Presidents* for mentions of veto threats. In a handful of instances, presidents stated specifically that they would veto a specific bill if it were not changed. A cursory reading suggests several points. First, presidents who make veto threats are likely to carry that threat out. Except in recent years when the margin of seats in Congress has been extraordinarily small, Congress usually had enough votes on hand to dismiss the president's threat outright. Second, presidents are generally reluctant to veto legislation or say that they might. If a president were to threaten a veto on most legislation that he did not prefer, his reputation and prestige might suffer. Indeed, many potential veto threats were actually prompted by media during press conferences. During question-and-answer periods, presidents usually refuse to give a threat, claiming that they need more information or that they need to read the bill first. Finally, presidents also make statements when they actually veto a bill. Vetoes are rare and important events, and they regularly involved a public statement of some sort. Only those threats made prior to the veto itself are counted as having a potential impact on legislators' voting decisions.

Media Attention

Media attention to an issue or an issue's public salience is important to the questions of whether and when a policy will positively condition the effects signals have on outputs. Salience is also a necessary control because either Congress or the bureaucracy could be responding to the public's interest in a policy, not to the president's signals. Although the percentage of respondents who claim that civil rights, clean air, or agriculture is the "most important problem" is a useful indicator of salience, Gallup has not asked about each policy area on a regular basis. Another measure is media attention. Most of what is salient to the public is first reported through magazines and other periodicals (see Baumgartner and Jones 1993; Edwards, Mitchell, and Welch 1995). The *Reader's Guide to Periodical Literature* lists articles devoted to a particular policy area each year. The number of such articles measures media attention to a policy area and indicates its salience to the public. A keyword list is included in Appendix C. At this writing, hardcover volumes of the *Reader's Guide to Periodical Literature* are available only through 2000. Counts from 2001 through 2004 are taken from the electronic version of the *Reader's Guide.*

Other available indicators of media attention include network news and newspaper coverage. The Vanderbilt News Archives houses time and subject data on network (and some cable television) evening news coverage. This is a particularly useful source of media attention data, primarily because agenda-setting research demonstrates that the evening news, particularly the top story, has a profound agenda-setting effect on the US public (Iyengar and Kinder 1987). Unfortunately, these data do not go as far back in time as my project, and they were only available since the early 1980s when I began this project. Stories on the front page of the *New York Times* have also been used to measure media attention. These data, available through Bryan Jones at the University of Washington, are useful but are also limited in that only a sample of stories is coded. This presents a problem for time series analyses, where random sampling may exclude relevant stories in several months or years of the analysis. Besides, *Reader's Guide to Periodical Literature* measures are comparable to these measures of media attention (Eshbaugh-Soha and Peake 2004).

Congressional Influence

Two measures tap congressional influence over the policy process. First, the minimum percentages of presidential party members in Congress indicate the support presidents are likely to receive from Congress. Presidents who have a more favorable proportion of party seats in Congress are simply more likely to be successful over roll-call votes. Moreover, signals may be more likely to be effective when the president's party controls Congress, as a favorable party-seat distribution increases the number of legislators who will listen to the president (Kingdon 1981). Presidential seats are the yearly percentage of seats in either the House of Representatives or the Senate controlled by the president's party. Measures of divided government produce similar results. I choose to use the percentage of the president's party's seats in each house of Congress because this ensures more variation in the models.

Second, congressional attention could limit the president's influence over the bureaucracy. Congress is an influential principal over bureaucratic activity (Aberbach 1990; McCubbins and Schwartz 1984; Ogul 1976; Weingast and Moran 1983). Therefore, the more congressional hearings, the more Congress will influence bureaucratic activity. A measure of congressional attentiveness to specific bureaucratic policies comes from the Congressional Information Service (CIS). This is the number of days Congress spends in committee hearings on a particular policy. I use an index of key words per policy area and then scan each entry to determine that each committee-hearing day addressed the policy area I am examining. Committee activity is particularly important to assess because policymaking and oversight occur predominately in committee, not on the floor. Because Congress can expand or contract an agency's authority through statute, dummy variables will control for theoretically important statutes.

Legislation

Several statutes are important to these policy areas. For civil rights, the 1957, 1964, and 1991 Civil Rights Acts are all relevant to the litigation of civil rights cases by the Civil Rights Division. I model the Civil Rights Act of 1964 as a pulse function, to account for its short-term and immediate impact on litigation, and as a step function, for its long-term impact. The pulse function is a one for 1964 and a zero for all other years, and the step function is ones from 1965 to 1990 and zeros for all other years. I code the Civil Rights Act of 1991 as a step function (ones between 1991 and 2002). Domestic farm policy models include several key price support statutes since the 1980s: 1983, 1985, 1990, 1996, and 2002. Reagan's 1983 Payment in Kind program is transitory, legislating immediate paybacks to farmers, and is coded as a pulse function. The other statutes are permanent renewals of the basic Agricultural Adjustment Act and are step functions.

Legislative Success

Success breeds success. Hence, presidents who are successful on past roll-call votes should be successful on present votes. Lacking a measure of legislative success during a president's first year, it is also likely that legislators will judge the president's capacity to govern more favorably if he received a large percentage of the popular vote. Past success is related theoretically to reputation but only marginally so. In brief, if presidents are successful in Congress and amid the electorate, they should be more successful on policy-specific floor votes.

My measure of success combines the president's yearly success on roll-call votes with the president's percentage of the popular vote during election years. First, *Congressional Quarterly Almanac* reports the president's yearly success on all position roll-call votes. Second, I also use the president's popular vote percentage during election years. Only measuring success in an election year is misleading. If a president is not reelected, then the president's past success is the last year's success rate of the previous president. A new president has his own reputation. Often he builds it upon another measure of political support, reputation, or capital: his electoral margin.

The following coding decisions explain my success variable for reelection years. First, I calculate the mean success rate of presidents included in this study, which is 67.3 percent, and assume that the mean popular vote is 50 percent. If the candidate won less than 50 percent of the popular vote, I then subtract the difference from the mean success rate; if the candidate won more than 50 percent, I add the difference to the mean success rate. For example, Kennedy's reputation measure for 1961 of 67 percent is reached by subtracting 0.3, his popular vote difference from 50 percent, from 67.3. In nonelection years, the president's roll-call success rate measures reputation.

Public Approval

Public approval has mixed effects on presidential success in Congress. Nevertheless, job approval may affect the president's legislative success, especially when public disapproval is high (see Ostrom and Simon 1985). High approval ratings also aid the president in his quest for legislative victories, at least at the margins (Edwards 1989), and help him influence public opinion (Page and Shapiro 1985). Approval could also aid the president's signals: popular presidents are more powerful, and their signals should be more influential than those sent by unpopular presidents. The president's approval ratings should also affect the bureaucracy's perception of the presidency's effects on their power. I code the president's job approval ratings according to Gallup's measure of public support for the president. Typically, I aggregate these numbers annually. In models where the vote is the unit of analysis, I take Gallup's measure of approval during the month prior to a roll-call vote in Congress.

Interest Group Influence

To assess interest group influence, I borrow from Schlozman and Tierney (1986) and code the total membership in interest groups that pertain to a policy area. I first examined the *Encyclopedia of Associations* by topic area. For civil rights, I examined the civil rights and civil liberties subsection of the Public Affairs listing. I found groups related to the environment and farmers' interests under various key words listed in Appendix C. As with any classification of this sort, not all entries under a broad heading fit my purposes. Clearly, Beer Drinkers of America have little to do with the civil rights of African Americans. As a result, I skimmed each interest group entry to make sure that the group's mission related to civil rights, the environment, or farmers.

Civil rights groups clearly had some influence over the adoption and implementation of civil rights policy, particularly in the 1960s (Rosenberg 1991). African American groups lobbied Congress and the presidency, whether directly or indirectly, to pass or sign civil rights legislation. Group interactions ranged from private meetings between Dr. Martin Luther King Jr. and Lyndon Johnson over 1960s civil rights legislation to public criticism of Reagan's lack of support for the voting rights act extension pushed by African American leadership. I difference the number of members of all civil rights groups to control for interest group effects on the adoption and implementation of civil rights policy. A significant increase or decrease in membership provides a better sense than absolute membership of the waxing or waning influence of interest groups over the adoption or implementation of policy.

Second, groups on both sides of the clean air debate have a vested interest in supporting or opposing its adoption and implementation. The environmental lobby regularly speaks out in favor of strict clean air regulations. The environmental lobby is diverse, and an accurate measure of its influence is difficult to attain. Relative to industrial interests, the environmental lobby has fewer resources and less influence over legislation (R. Cohen 1995). Industry has a vested interest in opposing government regulations and has the resources to influence the policy decisions of many members of Congress and the president.

One measure that acts as a proxy for both sides' relative influence on clean air policy is the economy. When the economy is doing poorly, industry is more likely to complain about regulations on air pollution and either resist further legislation or ask for the repeal of existing regulations. Change in real gross domestic product measures the strength of the economy. When in recession, industry is more likely to push Congress or the EPA to avoid regulating air pollution. Indeed, industrial influence will vary by the state of the economy. During a soft economy, industries pressure their agency contacts, the president, and Congress to limit enforcement of environmental regulations. As the economy improves, the EPA should be less constrained by economic conditions and regulate air pollution more vigorously. This measure is particularly useful because GDP is available by quarter.

Finally, agricultural interest groups have measurable impacts on policy in Congress. The dominant interest group, the American Farm Bureau Federation, maintained a sizable role over farm policy through the 1960s, but its influence has since declined, as agriculture policy has become less of a congressional and presidential priority (Hansen 1991). Agriculture interest groups are many and diverse. There is no single agricultural interest (Schlozman and Tierney 1986: 43), and a reliable and complete measure of farm groups is unavailable. The *Encyclopedia of Associations* begins in 1956. Nevertheless, the number of farms should be proportional to the level of interest group activity on farm policy. Simply put, if there are more farms, there are more farmers who can pay dues or participate in farm group activities. Therefore, total number of farms acts as a proxy for the level of lobby interest in agriculture policy; more farms generally means more interest group influence over farm policy (see Moyer and Josling 1990: 108).

Despite the potential usefulness of membership data for assessing the impact of interest groups on policy outputs, these data are limited in several respects. First, as I mentioned, they do not go back far enough in time to be useful for farm policy models or for much of the congressional models. Second, the numbers themselves are suspect. It is unclear that the groups update membership numbers regularly. For example, the Urban League has had 50,000 members since the 1960s and the National Association for the Advancement of Colored People (NAACP) had exactly 450,674 members from 1970 to 1980. Nevertheless, these data are the only measure available, and besides, they are only a control.

Budgets

The president's control over the bureaucracy's budget is a clear and effective source of presidential power (Wood and Waterman 1994). Budget requests may affect presidential influence in the bureaucracy, especially if they operate in tandem with Congress (Krause 1996). Budget data for each agency have been coded from successive years of the *Budget of the United States*. They have been corrected for inflation and differenced when appropriate. Because budget data are annual, I model a pulse function dummy to account for the clear negative intervention that the 1982 fiscal year budget should have on the EPA's enforcement activities (Wood 1988).

Appointments

Appointments could also affect the president's influence in the bureaucracy. Wood and Waterman (1994) showed many instances in which political appointments affected the direction of bureaucratic outputs. The appointments of Anne Burford and William Ruckelshaus to head the EPA during the Reagan administration are of particular interest for my clean air policy chapter. These appointments are step-function dummy variables, with ones denoting when they are employed and zeros when they are not. As past research demonstrates, we should see a decrease in EPA enforcements under the tutelage of Anne Burford and a subsequent rise in enforcement activity during Ruckelshaus's tenure. Because my other bureaucracy models are annual time series, a step function for appointments is not appropriate. The usefulness of intervention models hinges on the frequency of time points. One can accurately assess the impact of a bureaucratic appointee using step functions only when time points are refined enough to model when a director was appointed. Annual analyses cannot differentiate exactly when a new appointee may have had an impact, so measures of appointments are not included in the civil rights and agriculture policy models.

Judicial Influence

The Supreme Court has rendered several important decisions over the past fifty years, especially in the area of civil rights. These specific Court decisions may affect the litigation of civil rights policy. In other words, Court decisions that uphold or further civil rights law may increase the legal jurisdiction of the CRD to litigate civil rights cases; decisions that strike down civil rights laws may limit CRD activity.

Court decisions that uphold or strike down civil rights laws, measured as the number of liberal or conservative civil rights cases per year, will pick up any subtle changes in the CRD's legal authority. I have coded these from the Segal and Spaeth online dataset.[1]

Dependent Variables

Several dependent variables measure bureaucratic and congressional outputs by specific policy area. The bureaucratic outputs are measures related to specific federal agencies. These vary widely by policy type. Legislative outputs only differ by policy area; the coding and data sources are identical.

There are many measures of presidential success in Congress, each of which has its own benefits and detractions (see Bond and Fleisher [1990: chap. 3] for a complete discussion). For this study, I measure presidential success in Congress using roll-call votes on which presidents took discernible public positions. I include both those roll-call votes noted by *Congressional Quarterly* (*CQ*) and roll-call votes related to a policy area on which *CQ* does not denote a public position. There are many votes on which I could clearly determine, from the president's statements, that the president would unequivocally support or oppose the rendered vote. Contrary to the perceived ability of *CQ* to determine accurately each public position roll call (see Covington 1987), *CQ* makes many mistakes. For instance, in 1974, *CQ* credited President Nixon with a public position on Senate vote number 314, but not on an identical vote in the House (number 298). Edwards (1989: chap. 2) recoded his support scores because *CQ* often missed many votes. In addition, because *CQ* does not indicate a presidential position on roll calls prior to 1956, I used my own judgment on these votes consistent with the president's public statements.

In some models, I use the vote as the unit of analysis and therefore code the president's success on each roll-call vote. For the time series models, I first determine the president's success on each roll-call vote and then divide the number of votes per roll-call vote in the president's favor by the total number of legislators voting. For example, if the president's position on a House vote is "nay," but the measure passed 263–142, then the president's percentage of the vote is 142 divided by 405, or 35 percent. I then average the votes by policy area, year, and house of Congress and assess the influences on the president's average success on selected roll-call votes.

Data limitations preclude a more refined inspection of the direction of presidential signals on the president's success in Congress. Assessing a directional impact would require me to split my already small samples of individual roll-call votes. A larger sample of congressional roll-call votes (see Chapter 7) will facilitate an exploration into the differing effects of supportive and opposition signals and their influence over the adoption of public policy.

Civil Rights

To test the president's influence over the bureaucracy, I have selected outputs from the Civil Rights Division of the Department of Justice. Both civil and criminal cases are available over time and provide a specific measure of bureaucratic civil rights outputs. These data are available by fiscal year, which runs July through June (except after 1993, when the fiscal year became October 1 through September 30). This allows for a convenient six-month lag for all independent variables on most litigated cases in this time series. The president's signals for 1963, for example, affect cases filed from July of 1963 through June of 1964. This lag controls for the time required to file a case and ensures that at least one assumption of causality is met, that the independent variable occurs prior in time to the dependent variable. The models only run through 2002 because data after then are not comparable with previous years. According to Department of Justice statistics, "In 2003, a change in coding caused some cases that previously would have classified as homicide cases to be reported as aggravated assault cases; therefore, the data for 2003 and thereafter are not comparable to previous years" (*Sourcebook of Criminal Justice Statistics* 2003: 410, table 5.10). Legislative outputs are the average percentage of success presidents have on civil rights roll-call votes or the president's success per vote, depending on the model.

Clean Air

Clean air policy data come from two sources. First, the level of EPA monitoring activity runs quarterly from 1977 to 1989. This dependent variable, supplied by Wood (1988), is the number of monitoring activities undertaken by the EPA from 1977 to 1989. The second data source contains similar data supplied directly to me by the EPA. These are compliance and violation enforcement data from 1989 to 1998. I analyze these series separately for reasons explained in Chapter 5. As for civil rights policy, clean air success in Congress is the average success presidents have on clean air roll-call votes.

Agriculture

Presidential success on agriculture roll-call votes measures the legislative dependent variable. Like civil rights and clean air policy data, this is the average percentage of success presidents have on agriculture roll-call votes in Congress by year. The bureaucratic-agriculture policy dependent variable is a measure of yearly gross payments to farmers. Dollar amounts have been corrected for inflation. These data are available from the USDA National Agricultural Statistics Service at the USDA government Web page. Government payments to farmers have been a mainstay of the agriculture program, even though the substance of the payments has changed. Since 1996, for example, most government payments to farmers have been fixed payments set by Congress. These payments totaled $5.6 billion in 1996, $5.4 billion in 1997, and $5.8 billion in 1998. Total payments included other payments, such as disaster assistance payments and aid to farmers whose wheat experienced karnal bunt fungus. In years prior to 1996, payments comprised deficiency payments from the target price program, commodity surplus payments to farmers (under Reagan's 1983 Payment in Kind program), and aid to farmers who stored surplus commodities.

Note

1. The Segal and Spaeth dataset was available online at http://polisci.msu. edu/~pljp/sctdata1.html. As of September 2005, this link no longer appears to be active. I had previously downloaded and saved the Supreme Court database through 2000 and am happy to provide these data.

APPENDIX B

METHODS

THE POLICY PROCESS IS VIRTUALLY NEVER ENDING, DYNAMIC, AND cyclical at times (see Anderson 2000). Because presidents signal in an attempt to influence the policy process, the signaling process itself must change and evolve over time. Signaling, like several sources of presidential power (Wood 1988; Wood 2000a), is a dynamic process. Administration priorities and political environments all vary over time, as does each variable in this study. The most appropriate way to consider these data therefore is through time series analysis. Unfortunately, data limitations mean that only bureaucratic outputs may be modeled according to strict assumptions of dynamic methodology. Congressional outputs are modeled using one of two techniques.

Bureaucratic Outputs

Outputs from the Civil Rights Division, Environmental Protection Agency, and US Department of Agriculture comprise bureaucratic dependent variables. All three of these series vary over time and require modeling by some type of dynamic methodology. Box-Jenkins time series analysis follows a series of diagnostic steps crucial to appropriate dynamic modeling. Stationarity and autocorrelation are problems of particular interest. A series is stationary when its mean and variance are invariant with respect to time. In the presence of nonstationarity, the problem of spurious regression arises. Autocorrelation, or correlated errors in a model, violates a basic assumption of the classic linear regression model. If present, autocorrelation renders parameter estimates unreliable. Correlograms and Augmented–Dickey Fuller tests check for stationarity and autocorrelation in each variable.

Each bureaucratic output model follows a basic equation, whereby a selection of independent variables influences the policy outputs of the Civil Rights Division, Environmental Protection Agency, or US Department of Agriculture (see Equation B.1).

$$Y_t = b_0 + (1-\omega_{0n}B)X_{n-k} + \ldots + (1-\omega_{0n})X_{n-k} + \varepsilon_t \qquad \textbf{B.1}$$

Given unique characteristics, the criminal cases and clean air enforcement models have specific variations on this basic equation.

Criminal Cases

Heteroskedasticity presents a unique methodological problem for the criminal civil rights cases series. Most time series violate standard assumptions of ordinary least squares regression with correlated errors over time. Some series, such as this criminal cases series, display heteroskedasticity or disproportional error variance over time. Heteroskedastic errors mean that estimators are not efficient, and parameter estimates are not reliable.

There are several means of correcting for heteroskedasticity. One approach is to "dummy out" the influential observation. This controls for the year that induces heteroskedasticity in the model. Although this may be an effective diagnostic, it may cause other complications such as autocorrelation and is limited in time series methodology given its sensitivity to cases.

Another method is by modeling the conditional variance of an autoregressive time series that displays short bursts of volatility. This technique, known as either Autoregressive Conditional Heteroskedasticity (ARCH) or Generalized Autoregressive Conditional Heteroskedasticity (GARCH), is appropriate when the variance changes as a function of time (see Bollerslev 1986; Engle 1982). An ARCH or GARCH technique is not appropriate for the criminal cases series from 1958 to 2002, however, as demonstrated by an insignificant ARCH–Lagrange Multiplier test.

Transforming those variables that induce a model's heteroskedasticity is another means to correct for nonconstant variance. Logging or taking the square root of each observation is a standard transformation. By logging the criminal cases series—the dependent variable—I correct for nonconstant variance over time.[1] In this case, a logged dependent variable eliminates the problem of unequal error variance and translates my inefficient and unreliable estimators into estimators that are efficient and open to reliable interpretation. The only other peculiarity of a semi-log model is that a coefficient is interpreted as a percentage change or growth in the dependent variable.

Clean Air Activity

The dynamic nature of EPA enforcement data requires a dynamic methodology (see Wood 1988). Hence, I use Box-Jenkins time series methodology to analyze the data. Multivariate, transfer function ARMA models test hypothetical relationships among several variables and EPA activity. Because ARMA models require controls for history, identification of each series is first necessary. Indeed, a first-order autoregressive term and a moving average coefficient at the fourth lag express the history of EPA monitoring activity quite well. I also model EPA monitoring activity from 1977 to 1989 quarterly, as a function of several key theoretical variables.

Congressional Outputs

Roll-call votes for each policy area comprise the congressional dependent variables. Dynamic time series models are inappropriate for these data primarily because civil rights, clean air, and agriculture policies are not measurable each year. For many years, Congress does not vote on these policies, leaving no measurable indication of presidential success. There are two solutions to this problem. The first applies to civil rights and agriculture data, the other to clean air policy.

Congress has not voted on civil rights and agriculture policy every year since the late 1940s. This means that, for several years, legislative outputs are zero. Modeling these outputs according to some standard variant of time series analysis would lead to bias in the results. Simply put, no signals on a policy area in 1985 leads to a perfect relationship without any success in Congress for that same year. The lack of a relationship could actually drive the statistical result.

Heckman (1976) wrote a very influential methodological piece that suggests a way to account statistically for missing data bias. He argued that an omitted variable model could be estimated according to the following steps:

1. Run a probit model, estimating those on sample against those missing values.
2. Use these estimates to construct a ratio of predicted values from the probit model.
3. Run an OLS model with the appropriate dependent and independent variables, including the ratio of predicted values as an additional regressor.

Equations B.2, B.3, and B.4 express mathematically the Heckman selection procedure for both houses of Congress, which models the agenda-setting impact of signals on each house of Congress.

$$\text{Success} = X_i B + [\phi(Z_i \gamma / \sigma_0) / \Phi(Z_i \gamma / \sigma_0)] \overline{\sigma} \qquad \textbf{B.2}$$

Where

$$X_i B = B_0 + B_1 \text{Signals} + B_2 \text{Success}_{t-1} + B_3 \text{Approval} + \qquad \textbf{B.3}$$
$$B_4 \text{Media Attention} + B_5 \% \text{Seats} + B_6 \text{Honeymoon} + B_7 \text{Veto Threat} + \varepsilon$$

$$Z_i \gamma_0 = B_0 + B_1 \text{Signals} + B_2 \text{Media Attention} + B_3 \text{Approval} + \qquad \textbf{B.4}$$
$$B_4 \% \text{Seats} + B_5 \text{Success}_{t-1} + \varepsilon$$

One difficulty with this technique appears to be the ratio of zeros to nonzeros in the estimation: the closer the number of zeros is to nonzeros, the more reliable the correction.[2] Both civil rights and agriculture policy are on the legislative agenda for roughly half of the years in this study, so a Heckman correction may be used. For these policy areas, I model the average percentage in favor of the president's vote position.

Clean air policy, conversely, has been on the congressional agenda only a handful of times. Trying to employ a Heckman correction on these data brings into question the reliability of these data as well. For clean air policy outputs in Congress, I do not assume that the process is dynamic. Instead, I use the percentage of success presidents have on each clean air roll call as the dependent variable and use Ordinary Least Squares regression to analyze the effect signals have.

The Heckman selection models allow me to test one of my hypotheses, that signals affect the legislative agendas of Congress. Yet the specification bias present in annual data renders a direct test of presidential success in Congress problematic. Because of this, I also employ regression models with the vote as the unit of analysis. This effectively pools all roll-call votes and allows me to determine what impact presidential signals and other theoretically relevant control variables have on the president's legislative success by policy area.

Notes

1. A problem arises if one takes the log of zero. In 1958 and 1959, the Civil Rights Division did not file any criminal cases in US district court. To log the series, I changed these zeros to a constant one. These changes are unlikely to have a major impact on the final model. The log of one, after all, is zero.

2. Kennedy (1998: 256) noted that the Heckman correction is not appropriate when the sample size is small and when the collinearity is high. Hence, I do not run a Heckman selection model on clean air roll-call votes.

APPENDIX C Key Words for Content Analyses

Reader's Guide to Periodical Literature	Public Papers of the Presidents	Congressional Information Service Index	Judicial Database
Civil Rights			
Desegregation, racial discrimination, blacks (negroes), discrimination, segregation, civil rights, busing, integration	Civil rights, desegregation, discrimination, integration, voting rights, segregation, racism, affirmative action, busing	Civil rights, discrimination, desegregation, segregation, voting rights, affirmative action, integration, busing	Desegregation (220),[a] desegregation schools (221), employment discrimination (222), voting rights act (211)
Clean Air			
Acid rain, air pollution, clean air, Clean Air Act, emissions credits, smog	Air pollution, clean air, Clean Air Act, environment, Environmental Protection Agency, pollution, pollution prevention, regulation	Air pollution, clean air	Environmental protection (933), pollution (934) conservation,
Agriculture			
Agriculture, Agricultural Administration, farm legislation, price supports	Agriculture, Agricultural Adjustment Act, butter, corn, cotton, wheat, farms, farming, price supports	Agriculture, Agricultural Act, farm payments, price supports	n/a

Note: a. Numbers in parentheses are category numbers from the Segal and Spaeth judicial database (Spaeth 1999).

REFERENCES

Aberbach, Joel D. 1990. *Keeping a Watchful Eye: The Politics of Congressional Oversight.* Washington, DC: The Brookings Institution.

Agency director interview. 2005. August 29.

Anderson, James E. 2000. *Public Policymaking: An Introduction.* 4th ed. New York: Houghton Mifflin.

Arnold, R. Douglas. 1979. *Congress and the Bureaucracy: A Theory of. Influence.* New Haven, CT: Yale University Press.

———. 1990. *The Logic of Congressional Action.* New Haven, CT: Yale University Press.

Barber, David J. 1972. *The Presidential Character: Predicting Performance in the White House.* Englewood Cliffs, NJ: Prentice-Hall.

Barilleaux, Ryan J. 1988. *The Post-Modern Presidency: The Office After Ronald Reagan.* New York: Praeger.

Barnard, Chester I. 1938. *Functions of the Executive.* Cambridge: Harvard University Press.

Barrett, Andrew. 2000. "Gone Public: The Impact of Presidential Rhetoric in Congress." Ph.D. diss., Texas A&M University.

———. 2004. "Gone Public: The Impact of Going Public on Presidential Legislative Success." *American Politics Research* 32, no. 3 (May): 338–370.

Baum, Matthew A., and Samuel Kernell. 1999. "Has Cable Ended the Golden Age of Presidential Television?" *American Political Science Review* 93, no. 1 (March): 99–114.

Baumgartner, Frank, and Bryan D. Jones. 1993. *Agendas and Instability in American Politics.* Chicago: University of Chicago Press.

Bernstein, Marver. 1955. *Regulating Business by Independent Commission.* Princeton, NJ: Princeton University Press.

Bohte, John. 1997. "Critical Institutional Events and Agenda Setting in American Politics." Ph.D. diss., Texas A&M University.

Bollerslev, T. 1986. "Generalized Autoregressive Conditional Heteroskedasticity." *Journal of Econometrics* 31, no. 3 (August): 307–326.

Bond, Jon R., and Richard Fleisher. 1990. *The President in the Legislative Arena.* Chicago: University of Chicago Press.

————, eds. 2000. *Polarized Politics: Congress and the President in a Partisan Era.* Washington, DC: CQ Press.

Bond, Jon R., Richard Fleisher, and B. Dan Wood. 2003. "The Marginal and Time-Varying Effect of Public Approval on Presidential Success in Congress." *Journal of Politics* 65, no. 1 (February): 92–110.

Bose, Menna. 1998. *Shaping and Signaling Presidential Policy.* College Station: Texas A&M University Press.

Brace, Paul, and Barbara Hinckley. 1992. *Follow the Leader: Opinion Polls and the Modern Presidents.* New York: Basic Books.

Brady, David W. 1988. *Critical Elections and Congressional Policymaking.* Palo Alto, CA: Stanford University Press.

Browne, William P. 1988. *Private Interests, Public Policy, and American Agriculture.* Lawrence: University Press of Kansas.

Bryner, Gary C. 1995. *Blue Skies, Green Politics: The Clean Air Act of 1990 and Its Implementation.* 2nd ed. Washington, DC: CQ Press.

Cameron, Charles M. 2000. *Veto Bargaining: Presidents and the Politics of Negative Power.* Cambridge: Cambridge University Press.

Canes-Wrone, Brandice. 2001. "The President's Legislative Influence from Public Appeals." *American Journal of Political Science* 45, no. 2 (April): 313–329.

Canes-Wrone, Brandice, and Scott de Marchi. 2002. "Presidential Approval and Legislative Success." *Journal of Politics* 64, no. 2 (May): 491–509.

Carmines, Edward, and James Stimson. 1989. *Issue Evolution: Race and the Transformation of American Politics.* Princeton, NJ: Princeton University Press.

Carpenter, Daniel P. 1996. "Adaptive Signal Processing, Hierarchy, and Budgetary Control in Federal Regulation." *American Political Science Review* 90, no. 2 (June): 283–302.

Carson, Rachel. 1962. *Silent Spring.* Boston: Houghton Mifflin.

Clausen, Aage. 1973. *How Congressmen Decide: A Policy Focus.* New York: St. Martin's Press.

Cohen, Jeffrey E. 1995. "Presidential Rhetoric and the Public Agenda." *American Journal of Political Science* 39, no. 1 (February): 87–107.

————. 1997. *Presidential Responsiveness and Public Policy-Making.* Ann Arbor: University of Michigan Press.

Cohen, Richard E. 1995. *Washington at Work: Back Rooms and Clean Air.* Boston: Allyn and Bacon.

Congressional Quarterly Almanac. 1974. Washington, DC: Congressional Quarterly.

————. 1981. Washington, DC: Congressional Quarterly.

————. 1996. Washington, DC: Congressional Quarterly.

Cooper, Joseph, David W. Brady, and Patricia A. Hurley. 1977. "The Electoral Basis of Party Voting: Patterns and Trends in the U.S. House of Representatives." In *The Impact of the Electoral Process,* ed. Louis Maisel and Joseph Copper. Beverly Hills, CA: Sage Publications.

Cooper, Joseph, and William F. West. 1988. "Presidential Power and Republican Government: The Theory and Practice of OMB Review of Agency Rules." *Journal of Politics* 50, no. 4 (November): 864–895.

Corrigan, Matthew. 2000. "The Transformation of Going Public: President Clinton, the First Lady, and Health Care Reform." *Political Communication* 17, no. 2 (April): 149–168.

Costain, Anne N., and Steven Majstorovic. 1994. "Congress, Social Movements, and Public Opinion: Multiple Origins of Women's Rights Legislation." *Political Research Quarterly* 47, no. 1 (March): 111–135.

Covington, Cary. 1987. "Staying Private: Gaining Congressional Support for Unpublicized Presidential Preferences on Roll Call Votes." *Journal of Politics* 49, no. 3 (August): 737–755.

Covington, Cary R., J. Mark Wrighton, and Rhonda Kinney. 1995. "A 'Presidency-Augmented' Model of Presidential Success on House Roll Call Votes." *American Journal of Political Science* 39, no. 4 (November): 1001–1024.

Cox, Gary W., and Mathew D. McCubbins. 1993. *Legislative Leviathan: Party Government in the House.* Berkeley: University of California Press.

Dahl, Robert A. 1957. "The Concept of Power." *Behavioral Science* 2: 201–215.

Davies, J. Clarence, and Barbara S. Davies. 1975. *The Politics of Pollution.* 2nd ed. Indianapolis, IN: Pegasus.

Davis, Julie Hirschfeld. 2001. "Getting Government Back into the Farm Business." *Congressional Quarterly Weekly* 59 (July 7): 1630–1636.

Destler, I. M. 1980. *Making Foreign Economic Policy.* Washington, DC: The Brookings Institution.

Downs, Anthony. 1972. "Up and Down with Ecology: The Issue-Attention Cycle." *The Public Interest* 28, no. 1 (Spring): 38–50.

Drees, Caroline. 2005. "Civil Liberties Panel Is Off to a Sluggish Start," *Washington Post,* August 8, A13.

Dunlap, Riley E. 1989. "Public Opinion and Environmental Policy." In *Environmental Politics and Policy,* ed. James P. Lester. Durham, NC: Duke University Press.

Durant, Robert F. 1992. *The Administrative Presidency Revisited: Public Lands, the BLM, and the Reagan Revolution.* Albany: State University of New York Press.

Edsall, Thomas Byrne, and Mary D. Edsall. 1992. *Chain Reaction: The Impact of Race, Rights, and Taxes on American Politics.* New York: Norton.

Edwards, George C., III. 1980. *Presidential Influence in Congress.* San Francisco: W. H. Freeman.

———. 1983. *The Public Presidency: The Pursuit of Popular Support.* New York: St. Martin's Press.

———. 1989. *At the Margins: Presidential Leadership of Congress.* New Haven, CT: Yale University Press.

———. 1997. "Aligning Tests with Theory: Presidential Influence as a Source of Influence in Congress." *Congress and the Presidency* 24, no. 2 (Autumn): 113–130.

———. 2000. "Why Not the Best? The Loyalty-Competence Trade-Off in Presidential Appointments." In *The Merit and Reputation of an Administration: Presidential Appointees on the Appointment Process,* ed. Paul C. Light and Virginia L. Thomas. Washington, DC: The Brookings Institution and Heritage Foundation.

———. 2003. *On Deaf Ears: The Limits of the Bully Pulpit.* New Haven, CT: Yale University Press.

Edwards, George C., III, and Andrew Barrett. 2000. "Presidential Agenda Setting in Congress." In *Polarized Politics,* ed. Jon R. Bond and Richard Fleisher. Washington, DC: CQ Press.

Edwards, George C., III, Andrew Barrett, and Jeffrey Peake. 1997. "The Legislative Impact of Divided Government." *American Journal of Political Science* 41, no. 2 (April): 545–563.

Edwards, George C., III, and Matthew Eshbaugh-Soha. 2001. "Presidential Persuasion: Does the Public Respond?" Paper presented at the annual meeting of the Southern Political Science Association, Atlanta, GA.

Edwards, George C., III, William Mitchell, and Reed Welch. 1995. "Explaining Presidential Approval: The Importance of Issue Salience." *American Journal of Political Science* 39: 108–134.

Edwards, George C., III, and Stephen J. Wayne. 1999. *Presidential Leadership: Politics and Policymaking.* 5th ed. New York: Worth Publishers.

Edwards, George C., III, and B. Dan Wood. 1999. "Who Influences Whom? The President, Congress, and the Media." *American Political Science Review* 93, no. 2 (June): 327–344.

Eisner, Marc Allen, and Kenneth J. Meier. 1990. "Presidential Control Versus Bureaucratic Power: Explaining the Reagan Revolution in Antitrust." *American Journal of Political Science* 34, no. 1 (February): 269–287.

Encyclopedia of Associations. 1956–2004. 48 vols. Detroit, MI: Gale Research.

Enders, Walter. 1995. *Applied Econometric Time Series.* New York: John Wiley and Sons.

Engle, R. 1982. "Autoregressive Conditional Heteroskedasticity with Estimates of Variance of United Kingdom Inflation." *Econometrica* 50, no. 4 (July): 987–1007.

Erikson, Robert. 1978. "Constituency Opinion and Congressional Behavior: A Reexamination of the Miller-Stokers Representation Data." *American Journal of Political Science* 22, no. 3 (August): 511–535.

Eshbaugh-Soha, Matthew. 1999. "Presidential Control of the Bureaucracy: The Civil Rights Cases." Working paper, Texas A&M University.

———. 2001. "'Staying Private' in the Administrative Presidency." *Presidency Research Group Report* 26, no. 2 (Fall): 11–13.

———. 2003. "Presidential Press Conferences over Time." *American Journal of Political Science* 47, no. 2 (April): 348–353.

———. 2004. "Public Opinion and Presidents." In *Public Opinion and Polling Around the World: A Historical Encyclopedia,* ed. John G. Geer. Santa Barbara, CA: ABC-CLIO.

———. 2005. "The Politics of Presidential Agendas." *Political Research Quarterly* 58, no. 2 (June): 257–268.

Eshbaugh-Soha, Matthew, and Dunia Andary. 2004. "Speak Now: A Monthly Analysis of Presidential Speeches." Paper presented for delivery at the annual meeting of the American Political Science Association, Chicago.

Eshbaugh-Soha, Matthew, and Jeffrey S. Peake. 2004. "Presidential Influence over the Systemic Agenda." *Congress and the Presidency* 31, no. 2 (Autumn): 161–181.

———. 2005. "Presidents and the Economic Agenda." *Political Research Quarterly* 58, no. 1 (March): 127–138.

Fenno, Richard. 1978. *Home Style: House Members in Their Districts.* Glenview, IL: Scott, Foresman.

Fett, Patrick J. 1992. "Truth in Advertising: The Revelation of Presidential Legislative Priorities." *Western Political Quarterly* 45, no. 4 (December): 895–920.

———. 1994. "Presidential Legislative Priorities and Legislators' Voting Decisions: An Exploratory Analysis." *Journal of Politics* 56, no. 2 (May): 502–512.

Fleisher, Richard, and Jon R. Bond. 2000. "Partisanship and the President's Quest for Votes on the Floor of Congress." In *Polarized Politics: Congress and the President in a Partisan Era,* ed. Jon R. Bond and Richard Fleisher. Washington, DC: CQ Press.

Friedrich, Carl J. 1940. "Public Policy and the Nature of Administrative Responsibility." *Public Policy* 1, no. 1: 3–24.

Goldman, Sheldon. 1995. *Picking Federal Judges: Lower Court Selection from Roosevelt Through Reagan.* New Haven, CT: Yale University Press.

Gormley, William T. 1986. "Regulatory Issue Networks in a Federal System." *Polity* 18, no. 2 (Summer): 595–620.

Graham, Hugh Davis. 1990. *The Civil Rights Era: Origins and Development of National Policy, 1960–1972.* New York: Oxford University Press.

Granger, Clive, and P. Newbold. 1974. "Spurious Regressions in Econometrics." *Journal of Econometrics* 2, no. 2 (July): 111–120.

Grossman, Michael Baruch, and Martha Joynt Kumar. 1981. *Portraying the President: The White House and the News Media.* Baltimore: Johns Hopkins University Press.

Hager, Gregory L., and Terry Sullivan. 1994. "President-centered and Presidency-centered Explanations of Presidential Public Activity." *American Journal of Political Science* 38, no. 4 (November): 1079–1103.

Hall, Richard L. 1996. *Participation in Congress.* New Haven, CT: Yale University Press.

Hansen, John Mark. 1991. *Gaining Access: Congress and the Farm Lobby, 1919–1981.* Chicago: University of Chicago Press.

Hardin, Charles M. 1978. "Agricultural Price Policy: The Political Role of Bureaucracy" *Policy Studies Journal* 6, no. 4 (June): 467–471.

Hargrove, Erwin C. 1988. *Jimmy as President: Leadership and the Politics of the Public Good.* Baton Rouge: Louisiana State University Press.

Heckman, J. 1976. "The Common Structure of Statistical Models of Truncation, Sample Selection, and Limited Dependent Variables and a Simple Estimator for Such Models." *Annals of Economic and Social Measurement* 5: 475–492.

Henry, Gary T., and Craig S. Gordon. 2001. "Tracking Issue Attention: Specifying the Dynamics of the Public Agenda." *Public Opinion Quarterly* 65, no. 2 (Summer): 157–177.

Hill, Kim Quaile. 1998. "The Policy Agendas of the President and the Mass Public: A Research Validation and Extension." *American Journal of Political Science* 42, no. 4 (November): 1328–1334.

Hill, Kim Quaile, and Patricia A. Hurley. 1999. "Dyadic Representation Reappraised." *American Journal of Political Science* 45, no. 1 (February): 109–137.

Hinckley, Barbara. 1990. *The Symbolic Presidency: How Presidents Portray Themselves.* New York: Routledge.

Iyengar, Shanto, and Donald R. Kinder. 1987. *News that Matters: Television and American Opinion.* Chicago: University of Chicago Press.

Jackson, John E. 1971. "Statistical Models of Senate Roll Call Voting." *American Political Science Review* 65, no. 2 (June): 451–470.

Jacobs, Lawrence R., and Robert Y. Shapiro. 1995. "The Rise of Presidential Polling: The Nixon White House in Historical Perspective." *Public Opinion Quarterly* 59, no. 2 (Summer): 163–195.

———. 2000. *Politicians Don't Pander: Political Manipulation and the Loss of Democratic Responsiveness.* Chicago: University of Chicago Press.

Jacobson, Gary C. 1997. *The Politics of Congressional Elections.* 4th ed. New York: Longman.

Jones, Charles O. 1961. "Representation in Congress: The Case of the House Agriculture Committee." *American Political Science Review* 55, no. 2 (June): 358–367.

———. 1975. *Clean Air: The Policies and Politics of Pollution Control.* Pittsburgh: University of Pittsburgh Press.

———. 1994. *The Presidency in a Separated System.* Washington, DC: The Brookings Institution.

Kaufman, Herbert. 1960. *The Forest Ranger: A Study in Administrative Behavior.* Baltimore: Johns Hopkins University Press.

Kearns, Doris. 1976. *Lyndon Johnson and the American Dream.* New York: Harper and Row.

Kennedy, Peter. 1998. *A Guide to Econometrics.* 4th ed. Cambridge, MA: MIT Press.

Kernell, Samuel. 1997. *Going Public: New Strategies of Presidential Leadership.* 3rd ed. Washington, DC: CQ Press.

Kingdon, John W. 1977. "Models of Legislative Voting." *Journal of Politics* 39, no. 3 (August): 563–595.

———. 1981. *Congressmen's Voting Decisions.* New York: Harper and Row.

———. 1995. *Agendas, Alternatives, and Public Policies.* Boston: Little, Brown.

Kraft, Michael E. 1990. "Environmental Gridlock: Searching for Consensus in Congress." In *Environmental Policy in the 1990s,* ed. Norman J. Vig and Michael E. Kraft. Washington, DC: CQ Press.

Kraft, Michael E., and Norman J. Vig. 1984. "Environmental Policy in the Reagan Presidency." *Political Science Quarterly* 99, no. 3 (Autumn): 415–439.

———. 1990. "Environmental Policy from the Seventies to the Nineties: Continuity and Change." In *Environmental Policy in the 1990s,* ed. Norman J. Vig and Michael E. Kraft. Washington, DC: CQ Press.

———. 2000. "Environmental Policy from the 1970s to 2000: An Overview." In *Environmental Policy: New Directions for the Twenty-first Century,* 4th ed., ed. Michael E. Kraft and Norman J. Vig. Washington, DC: CQ Press.

Krause, George A. 1996. "The Institutional Dynamics of Policy Administration: Bureaucratic Influence over Securities Regulation." *American Journal of Political Science* 40, no. 4 (November): 1083–1121.

Krehbiel, Keith. 1991. *Information and Legislative Organization.* Ann Arbor: University of Michigan Press.

Kriz, Margaret, and Gregg Sangillo. 2005. "Clean Air Act: A Cloudy Outlook for 'Clear Skies.'" *National Journal,* April 9.

Landsberg, Brian K. 1997. *Enforcing Civil Rights: Race Discrimination and the Department of Justice.* Lawrence: University Press of Kansas.

Landy, Marc K., Marc J. Roberts, and Stephen R. Thomas. 1994. *The*

Environmental Protection Agency: Asking the Wrong Questions from Nixon to Clinton. New York: Oxford University Press.

Lewis, David Allen. 1997. "The Two Rhetorical Presidencies: An Analysis of Televised Presidential Speeches, 1947–1991." *American Politics Quarterly* 25, no. 3 (July): 380–395.

Light, Paul C. 1993. "Presidential Policy Making." In *Researching the Presidency: Vital Questions, New Approaches,* ed. George C. Edwards, John H. Kessel, and Bert A. Rockman. Pittsburgh: University of Pittsburgh Press.

———. 1995. *Thickening Government: Federal Hierarchy and the Diffusion of Accountability.* Washington, DC: The Brookings Institution.

———. 1999. *The President's Agenda: Domestic Policy Choice from Kennedy to Clinton.* Baltimore: Johns Hopkins University Press.

Long, Norton. 1949. "Power and Administration." *Public Administration Review* 9, no. 4 (July/August): 257–264.

Lowi, Theodore J. 1972. "Four Systems of Policy, Politics and Choice." *Public Administration Review* 32, no. 4 (July/August): 298–310.

———. 1979. *The End of Liberalism: The Second Republic of the United States.* 2nd ed. New York: Norton.

———. 1985. *The Personal President: Power Invested, Promise Unfulfilled.* Ithaca, NY: Cornell University Press.

Lowry, William R. 1992. *The Dimensions of Federalism: State Governments and Pollution Control Policies.* Durham, NC: Duke University Press.

Macey, Jonathan R. 1992. "Organizational Design and Political Control of Administrative Agencies." *Journal of Law, Economics, and Organization* 8, no. 1 (March): 93–110.

MacRae, Duncan, Jr. 1970. *Issues and Parties in Legislative Voting: Methods of Statistical Analysis.* New York: Harper and Row.

Maltese, John Anthony. 1994. *Spin Control: The White House Office of Communications and the Management of Presidential News.* Chapel Hill: University of North Carolina Press.

March, James G., and Herbert A. Simon. 1958. *Organizations.* New York: Wiley.

Marcus, Alfred. 1980. *Promise and Performance: Choosing and Implementing an Environmental Policy.* Westport, CT: Greenwood Press.

Matthews, Donald R., and James A. Stimson. 1970. "Decision-Making by U.S. Representatives: A Preliminary Model." In *Political Decision-Making,* ed. Sidney Ulmer. New York: Reinhold.

———. 1975. *Yeas and Nays: Normal Decision-Making in the US House of Representatives.* New York: John Wiley and Sons.

Mayhew, David R. 1974. *Congress: The Electoral Connection.* New Haven, CT: Yale University Press.

———. 1991. *Divided We Govern: Party Control, Lawmaking, and Investigations, 1946–1990.* New Haven, CT: Yale University Press.

McCleary, Richard, and Richard Hay. 1980. *Applied Time Series Analysis.* Beverly Hills, CA: Sage Publications.

McCrone, Donald J., and James H. Kuklinski. 1979. "The Delegate Theory of Representation." *American Journal of Political Science* 23, no. 2 (May): 278–300.

McCubbins, Matthew D., and Thomas Schwartz. 1984. "Congressional

Oversight Overlooked: Police Patrols and Fire Alarms." *American Journal of Political Science* 84, no. 1 (February): 165–179.

McCubbins, Matthew D., Roger G. Noll, and Barry R. Weingast. 1989. "Structure and Process, Politics and Policy: Administrative Arrangements and the Political Control of Agencies." *Virginia Law Review* 75 (March): 431–482.

McMahon, Kevin J. 2004. *Reconsidering Roosevelt on Race.* Chicago: Chicago University Press.

Meier, Kenneth J. 1985. *Regulation: Politics, Bureaucracy, and Economics.* New York: St. Martin's Press.

———. 1993. *Politics and the Bureaucracy: Policymaking in the Fourth Branch of Government.* Belmont, CA: Wadsworth Publishing.

———. 1995. "Regulating Agriculture." In *Regulation and Consumer Protection,* ed. Kenneth J. Meier and E. Thomas Garman. Houston, TX: Dame Publications.

Meier, Kenneth J., J. L. Polinard, and Robert D. Wrinkle. 1999. "Politics, Bureaucracy, and Farm Credit." *Public Administration Review* 59, no. 4 (July/August): 293–302.

Meier, Kenneth J., Robert D. Wrinkle, and J. L. Polinard. 1995. "Politics, Bureaucracy, and Agricultural Policy: An Alternative View of Political Control." *American Politics Quarterly* 23, no. 4 (October): 427–460.

Melnick, R. Shep. 1983. *Regulation and the Courts: The Case of the Clean Air Act.* Washington, DC: The Brookings Institution.

Member of Congress (Texas) interview. 2005. September 7.

Miller, W., and Donald Stokes. 1963. "Constituency Influence in Congress." *American Political Science Review* 57, no. 1 (March): 45–56.

Moe, Terry. 1982. "Regulatory Performance and Presidential Administration." *American Journal of Political Science* 26, no. 2 (May): 197–224.

———. 1985. "Control Feedback in Economic Regulation: The Case of the NLRB." *American Political Science Review* 79, no. 4 (December): 1094–1116.

———. 1989. "The Politics of Bureaucratic Structure." In *Can the Government Govern?* ed. John E. Chubb and Paul E. Peterson. Washington, DC: The Brookings Institution.

Mondak, Jeffrey J. 1993. "Source Cues and Policy Approval: The Cognitive Dynamics of Public Support for the Reagan Agenda." *American Journal of Political Science* 37, no. 1 (February): 186–212.

Moyer, H. Wayne, and Timothy E. Josling. 1990. *Agricultural Policy Reform: Politics and Process in the EC and the USA.* Ames: Iowa State University Press.

Nathan, Richard P. 1983. *The Administrative Presidency.* New York: Wiley.

Neustadt, Richard E. 1990. *Presidential Power and the Modern Presidents.* New York: The Free Press.

Ogul, Morris. 1976. *Congress Oversees the Bureaucracy.* Pittsburgh: University of Pittsburgh Press.

Ostrom, Charles W., and Dennis M. Simon. 1985. "Promise and Performance: A Dynamic Model of Presidential Popularity." *American Political Science Review* 79, no. 2 (June): 334–358.

Page, Benjamin, and Robert Shapiro. 1985. "Presidential Leadership Through Public Opinion." In *The Presidency and Public Policy Making,* ed. George

C. Edwards III, Steven A. Shull, and Norman C. Thomas. Pittsburgh: University of Pittsburgh Press.

————. 1992. *The Rational Public: Fifty Years of Trends in Americans' Policy Preferences.* Chicago: University of Chicago Press.

Pauley, Garth E. 1999. "Harry Truman and the NAACP: A Case Study in Presidential Persuasion on Civil Rights." *Rhetoric and Public Affairs* 2, no. 2 (Summer): 211–242.

Peake, Jeffrey S. 2001. "Presidential Agenda Setting in Foreign Policy." *Political Research Quarterly* 54, no. 1 (March): 69–86.

Peake, Jeffrey S., and Matthew Eshbaugh-Soha. 2002. "Presidential Agenda Setting and the Salience of Economic Issues." Paper presented at the annual meeting of the Midwest Political Science Association, Chicago, IL.

————. 2003. "The Limits of Presidential Rhetoric: The Agenda-Setting Impact of Major Television Addresses." Paper presented at the Annual Meeting of the American Political Science Association, Philadelphia, PA.

Perry, H. W. 1991. *Deciding to Decide: Agenda Setting in the United States Supreme Court.* Cambridge: Harvard University Press.

Peterson, Mark A. 1990. *Legislating Together: The White House and Capitol Hill from Eisenhower to Reagan.* Cambridge: Harvard University Press.

Pfiffner, James A. 1988. *The Strategic Presidency: Hitting the Ground Running.* Chicago: Dorsey Press.

Polsby, Nelson. 1978. "Presidential Cabinet Making: Lessons for the Political System." *Political Science Quarterly* 93, no. 1 (Spring): 15–25.

Porter, Laurellen. 1978. "Congress and Agriculture Policy." *Policy Studies Journal* 6, no. 4 (June): 472–478.

Portney, Paul R. 1990. *Public Policies for Environmental Protection.* Washington, DC: Resources for the Future.

Powell, Richard J. 1999. "'Going Public' Revisited: Presidential Speechmaking and the Bargaining Setting in Congress." *Congress and the Presidency* 26, no. 2 (Fall): 153–170.

Public Papers of the Presidents: Truman, 1948–1953. 5 vols. Washington, DC: Government Printing Office.

Public Papers of the Presidents: Eisenhower, 1953–1961. 8 vols. Washington, DC: Government Printing Office.

Public Papers of the Presidents: Kennedy, 1961–1963. 3 vols. Washington, DC: Government Printing Office.

Public Papers of the Presidents: Johnson, 1963–1969. 5 vols. Washington, DC: Government Printing Office.

Public Papers of the Presidents: Nixon, 1969–1974. 6 vols. Washington, DC: Government Printing Office.

Public Papers of the Presidents: Ford, 1974–1977. 3 vols. Washington, DC: Government Printing Office.

Public Papers of the Presidents: Carter, 1977–1981. 4 vols. Washington, DC: Government Printing Office.

Public Papers of the Presidents: Reagan, 1981–1989. 8 vols. Washington, DC: Government Printing Office.

Public Papers of the Presidents: Bush, 1989–1993. 4 vols. Washington, DC: Government Printing Office.

Public Papers of the Presidents: Clinton, 1993–2000. 8 vols. Washington, DC: Government Printing Office.

Public Papers of the Presidents: Bush, 2001–2004. 4 vols. Washington, DC: Government Printing Office.

Ragsdale, Lyn. 1984. "The Politics of Presidential Speechmaking, 1949–1980." *American Political Science Review* 78, no. 4 (December): 971–984.

———. 1998. *Vital Statistics on the Presidency: Washington to Clinton.* Washington, DC: CQ Press.

Ramsey Clark Oral History Interview I. October 30, 1968. Transcript by Harri Baker. LBJ Library, Austin, Texas.

Redford, Emmette Shelburn. 1969. *Democracy in the Administrative State.* New York: Oxford University Press.

Regan, Donald T. 1988. *For the Record.* San Diego: Harcourt Brace Jovanovich.

Ringquist, Evan J. 1993. *Environmental Protection at the State Level: Politics and Progress in Controlling Pollution.* Armonk, NY: M. E. Sharpe.

———. 1995. "Environmental Protection Regulation." In *Regulation and Consumer Protection,* ed. Kenneth J. Meier and E. Thomas Garman. Houston, TX: Dame Publications.

Ripley, Randall B., and Grace A. Franklin. 1991. *Congress, the Bureaucracy, and Public Policy.* Chicago: Dorsey Press.

Rivers, Douglas, and Nancy L. Rose. 1985. "Passing the President's Program: Public Opinion and Presidential Influence in Congress." *American Journal of Political Science* 29, no. 2 (May): 183–196.

Rockman, Bert A. 1984. *The Leadership Question: The Presidency and the American System.* New York: Praeger.

Rosenbaum, Walter A. 1989. "The Bureaucracy and Environmental Policy." In *Environmental Politics and Policy,* ed. James P. Lester. Durham, NC: Duke University Press.

———. 1991. *Environmental Politics and Policy.* 2nd ed. Washington, DC: CQ Press.

———. 2002. *Environmental Politics and Policy.* 5th ed. Washington, DC: CQ Press.

Rosenberg, Gerald N. 1991. *The Hollow Hope: Can Courts Bring About Social Change?* Chicago: University of Chicago Press.

Rourke, Francis E. 1969. *Bureaucracy, Politics, and Public Policy.* Boston: Little, Brown.

Rozell, Mark J. 1990. "President Carter and the Press: Perspectives from White House Communications Advisers." *Political Science Quarterly* 105, no. 3 (Autumn): 419–434.

Schlozman, Kay Lehman, and John T. Tierney. 1986. *Organized Interests and American Democracy.* New York: Harper and Row.

Shull, Steven A. 1983. *Domestic Policy Formation: Presidential-Congressional Partnership?* Westport, CT: Greenwood Press.

———. 1989. *The President and Civil Rights Policy: Leadership and Change.* Armonk, NY: M. E. Sharpe.

———. 1993. *A Kinder, Gentler Racism? The Reagan-Bush Civil Rights Legacy.* Armonk, NY: M. E. Sharpe.

Shull, Steven A., and David Garland. 1995. "Presidential Influence Versus Agency Characteristics in Explaining Policy Implementation." *Policy Studies Review* 14, no. 2 (Summer): 49–70.

Simon, Herbert A. 1957. *Administrative Behavior: A Study of Decision-Making Processes in Administrative Organization.* 2nd ed. New York: Macmillan.

Skowronek, Stephen. 1993. *The Politics Presidents Make: Leadership from John Adams to George Bush.* Cambridge, MA: Belknap Press

Sourcebook of Criminal Justice Statistics. 31st ed. 2003. US Department of Justice, Bureau of Justice Statistics. Washington, DC: US Government Printing Office.

Spaeth, Harold J. 1999. "United States Supreme Court Database," 9th ICPSR version. East Lansing: Michigan State University, Department of Political Science.

Stimson, James A., Michael B. MacKuen, and Robert S. Erikson. 1995. "Dynamic Representation." *American Political Science Review* 89, no. 3 (September): 543–565.

Suskind, Ron. 2004. *The Price of Loyalty: George W. Bush, the White House, and the Education of Paul O'Neill.* New York: Simon and Schuster.

Sussman, Glen, and Mark Andrew Kelso. 1999. "Environmental Priorities and the President as Legislative Leader." In *The Environmental Presidency,* ed. Dennis L. Soden. Albany: State University of New York Press.

Switzer, Jacqueline Vaughn. 1998. *Environmental Politics: Domestic and Global Dimensions.* New York: St. Martin's Press.

Tulis, Jeffrey K. 1987. *The Rhetorical Presidency.* Princeton, NJ: Princeton University Press.

———. 1998. "The Two Constitutional Presidencies." In *The Presidency and the Political System,* 5th ed., ed. Michael Nelson. Washington, DC: CQ Press.

Tweeten, Luther G. 1979. *Foundations of Farm Policy.* 2nd ed. Lincoln: University of Nebraska Press.

Ulrich, Hugh. 1989. *Losing Ground: Agricultural Policy and the Decline of the American Farm.* Chicago: Chicago Review Press.

Vig, Norman J. 2000. "Presidential Leadership and the Environment: From Reagan to Clinton." In *Environmental Policy: New Directions for the Twenty-first Century,* 4th ed., ed. Michael E. Kraft and Norman J. Vig. Washington, DC: CQ Press.

Vogel, David. 1986. *National Styles of Regulation: Environmental Policy in Great Britain and the United States.* Ithaca, NY: Cornell University Press.

Waterman, Richard W. 1989. *Presidential Influence and the Administrative State.* Knoxville: University of Tennessee Press.

———. 1999. "Bureaucratic Views of the President." In *Presidential Policymaking: An End-of-Century Assessment,* ed. Steven A. Shull. Armonk, NY: M. E. Sharpe.

Waterman, Richard W., Hank C. Jenkins-Smith, and Carol L. Silva. 1999. "The Expectations Gap Thesis: Public Attitudes Toward an Incumbent President." *Journal of Politics* 61, no. 4 (November): 944–966.

Wayne, Stephen. 1982. "Great Expectations." In *Rethinking the Presidency,* ed. Thomas E. Cronin. Boston: Little, Brown.

Weingast, Barry R., and Mark J. Moran. 1983. "Bureaucratic Discretion or Congressional Control? Regulatory Policymaking by the Federal Trade Commission." *Journal of Political Economy* 83, no. 5 (October): 765–800.

Wenner, Lettie McSpadden. 1989. "The Courts and Environmental Policy." In *Environmental Politics and Policy,* ed. James P. Lester. Durham, NC: Duke University Press.

West, William F. 1995. *Controlling the Bureaucracy: Institutional Constraints in Theory and Practice.* Armonk, NY: M. E. Sharpe.

Whitford, Andrew B., and Jeff Yates. 2003. "Policy Signals and Executive Governance: Presidential Rhetoric in the War on Drugs." *Journal of Politics* 65, no. 4 (November): 995–1012.

Wildavsky, Aaron B. 1984. *Politics of the Budgetary Process.* 4th ed. Boston: Little, Brown.

Wilson, Woodrow. 1885. *Congressional Government: A Study in American Politics.* Boston, MA: Houghton Mifflin.

Wood, B. Dan. 1988. "Principals, Bureaucrats, and Responsiveness in Clean Air Enforcements." *American Political Science Review* 82, no. 1 (March): 213–234.

———. 1990. "Does Politics Make a Difference at the EEOC?" *American Journal of Political Science* 34, no. 2 (May): 503–530.

———. 2000a. "Weak Theories and Parameter Instability: Using Flexible Least Squares to Take Time Varying Relationships Seriously." *American Journal of Political Science* 44, no. 3 (July): 603–618.

———. 2000b. "The Federal Balanced Budget Force: Modeling Variations from 1904–1996." *Journal of Politics* 62, no. 3 (August): 817–845.

Wood, B. Dan, and James E. Anderson. 1993. "The Politics of U.S. Antitrust Regulation." *American Journal of Political Science* 37, no. 1 (February): 1–39.

Wood, B. Dan, and Richard W. Waterman. 1993. "The Dynamics of Political-Bureaucratic Adaption." *American Journal of Political Science* 37, no. 2 (May): 497–528.

———. 1994. *Bureaucratic Dynamics: The Role of Bureaucracy in a Democracy.* Boulder, CO: Westview Press.

INDEX

Acid rain, 95
Adarand Constructors, Inc. v. Pena, 78
Administrative clearance, 35
Affirmative action, 73, 76, 78, 94*n13,*
94*n14*
African Americans. *See* Civil rights
policy
Agenda setting, 42, 44; and civil rights,
80, 84, 161; and clean air policy,
160–161; and drug crime prosecu-
tions, 17; and farm policy, 145; tele-
vised addresses as signals of high
priority, 37, 111. *See also* Signaling,
as indication of priorities and com-
mitment
Agricultural Act of 1949, 128, 134, 143
Agricultural Act of 1965. *See* Food and
Agricultural Act of 1965
Agricultural Act of 1985. *See* Food
Security Act of 1985
Agricultural Adjustment Act of 1933,
128
Agricultural Adjustment Act of 1938,
128, 134
Agricultural Adjustment Act, renewal
cycle, 144–145, 149, 153*n9*
Agricultural Adjustment
Administration, 128
Agricultural policy. *See* Farm policy
Agriculture and Consumer Protection
Act of 1973, 130
Air Pollution Control Act of 1955, 96,
100

Air Quality Act of 1967, 97
Appointments/removals, bureaucratic,
20–21, 51–53; effectiveness as
means of control, 21, 116–118,
167–168; and effects of absent presidential leadership, 22; research
methodology, 185; unfavorable
appointments, 52, 77–78, 98

Bargaining, decline of, 30, 33
Barrett, Andrew, 14
Bond, Jon R., 6
Brace, Paul, 5
Browner, Carol, 111
Budget of the United States, 185
Budgets: and civil rights, 86*tab,* 91*tab;*
and clean air policy, 119–120*tabs,*
124; effectiveness as means of con-
trol, 21, 50, 53, 169, 185; and farm
policy, 151–152*tabs;* and going-
public model, 13, 14; and presiden-
tial influence over bureaucracy, 17,
20–22, 52, 116–118, 169; Reagan's
EPA budget cuts, 98, 117–118;
Reagan's use of speeches and
Gramm-Latta budget reconciliation,
13; research methodology, 185
Buford, Anne, 21
Bureaucracy: conflicting incentives for
salient, complex issues, 105; and
Congress, 53, 72–73; and interest
groups, 53, 106; and judicial system, 53; "policy drift," 106; "thick-

209

About the Book

WHY DO PRESIDENTS BOTHER TO GIVE SPEECHES WHEN THEIR WORDS rarely move public opinion? Arguing that "going public" isn't really about going to the public at all, Matthew Eshbaugh-Soha explores to whom presidential speeches are in fact targeted and what—if any—influence they have on public policy.

Eshbaugh-Soha shows that, when presidents speak, their intent is to provide legislators and bureaucrats with cues pointing to particular policy decisions. Analyzing fifty years of presidential rhetoric, he demonstrates the impact of such "presidential signaling" vis-à-vis a range of policy areas. He finds that, although citizen support may increase the likelihood that a legislator will respond to presidential signals, it is not essential to a president's legislative success.

Matthew Eshbaugh-Soha is assistant professor of political science at the University of North Texas.

DATE DUE

HIGHSMITH 45230